Sports Marketing

Any sports marketing student or prospective sports marketer has to understand in detail genuine industry trends and be able to recognize solutions to real-world scenarios. *Sports Marketing: A practical approach* is the first textbook to offer a comprehensive, engaging, and practice-focused bridge between academic theory and real-life, industry-based research and practice. Defining the primary role of the sports marketer as revenue generation, the book is structured around the three main channels through which this can be achieved – ticket sales, media, and sponsorship – and explores key topics such as:

- Sports markets and business markets (B2B)
- Fan development
- Brand management
- Media audiences, rights, and revenue
- Live sports events
- Sponsorship
- Merchandise and retail.

Integrating real industry-generated research into every chapter, the book also includes analyses of industry job descriptions and guidance for developing and preparing for a career in sports marketing. It goes further than any other sports marketing textbook in surveying the international sports market, including international cases and detailed profiles of international consumer and business markets throughout. A companion website offers multiple choice questions for students, editable short answer and essay questions, and lecture slides for instructors.

No other textbook offers such a relevant, practice-focused overview of contemporary sports marketing. It is the ideal companion to any sports marketing course.

Larry DeGaris is a leading research consultant to the sponsorship and sports marketing industries, and Professor of Marketing at the University of Indianapolis, USA. He has personally conducted over 100 research studies for sports organizations funded to well over $3 million, and is a sought after expert for the media.

www.routledge.com/cw/degaris

Sports Marketing

A practical approach

Larry DeGaris

Routledge
Taylor & Francis Group

LONDON AND NEW YORK

First published 2015
by Routledge
2 Park Square, Milton Park, Abingdon, Oxon OX14 4RN

and by Routledge
711 Third Avenue, New York, NY 10017

Routledge is an imprint of the Taylor & Francis Group, an informa business

British Library Cataloguing-in-Publication Data
A catalogue record for this book is available from the British Library

Library of Congress Cataloging in Publication Data
DeGaris, Larry.
Sports marketing : a practical approach / Larry DeGaris.
   pages cm
   Includes bibliographical references and index.
   1. Sports–Marketing. 2. Sports–Economic aspects. I. Title.
   GV716.D42 2015
   796.06'88–dc23   2014032424

ISBN: 978-0-415-63046-7 (hbk)
ISBN: 978-0-415-63047-4 (pbk)
ISBN: 978-0-203-09761-8 (ebk)

Typeset in Perpetua & Bell Gothic
by Wearset Ltd, Boldon, Tyne and Wear

Aim high. You're better than you think you are.

In memory of...
Don "Sonny Boy Hinko" Hinchey. The best wingman ever, in and
out of the office.

And dedicated to...
Lani, both a distraction from writing and an inspiration for
finishing.

Contents

Figures

Tables

Preface

I learned marketing on the job. The first marketing class I was ever in was one that I taught. In reading leading sports marketing textbooks, I found little resemblance to my experiences working in sports marketing. This book is an attempt to bridge that gap.

I thank my editors at Routledge for providing the impetus for putting this book together. After criticizing sports marketing textbook proposals because they largely fail to reflect sports marketing practice, my editors at Routledge, Simon Whitmore in particular, provided me with the opportunity to do something different. That proved to be more of a challenge than I had anticipated. Most sports marketing textbooks follow the template set by leading marketing textbooks and apply marketing principles to sports examples, with a focus on the principles not the practice.

Marketing practice is more goal-driven than process-oriented. Therefore, this book attempts to focus on how sports marketing can be tied to larger business goals, especially sales and profits. In organizing the book, I "followed the money." This book tries to "follow the money" by (1) structuring chapters around revenue generation; and (2) emphasizing areas in which there are employment opportunities.

First, I look at revenue opportunities in sports marketing. Globally, the sports industry generates revenues from (1) live events, (2) media, and (3) commercial (e.g., sponsorship and licensing/merchandising). The first part of the book discusses marketing goals and strategies. The remaining three parts of the book discuss specific marketing tactics to generate revenue in each of the three revenue domains.

The book is also structured around revenue opportunities for readers of the book, i.e., jobs. Not surprisingly, the greatest number of job opportunities in sports marketing can be found in the areas which generate the greatest revenue. One of the features of this book is that it links strategies and tactics to job descriptions from actual job ads.

The sports business is a sales-based industry. "Sell or die" is the common mantra among sports executives. Consequently, the book is very sales-oriented, with four chapters devoted exclusively to the sales process as applied to specific sports domains.

One of the unique features of this book is its emphasis on sports' use in business-to-business marketing. The contribution of client entertainment and corporate hospitality is substantial with respect both to ticket sales and sponsorships. Both academics and practitioners have paid far too little attention to the B2B component of sports marketing. With this book, I hope to promote a more rigorous approach to this part of the business.

At the very least, I hope this book helps to further the conversation between academics and practitioners. I hope academics can use the books to better understand what practitioners are looking for; and I hope practitioners will start to look toward academia as a potential resource.

I'd also like to say a few words about "learning objectives" for the book. The main goal of this book is to provide readers with enough of a framework to think about sports marketing, and enough interesting examples to spur thought. Readers will notice that I used a lot of examples from reports in the *SportsBusiness Journal*. I highly recommend a subscription to the SBJ as a companion to the book. Sports marketing is a rapidly evolving discipline. As readers will note, there is a premium placed on innovation and creativity in sports marketing, especially with respect to identifying new sources of revenue. Rather than reaching conclusions, I hope this book helps readers formulate some good questions.

Acknowledgments

I've been lucky.

I've had great teachers and coaches. They taught me both to love sports and to love school.

I've had great bosses. I'm grateful for the opportunity to have worked in the industry full-time. For that, I thank Tracy Schoenadel for taking a chance on a grad student in sport sociology and giving me my start with ROI Research at the Interpublic Group. Tim Taylor at the Bonham Group took a chance on hiring me despite concerns about my work being "too theoretical," and was gracious enough to provide me with opportunities to manage client projects, sharing successes when things went well and blame when they didn't. Marjorie White gave me the opportunity to work in areas beyond sports and gain exposure to public relations at Ogilvy Public Relations Worldwide. Thanks for the opportunity.

I've had great colleagues. Don Hinchey, in whose memory this book was written and who was taken from us too soon, was an enthusiastic advocate and a great sparring partner in internal strategy sessions. Don's genuine desire to see other people succeed continues to be humbling. I miss you, Donnie. Corrie West, my longtime colleague, business partner, and friend afforded me the luxury of having time to think about research design and results. I'm delighted to have had the opportunity to work together, grateful for her diligence and hard work, and proud of the work we've done. Thanks, CJ.

I've had great clients. I've had the privilege of working with clients across the sports marketing spectrum: properties/brands, big/small. I've worked with well over a hundred different clients in the sports industry who have provided collegiality, guidance, and funding. Thanks for the business and let me know if you need anything else!

I've had great students. Thanks for taking my classes. I hope you got as much out of them as I have.

Most importantly, I have great family and friends, and a special "special someone." Like I said, I'm lucky.

Part I
Strategy

Chapter 1

A practical approach to sports marketing

CHAPTER OUTLINE

1 Bridging theory and practice

2 A practical approach to sports marketing
   a Goals
      i Organizational goals
      ii Marketing goals
   b Strategies
   c Tactics

3 Data and measurement
   a Goals
      i Marketing intelligence
      ii Customer analytics
      iii Market research

BRIDGING THEORY AND PRACTICE

The relationship between the academic study of sports business and sports business practitioners historically has not been close or productive, more often ranging from distant to downright adversarial. The *Wall Street Journal* (WSJ) gave college sport management programs a "failing" grade in preparing students for work in the sports business.[1] The WSJ article recounted a speech to an association of academics by Andy Dolich in 2004, in which Dolich sharply criticized academic sports business programs for their lack of relevant course offerings.[2] The WSJ article recommends that students look for a program which offers "real-world experience" provided by faculty who are "real-life practitioners."

The dilemma of the academic study pitted against practical relevance is not limited to the sports business but extends to the broader fields of marketing and business. The gap between academic marketers and the needs of marketing executives has been described as "alarming" and "growing."[3] The WSJ does not place the blame on the gap between academics and practitioners solely on academia, noting that the sports industry has not invested in or nurtured sport management programs.

One of practitioners' main criticisms of the academic study of sports marketing is that it is "too theoretical." But what does it mean to be "too theoretical" and what would it mean to have a "practical" approach to sports marketing? In the common use, the term "theoretical" is meant as something which is abstract, which may or may not be relevant to a real-world situation. Practical, on the other hand, means performing or doing something. In this sense, a theoretical approach to sports marketing means looking at abstract principles or processes which may or may not be actively practiced. A theoretical approach focuses on *what sports marketing "is."* In contrast, *a practical approach to sports marketing focuses on what sports marketers do*.

In general, academic research and textbooks tend to take a more theoretical approach to sports marketing, focusing on marketing principles and providing examples from the sports business. Academics and practitioners even differ with respect to the name of the field: academics study "sport" marketing; practitioners do "sports" marketing. The terminologies represent different approaches: "sport" marketing as a field of academic study attempts to create a "general theory of sport marketing," which can be applied across industry segments.[4] One of the main criticisms of the academic approach to marketing is that it lacks context: what works in one research study might not work under different circumstances.[5] Practitioners are more concerned with what works than finding a unifying theory of the field, and they are concerned that what might work in one situation might not work in another.

Understandably, sports marketing practitioners' primary concern is with marketing problems which are "here and now,"[6] but by focusing on relevant practical problems, sports marketers often fail to take a systematic, rigorous approach. The academic study of "sport" marketing is characterized by a rigorous, systematic approach. Rigor can be both conceptual, or well thought out, and methodological, systematically analyzing empirical data. Academic research tends to focus on rigor to the exclusion of relevance. In contrast, sports marketing practice tends to maintain a laser-like focus on relevance, often at the expense of rigor.

Critics of the "academic" or "theoretical" approach to sports marketing overlook the benefits of a more rigorous approach which is informed by data. Practice-oriented sports marketers also tend to overlook a big weakness in the sports industry relative to other industries: as an industry, sports lags woefully behind other industries in its use of research and data. According to a recent industry study,[7] sponsors give properties (e.g., teams, leagues, and events) a failing grade for measurement and research. Table 1.1 provides some results from the study: nearly two-thirds (67%) of sponsors say properties are not meeting their expectations in delivering return-on-investment (ROI) measurement or research information; more than half (55%) do not have a standardized measurement process; nearly half (45%) spend 0% of their sponsorship budgets on pre-selection research; and about a third (32%) spend nothing on concurrent/post-event research. Sponsors are more likely to rely on their guts than hard data as "internal feedback" is considered to be a more important type of sponsorship analysis than "primary consumer research." The numbers are not good to begin with and might be worse, as respondents might be prone to overestimating their use of research because that would be the more desirable response. Most marketing practitioners would not like to admit that they make decisions about million dollar deals without rigorous, fact-based support.

Table 1.1 Sponsors' use of research

- 67% of sponsors say properties are NOT meeting their expectations in delivering ROI measurement or research information

- 55% of sponsors do not have a standardized process for measuring return from sponsorships

- 45% of sponsors spend 0% of their sponsorship budgets on pre-selection research

- 32% of sponsors spend NOTHING on concurrent/post-event research, despite 86% saying the need for validated results from sponsorship has increased during the past 1–2 years

- "Internal feedback" is the most important type of sponsorship analysis (42% 9–10 on a 10-pt. scale), more than "primary consumer research" (29%)

Source: 12th Annual IEG/Performance Research Sponsorship Decision-Makers Survey.

It's not surprising that sponsorship properties get a failing grade from sponsors on research and measurement. Sports marketers have long had a skeptical and somewhat dubious view of research. Jon Spoelstra, a highly influential figure in helping to professionalize sports marketing as a discipline, eschews research conducted by "big professional research firms" – the type often used by "megacorporations" – in favor of "free research," or "going to your customers and talking to them one-to-one."[8] Along these lines, other sports marketers suggest executives "gather your own research," "walk around the arena and observe what's happening," and "introduce yourself as a team executive and ask random fans to share their experiences with you."[9] But while research by walking around might add insight to more systematic, rigorous data, on its own it's a terrible method of collecting information, prone to all sorts of individual biases and measurement errors. One of the main benefits of using rigorous methods to conduct research is to reduce biases of individuals and reduce risk in decisions.

There is, however, recognition of the importance of rigorous research, measurement, and data in the sports industry, although sports-related organizations tend to lag far behind their "megacorporation" counterparts. Table 1.2 provides some examples of research-related job responsibilities in job ads posted by sports organizations. The Special Olympics sees a Vice President who will build "off the data, research, and evaluation findings." Churchill Downs Racetrack, home of the Kentucky Derby, seeks a Vice President who will develop a "comprehensive data driven marketing strategy." The Chicago Fire, a Major League Soccer (MLS) team, seeks a Senior Director of Marketing who will oversee research initiatives, which will "heighten Fire's awareness of current business activity and grow/ develop future business opportunities."

So, practitioners criticize academics for a lack of relevance and academics criticize practitioners for a lack of rigor. To a certain extent, they're both right. The main goal of this book, therefore, is to provide a systematic and rigorous approach to the sports marketing practice, which is informed by data. This book adopts a practical approach to sports marketing and takes what sports marketers do and how you might learn how to do it as the starting points. That's not to say that there are no theories or principles involved in the practice of sports marketing. Theory and practice are not mutually exclusive, nor are relevance and rigor. Sports marketing practitioners don't make choices randomly; they operate from theoretical frameworks, though most practitioners would probably use the term "strategies."

5

Table 1.2 Research-related duties for sports marketers

Job description	Comments
VP, Special Olympics position summary[1] ■ "The Vice President, Global Youth Activation and Education Policy will lead the global expansion and implementation of youth activation in each of seven Special Olympics regions around the world, as a core component of the community building pillar of the Movement's strategic plan. S/he will create an integrated overarching global blueprint for youth activation and school and education policy *building off the data, research and evaluation findings*, key characteristics and principles that ensure Project UNIFY remains a successful US youth activation program." (emphasis added)	Many sports marketing job descriptions seek candidates who can develop evidence-based programs. The Special Olympics sought a candidate who would build programs off data, research, and evaluation findings.
Senior Director of Marketing – Chicago Fire Soccer Club responsibilities[2] ■ "*Oversee development of all research initiatives* including surveys, questionnaires, focus groups, etc. Use such data to heighten Fire's awareness of current business activity and grow/develop future business opportunities." (emphasis added)	Major League Soccer's Chicago Fire sought a marketing director who would oversee research initiatives. Heightening awareness involves developing a more informed and intentional approach to marketing activities. The Fire also sought a Director who would use data to support business development. Research is often undervalued by sports organizations, especially on the property side, because it is difficult to establish a direct link between research and revenue, but many organizations endeavor to use research for sales support and product development.
Vice President of Marketing – Churchill Downs Racetrack essential duties[3] ■ "Leading and managing efforts to integrate technology, advertising, and other business intelligence into a comprehensive data driven marketing strategy. Analyzing demographic, geographic, behavioral and other data to effectively target and engage desired audience while quantifying results. *Conducting marketing surveys on new concepts, products, and innovations*." (emphasis added)	Churchill Downs, home of the Kentucky Derby, sought a candidate who would not only analyze existing data but actually conduct marketing surveys, which would inform new product development.

Notes
1 Vice President, Global Youth Activation and Education Policy. www.sportbusiness.com/marketplace/jobs/vice-president-global-youth-activation, accessed 1/11/2012.
2 Major League Soccer Job Board. http://mls.teamworkonline.com/teamwork/r.cfm?i=47233, accessed 8/9/2012.
3 Job Opportunities Churchill Downs Incorporated. http://churchilldownsincorporated.teamworkonline.com/teamwork/r.cf, accessed 8/9/2012.

While sports marketers use theoretical frameworks, they tend not to draw on academic research for their theories, developing "theories on the ground" based on experience or, less often, using market research.

A PRACTICAL APPROACH TO SPORTS MARKETING

> Sports marketers develop strategies and implement tactics to achieve goals.

What do sports marketers do? And where do they do it? Broadly speaking, sports marketers develop strategies and tactics to achieve goals. Sports marketers work for a property, sponsor, media rights holder, or agency.[10]

A sports *property* is a team, league, venue, event, governing body, or association. Sports marketing executives at sports properties are primarily concerned with the **marketing of sports** with the goal of generating sports consumers, fans, and/or participants. Manchester United and the New York Yankees are sports properties as are the leagues in which they compete – Barclays Premier League (BPL) and Major League Baseball (MLB) – respectively, and these organizations are concerned primarily with building their fan bases. National governing bodies for Olympic sports and your local gym are sports properties also concerned with building sports audiences but more focused on participants than fans.

Sponsors are companies or brands, whether sports-related or not, who pay sports properties for exploitable marketing assets, whether as official sponsors or as advertisers on sports-related content. Sports marketing executives working for or on behalf of sponsors are primarily concerned with **marketing through sports** with the goal of using sports to gain access to audiences of fans and/or participants. Sports properties build audiences which they can then deliver to sports sponsors.

Media rights holders, such as television, radio, and digital companies, play a vital role both in distributing sports products, especially event broadcasts to fans, and providing a vital source of revenue for sports properties. Media companies are appropriately named because they mediate the role between sports properties, playing a role in both building audiences and delivering them to corporate sponsors. Sports marketing executives at media rights holders are concerned with both building audiences, such as television viewers, radio listeners, or website visitors, AND monetizing those audiences through subscription fees and/or advertising.

Agencies perform specialized functions across sports properties, sponsors, and media companies. Sports marketers employed by an agency can represent a sports property, selling tickets or sponsorships, for example; they can represent sponsors, such as by developing and implementing sponsorship programs; or they can represent media companies. Some agencies specialize in sports marketing or a specialization within sports marketing, such as sponsorship or athlete representation. Other agencies offer sports-related services as one industry category among many. Typically, however, agencies offer a specialized expertise and capabilities in an area not possessed by their clients.

Goals

One of the biggest challenges marketers face day-to-day is how to allocate their time, energy, and resources. Marketers are faced with a dizzying array of choices about how to market their products and brands. Sports organizations as different as the Ultimate Fighting

Championships (UFC) and Ladies Professional Golf Association (LPGA) share the challenge of deciding how to spend their precious marketing dollars. As UFC President Dana White says, "Our biggest challenge is one of focus and resources."[11] LPGA Commissioner Gary Whan echoes the sentiment, saying his "biggest challenge on the job ... has been focus." "If you're not careful," Whan warns, "you can actually finish a 10-, 12-hour day and realize you spent zero amount of time focusing on the most important thing: that is our business partners, who get our players on the golf course."[12]

For the UFC, given that pay-per-view broadcasts generate the most revenue, how much time, energy, and money do you spend on other activities? Other types of TV shows, such as reality shows on Spike? Video games? A UFC magazine? UFC gyms? These are big questions and we haven't yet touched on strategic questions, such as who UFC would want to reach (i.e., their targets) and what they would want to say (i.e., brand positioning). At some point, all marketers need to decide how much money they are going to spend and where they are going to spend it. And they'll need to spend it well. Determining and allocating budgets is where the rubber meets the road, especially in the face of increasing demands for accountability for marketers, as will be discussed later in this chapter. As Beth Hirschhorn, EVP, Global Brand, Marketing and Communications at Metlife says, "the challenge is to spend smart. Anyone can spend more."[13]

Most sports marketers will tell you that sports marketing is more about marketing than it is about sports. But many of the skills required to be successful in sports are similar to those required for success in business. There is evidence, for example, that individuals who participated in sports in high school make more money later in life, even when controlling for ability.[14] There are many factors which could possibly explain higher wages for athletes: work ethic, time management, discipline, etc. Success in sports, as in business, requires setting clear goals and making a plan to attain them. Successful athletes are likely to have learned goal-setting skills which enhanced their performance. While not automatically transferred to business settings, goal-setting is an important skill for marketing success, so in this case there's a valuable lesson marketers can learn from sports.

Let's take an example of goal-setting from sports. Most athletes want to get stronger to improve performance. How would you recommend someone go about "getting stronger"? General goals like "get stronger" are not likely to facilitate changes in behavior. So you'd break it down into more specific goals, such as increasing number of repetitions at 225 lbs. on the bench press. If I can currently do eight reps at 225, what's a reasonable goal for my next workout? The end of the year? Where do I want to end up and how am I going to get there? The same principles apply to setting sports marketing goals. Most professional sports teams want to increase attendance. How would you go about increasing attendance? If current attendance is 12,000 fans per game, what's a good attendance goal for the next game? The next season? Again, where do I want to end up and how am I going to get there? Sports psychologist Daniel Gould reviewed related research and offers some guidelines for effective goal-setting:[15]

- **Set specific goals in measurable and behavioral terms.** If you want to get stronger, set specific goals, such as increasing the number of reps for 225 lbs. on the bench press. If a professional sports team wants to increase attendance, specific attendance goals must be set.

8

- **Set difficult but realistic goals.** The most effective goals are challenging but attainable. If an athlete currently bench presses 225 lbs. for eight repetitions, what would be a difficult but realistic goal for the next workout? For next year? When David Freeman bought the Nashville Predators of the National Hockey League (NHL), the team was averaging slightly under 14,000 attendees per game. Freeman set a goal of selling out the arena, which has a capacity of slightly more than 17,000.[16] Is that a realistic goal? Maybe long-term, but probably not for the next game.

- **Set short-range as well as long-range goals.** For Freeman and the Nashville Predators, increasing attendance by 20 percent to sell out their arena is attainable given an appropriate timeline and depending on the situation. You might not expect a huge increase over the course of a week or a month but over a season? Maybe. In order to reach long-term goals, such as selling out an arena or benching 225 for 15 reps, it's necessary to set more immediate short-term goals, such as getting one more rep on the bench in the next workout, or maybe selling a game on the schedule that's a potential sell-out date, maybe because of a popular opponent, and focusing resources and energy on that game.

- **Set process goals as opposed to outcome goals.** Ultimately, most sports marketers are interested in bottom-line results: increased ticket sales, and more sponsorship and advertising revenue. Setting outcome goals such as attendance, however, neglects to address the process by which outcomes are achieved. An account executive selling tickets, for example, setting an outcome goal of "selling more tickets" might distract the exec from the process involved, such as increasing the number of sales calls. Process goals help individuals, athletes, and businesspeople alike, to maintain focus on the tasks and procedures required for successful results.

- **Identify goal-achievement strategies.** Setting goals is meaningless if there is no plan to achieve them. As Jay Abraham, COO of NASCAR Media Group says, "The biggest challenge is making sure you have a clear strategic direction and that you focus your resources against those objectives, as opposed to chasing every opportunity that comes along just to make money."[17] A softball player trying to raise her batting average by 50 points might want to identify a goal achievement strategy of taking 50 extra practice swings after every practice. A professional sports team trying to increase attendance might identify a strategy of targeting more group sales and then hiring a full-time group sales executive and/or acquiring a list of 1000 additional community organizations for a direct marketing promotional offer.

- **Provide for goal evaluation.** With processes and strategies identified, sports marketers, like athletes, need feedback about how their performances relate to both short-term and long-term goals. Many sales offices, for example, post cumulative and weekly sales for each salesperson in a department, a practice which would be familiar to any athlete on a team with a depth chart for starters and reserves. Outcomes such as weekly and monthly sales, however, must be tied to the strategies and processes associated with those outcomes: increased sales calls, asking more open-ended questions, qualifying prospects more rigorously, etc.

Despite the importance of goal-setting in business environments, many executives don't spend a lot of time or energy planning and developing goals. If goals are not rigorously developed and vetted, they can have negative business consequences, such as a narrow focus, unethical behavior, a competitive environment, and reduced motivation, among other problems.[18] Poor goals lead to poor results. Since goals are used to guide behaviors, poor goals also lead to poor behaviors.

With respect to retail sales of licensed merchandise, some industry observers regard $100 million as the "hallmark" of a successful licensed merchandise program.[19] Why $100 million and not $80 million or $120 million? Likely because 100 is a nice, round number. "Double-digit" growth is a fairly common goal but the "digits" it refers to are our fingers. Suppose humans evolved with eight fingers instead of ten, like on *The Simpsons*. Would the hallmark of a successful licensing program be $80 million? Or what if baby Kaitlyn from reality show *Here Comes Honey Boo Boo*, who was born with an extra thumb and therefore has 11 digits, grows up to be a sports marketing executive? Would her goal be $110 million because of the extra digit? Would you want to plan your daily activities based on the fact that humans evolved with ten digits instead of eight or twelve?

Designing difficult but realistic goals requires a realistic analysis of the organization's current situation. Typically, a situation analysis, commonly called a SWOT analysis in marketing textbooks (strengths, weaknesses, opportunities, and threats), includes assessing an organization's capabilities and its external environment, such as competitors, technological developments, demographics, cultural trends, and the economy. Basically, everything. But conducting a situation analysis without tying it to goals fails to establish priorities that can guide action. In addition, analyzing what "is" ignores the more important question of what is possible.[20]

Sports marketers ask, where are we at now and where do we want to be? Sports marketers look to both understand and change reality. You can look at what competitors are doing, but just because they can't do it doesn't mean you can't. Conversely, because they *can* do it doesn't mean you *can*. After posting a 13.7 percent increase in commercial revenue at Manchester United, United's marketing manager said, "We don't know how far we can go. We certainly don't think we are reaching a limit," pointing to growth in fan-base numbers, engagement levels, and viewing figures.[21] Clubs such as Arsenal, Real Madrid, and Barcelona are reported to be attempting to replicate Manchester United's strategy, prompting greater investment from Man U in the area. What is required, then, is for sports marketers to take an integrated approach to developing goals, considering potential strategies and tactics, and environmental considerations. Inherently, goals are set in order to push current boundaries, establish new precedents, and create new realities.

Organizational goals

Goals must be developed specific to organizations and their environments, but there are certain goals which most business share. Most business executives want to increase the profitability of their business overall. Profitability can be broken down into:

- **Increase sales.** Few business executives are content for the businesses to remain stagnant; most want to grow their companies. For many sports marketers, increasing sales is the end goal and the ultimate measuring stick for performance.

- **Reduce costs.** Sports marketers spend a lot of time trying to figure out how to get more bang for the marketing dollars. Increasing sales is a common goal but not if it comes at the expense of profits.
- **Increase productivity.** Sports marketing managers spend a lot of time trying to figure out how they can create environments in which employees can maximize their performance.

When it comes to sports, it's not all just about the money. "Sport" is not only a business, it is a social institution and is deeply connected to other social institutions, such as religion, family, education, politics, and the media. I'm not sure that makes sport unique as I think music might share many characteristics, but it does introduce the idea that many sports goals can be social in nature and not just business. Sports marketers often engage in what's commonly called "social marketing," or using marketing principles and techniques for the benefit of society.

- **Sport as diplomacy.** The United States Department of State has a program of sports diplomacy, which attempts to improve relationships with other countries through sports.[22]
- **Sport for development.** The United Nations uses sports to promote development and peace. The UN attempts to harness sport's universal appeal in order to connect people and communities.[23]
- **Sport as an educational institution.** According to the President of the National Collegiate Athletic Association (NCAA), the organization which governs college sports in the US, the NCAA's mission is, "to be an integral part of higher education and to focus on the development of our student-athletes."

Marketing techniques are a tool, much like a hammer. You can use a hammer to build a house or to hit someone over the head. It just depends on what your objectives are. Marketing principles can be applied to a wide variety of sports settings in order to achieve a broad array of goals, whether they are profit-centered business goals or social goals. So sports marketers can use their skills to achieve goals ranging from selling more tickets to a game to working toward world peace.

Marketing goals

What do you want said about your company or property at the end of the Olympics?[24]

> . . . it's brand equity and sales.
>
> Chief Marketing Officer, Samsung Electronics America

> . . . at the end of the day it's outcomes. Did we change consumers' attitudes and behaviors towards our brand? And did we sell more of our product more profitably?
>
> Vice President, Worldwide Media, Sports and Entertainment
> Marketing, Coca-Cola

11

The ultimate goal for most sports businesses is to increase profits. As we've seen, though, focusing exclusively on outcome goals is an ineffective technique for setting goals. At the 2010 owners meeting, the NFL's commissioner set a goal of tripling the league's revenues over the course of an 18-year period, reaching $25 billion by 2027.[25] Certainly, it was an aggressive goal and as of 2013, the league is well off the pace to reach it. Setting aggressive goals can help improve performance but if you're focusing on financial outcomes, the question must be asked about processes required to achieve desired outcomes: How do you do it?

Ultimately, most businesses are concerned primarily with behaviors. Businesses want more people to spend money on their products and services and want people to spend more money. But people don't just *do*, they also *think* and *feel*. In order to promote behaviors, sports marketers attempt to influence people's thoughts and feelings. In academic terms, cognition (thinking) and affect (feeling) are closely related to conation (doing). Sports marketers want people to know about their brands, like their brands, and act upon that knowledge and feeling with behaviors, especially purchases.

The purchase funnel is a common conceptual tool used by sports marketers to break down marketing goals into different components. There are many versions of the funnel: try doing a Web search and see how many you find (see Table 1.3 for an example).[26] Most purchase funnels lay out the steps between awareness and purchase, though there is a lot of variation with respect to naming the different levels and/or stages. However, most funnels include some version of the following concepts:

- **Awareness.** Awareness is the extent to which a brand is recognized and/or remembered. Brand awareness is often an important goal for new brands and new products with existing brands. A new professional women's soccer league, for example, needs to first let people know they exist.
- **Knowledge.** Aflac is a well-known brand and most people who know the name also know that it's an insurance company. But Aflac sells "supplemental insurance," not the more familiar auto or health insurance that people buy. So, Aflac needs to explain what supplemental insurance is and why people might need it.
- **Liking.** Just because people know your brand doesn't mean they'll like it. Awareness and knowledge are cognitive outcomes but humans are not purely rational beings. Far from it. Emotions and feelings play an important and often dominant role in influencing human behaviors. More broadly, the goal might be described as developing favorable attitudes because it could include a broad range of feelings.

Table 1.3 The purchase funnel

Awareness
Knowledge
Liking
Purchase intent
Purchase

■ **Consideration.** The approach assumed by a purchase funnel is often referred to as a hierarchy of effects. The hierarchy of effects model has come under criticism because the stages don't follow an orderly sequence. Where the hierarchy is accurate, however, is in its importance because most businesses are ultimately concerned with the bottom line. One problem is that sales are influenced by numerous factors outside the purview of marketing, such as politics and the economy. In sports, most marketers don't have control over their products. Marketers can't control winning and losing. Therefore, purchase *intent* is often a goal for marketers because it is a more valid direct measure of their efforts.

■ **Purchase.** All roads lead to sales. For most sports marketers, cognition and affect are relevant to the extent that thoughts and feelings lead to behaviors. Purchase goals could include acquiring new customers, increasing retention rates for current customers, and/or increasing the volume of purchasing among current customers.

To summarize, it's about brand and sales, attitudes, and behaviors. "At the end of the day," it's about outcomes. Do people know who we are? Do they care? Will they buy our product? And how do we get there?

Table 1.4 Developing situation-based goals

Organization	Situation	Goal
Learfield Sports	Learfield Sports represents numerous college athletic departments in selling media rights. Digital technology allows colleges to create a lot of content inexpensively, but the challenge is driving traffic to the content. The first step is to generate awareness.	Generate awareness of digital content
Deutsche Eishockey Liga (DEL)	Germany's professional hockey league enjoys solid attendance. In order to increase awareness and knowledge of the league, it needs a bigger and better media presence.	Increase domestic media presence
Budweiser	Anheuser Busch developed Black Crown, a new upscale brand. Its challenge is to generate awareness for the new brand and knowledge about what the brand represents.	Introduce Black Crown
Formula 1 (F1)	F1 has lacked a consistent presence in the US. While most auto racing fans have heard of F1, they lack knowledge about the rules of the sanctioning body.	Educate US fans about rules
UFC	Known early on as "cage fighting" or a version of human cockfighting, mixed martial arts has been the subject of a lot of controversy. Ultimate Fighting Championships, therefore, set out to demystify the sport.	Combat misconceptions about the sport
EA Sports	EA Sports enjoys strong awareness and knowledge of their sports titles, but are challenged to get sports fans to want to experience their sports interactively.	Get sports fans to want to experience interactive sports

The funnel is often thought to depict a process, or stages, which individuals pass through on their way to becoming consumers. That's inaccurate, primarily because thinking, feeling, and doing are inter-related. People have stronger feelings for things they know about, and vice versa. They're more likely to buy things they like, and like things they buy. Sometimes people think, then feel, then do. Sometimes they feel, then do, then think. There's no set sequence or orderly process.

The funnel is, however, an effective visual representation of the number of individuals typically at each level. For example, just about everyone on the planet is aware of Coca-Cola. A smaller percentage like it. A yet smaller subset drink it. As such, a purchase funnel can be a useful conceptual tool in identifying opportunities and developing marketing goals.

Strategies

As we've seen, focusing solely on outcome goals is ineffective, so focusing on sales, even if that's the end goal, will not likely yield the desired results. Goals are achieved most effectively when they are broken down into their component parts and the processes needed to achieve goals successfully are identified. In marketing terms, processes are most often broken down into strategies and tactics. A strategy is an overall plan of action. A tactic is a specific action strategically planned to achieve a goal.

Broadly speaking in marketing, most strategy is guided by asking: Who do we want to reach? And, what do we want them to know about us? As a job ad for a marketing director for a MLS team states about responsibilities addressing strategy: "target audience, key message."[27] In traditional marketing terms, targeting is determining the audience you want to reach, and positioning is the key message. So, for example in Table 1.5, Coca-Cola wants to promote healthy, active living (key message) to moms (target audience).

Tactics

Tactics are the specific actions which are guided (hopefully) by strategies. In traditional marketing terms, tactics refer to the "4 p's" of marketing: product, price, place, and promotion.

Table 1.5 Sports marketing strategies

In their own words:

- ■ "Moms in the US are decision makers, and we want to continue to push the way our company promotes healthy, active living, and we want to continue to do that through moms."[1] Coca-Cola North America senior vice president of sports and entertainment marketing partnerships.

- ■ "We saw we had an Achilles heel – we weren't getting enough kids playing competitively at younger ages. If we really want to create lifetime tennis players ... and we also want to create future US Open champions, we need to get a bigger pool of kids playing tennis competitively."[2] Chief executive, USTA's community tennis division.

Notes
1 Mickle, T. (2012). Coke targets moms, along with teens, in Olympic marketing. www.sportsbusinessdaily. com/SB-Blogs/Olympics/London-Olympics/2012/07/cokeJuly16.aspx, accessed 1/9/2013.
2 Schultz, E.J. (2011). Tennis to market small-ball approach to find next pro star. *Advertising Age*, April 5. http://adage.com/article/news/tennis-market-small-ball-approach-find-pro-star/226799/, accessed 1/8/2013.

Table 1.6 Baltimore Ravens media summit[1]

Situation	Goal	Strategy	Tactic
Baltimore Ravens enjoy strong attendance but have gained control of local radio and TV rights for the first time	Create and sell media properties	"Take the game" to the New York media market	Invite local media execs to a team "summit" to showcase the club during the team's visit to New York to play the Giants

Note

1 Lefton, T. (2008). Ravens hosting NY summit to showcase team to media buyers. www.sportsbusinessdaily. com/Daily/Issues/2008/11/Issue-44/Sponsorships-Advertising-Marketing/Ravens-Hosting-NY-Summit-To-Showcase-Team-To-Media-Buyers.aspx, accessed 1/9/2013.

Tactics are the tools available to sports marketers to implement strategies. Sports marketers can create new or modify existing products; reduce or increase prices; invent new methods of distributing their products; and use advertising, public relations, sales promotions, and direct marketing to communicate their messages. With so many tools at sports marketers' disposal, however, the main challenge for many sports marketers is to find a way to bring all of these pieces together; to integrate tactics along a cogent strategy focused on achieving goals, which were developed based on an analysis of the situation.

The Baltimore Ravens, like most NFL teams, enjoy strong attendance (see Table 1.6). With consistent sell-outs at home, the growth in revenue from ticket sales is limited so opportunities for growth are likely to be found in media. Therefore, the team set a goal of creating and selling media properties associated with the team. Ravens executives developed a strategy of showcasing their offerings to New York-based "agency types and media buyers." In order to implement the strategy, Ravens executives created a "summit" featuring NFL Films narrator Steve Sabol, which attracted a crowd representing an estimated 34 agencies.

DATA AND MEASUREMENT

What industry execs are saying...

"Research helps us make choices"[28] Sports marketing executives should not rely on research to make decisions for them. Research does not provide definitive answers but can be helpful in assisting executives to make better decisions.

VP Media and Marketing Services, MillerCoors

According to the President and CEO of the Association of National Advertisers, an organization representing the biggest advertisers in the US, "Accountability reigns supreme in all aspects of marketing."[29] In the face of increased competition and decreased budgets, marketers are under pressure to demonstrate results. Does marketing work? That's a fair question, and one that marketers must answer. The increased pressure for accountability also increases the importance of making better decisions on the front end in planning marketing programs. Research doesn't make the decisions *for* sports marketers, but measurement and data can *help* sports marketers make choices. In fact, measurement and data can help to justify the very existence of a marketing department, the fundamental choice in marketing management. Research can help justify programs, plan and evaluate marketing efforts, and support sales.[30]

- **Program justification.** Suppose you are the owner of a professional sports team. Would you be better off financially investing money in marketing or players? Don't we need to just win some games? If we entertain this notion, we could follow it to its logical conclusion. Send everybody in the marketing department home, spend all available money on players, then print up the schedule and open the box office window. Or, suppose you manage a sports marketing program for a consumer goods company and a new chief marketing officer comes in who has a background in direct marketing and is skeptical about sports marketing programs. How could you prove that your programs are effective?
- **Evaluation and planning.** In order to decide how to best spend their marketing dollars, sports marketers need to understand what works and what doesn't. So, the evaluation of sports marketing programs helps to plan future strategies, forming a feedback loop from planning to implementation to evaluation.
- **Sales support.** Program justification is a form of internal sales, but sports businesses must also demonstrate their value to their customers. Sales support is probably the most common use for research and data in sports marketing because there is a direct connection between research and revenue.

Data types and sources

There are three main sources of data that sports marketers can draw upon to help them make better decisions: market intelligence, customer analytics, and market research.

Marketing intelligence

First, a lot of information about sports marketing is publicly available. Marketing intelligence consists of collecting and analyzing published information. Reading trade publications regularly and systematically helps to keep abreast of competitors' activities and identify ideas and practices which can be adapted to your own organization. A brief roster of important sources for marketing intelligence in sports marketing includes:

- *SportsBusiness Journal* (SBJ), *SportsBusiness Daily* (SBD), and *Sports Business Global Daily*. The SBD consists of aggregated news synopses and is published daily. The Global SBD is also published daily and covers international sports markets. The SBJ is published weekly and includes longer, in-depth analyses and editorials.
- *SportBusiness.* Similar to the SBJ but based in London and provides more international scope in sports business news.
- *IEG Sponsorship Report.* Not exclusive to sports but provides news and analysis for the sponsorship industry.

- *AdAge*, *Brandweek*, *MediaPost*. Advertising, marketing, and media trade publications for insight into marketing in general.
- Industry trade publications. Sport-related organizations that hope to sell their products and services to non-sports companies need to understand and track those industries. For example, a sports property wanting to sell a sponsorship to Coke or Pepsi might want to keep abreast of industry goings-on in the *Beverage Digest*.
- Web searches can be a good starting point.

Customer analytics

Technological advances have allowed sports organizations to collect and store huge amounts of data about their customers and members, especially with respect to purchase behaviors. These huge amounts of data present an opportunity to learn more about customers but also present a challenge in managing that customer data in a way that is useful. Businesses collect information about their customers from a variety of sources: personal information, purchases, communications history, and website visits. Customer analytics is the process of integrating and analyzing data to gain insights which can be leveraged into marketing strategies and tactics.

Market research

Sports marketers turn to market research when needed information cannot be found from published or internal sources. Market research is "the systematic design, collection, analysis, and reporting of data and findings relevant to a specific marketing situation facing an organization."[31] Technological advances, in particular user-friendly Web-based survey software, have allowed sports organizations to conduct market research on their own. That's a double-edged sword. For organizations that couldn't get data otherwise, it might be helpful, but poorly designed market research can lead to poor decisions. The sports industry is behind the curve as a *consumer* of market research, much less as a producer of it. The main goal here is to help sports marketers become better consumers of market research.

There's also been a blurring of lines between market intelligence, customer analytics, and market research. Some organizations, for example, use "surveys" to gather customer information which they later use for marketing purposes. One of the tenets of market research, however, is that participation is anonymous and confidential. Ethically, it's important to protect research participants, but anonymous participation also ensures honest responses and quality data. Think about the differences in responses among: (1) an "on-the-record" media interview, (2) an interview by a researcher who guarantees confidentiality but records the conversation, and (3) an interview by a researcher where the audio recorder is turned off. Which data would you trust?

The first step in market research is to identify the problem, or business issue. So, for example, a Major League Baseball (MLB) team analyzes their customer lists and finds that young adults aged 18–34 aren't attending games.[32] That's a problem. So, the team might set a goal that they want to increase attendance among 18–34-year-olds, but they don't know why young adults aren't coming to the ballpark. Should the team spend money marketing to young adults? If so, how could the team be successful? Or, should they skip that age cohort and just start marketing to eight-year-olds? What information would you need to decide? And how would you go about getting that information?

The business issue then needs to be formed into research questions with a focus on actionable results: "If we knew this, we could do that." The main research question here would be: Why aren't young adults coming to games? Is it too expensive? Do they have the money but other priorities? Do they not like baseball? Do they not like the team?

How would you answer these questions? Broadly speaking, data collection methods can be qualitative or quantitative. In qualitative research, the most common data collection techniques are personal interviews, especially focus groups. In a focus group, 8–10 participants are recruited based on specified characteristics. A moderator develops a discussion guide to prompt questions and potential follow-ups. The main strength of this approach is that questions are open-ended and interactive. Therefore, it's possible to gain more insight into participants' attitudes. The main weakness of qualitative research, and the most common mistake made from it, is that you can't generalize the results to a larger population. If six out of 10 young adult fans say they don't attend games because it's too expensive, you can't say with any level of confidence that 60 percent of all young adult fans feel that way.

In order to generalize to a larger population, quantitative research is required. The most common type of quantitative research is survey research, increasingly conducted online. The main strength of quantitative research is that, well, you can quantify results. So, you can identify market sizes and recommend marketing strategies and tactics. Quantitative and qualitative research methods can complement each other. In survey research, it's important to ask the right questions. Qualitative research conducted prior to quantitative research can help to generate survey items. Other times, quantitative research can yield interesting results but not explanations to which qualitative research can provide greater insight.

In order to generalize to a larger population, however, quantitative research must use a "scientific" sample. "Scientific" study is a term you might have seen in political polls. Suppose you're reading about your favorite team on a sports website and there's a "poll" at the end of the article. Could you generalize the results of that question to the public at large? Well, wouldn't people reading the article be more likely to be fans of the team? What are the characteristics of the people who visit the website? You'll likely see a disclaimer that results are not "scientific." What that means is that the results can be generalized to a larger population. In order to be "scientific," that is to be able to generalize from a smaller sample to a larger population, the sample must be a probability or random sample. There are different ways to accomplish this but the general principle is that each person in the population you want to study should have an equal chance of participating in the study. In interpreting research results, it's very important to look at the sample characteristics, especially sample sizes, and how that sample was collected.

Ultimately, the value of market research depends on the extent it can be used. If research is designed well, recommended actions should flow out of results: "we found this, so we should do that." Here, it helps to have market research suppliers who have specialized expertise in the field. I might be biased because I include myself in that number of specialized sports marketing researchers, and I recognize that big-name research suppliers can lend credibility to results to executives outside of sports. But market research suppliers specializing in sports and sponsorship research can provide valuable perspectives in the interpretation of results.

CASE: DETERMINING WHAT INFORMATION YOU NEED AND HOW TO GET IT

Writing an RFP

Sports marketers should use research to help them make decisions but, unless a sports marketing executive has formal research training, actually doing the research is better left to professional market researchers. Sports marketers still must be able to request proposals from market research suppliers. A clear statement of objectives for a research project is a helpful tool in requesting proposals from research suppliers. When writing a request for proposals (RFP), sports marketers must identify what they hope to get out of the proposed research so that market researchers can determine the appropriate methods (e.g., surveys, focus groups, etc.).

Research should be designed keeping in mind how sports marketers will use it. Former Ladies Professional Golf Association (LPGA) marketing executive Sharlene Sones suggests research be designed for the following uses to help sports properties increase their marketing effectiveness:

- "Measurement of our fan base growth;
- Quantifiable means of assessing the success of our strategic plan (i.e., brand perception and awareness);
- Identification of proper marketing messages and tools to communicate to the fan;
- Assistance in determining strategic direction;
- Identification of logical corporate sponsors; with information to provide in a sales pitch on the strengths of our brand and fan base."[33]

According to Sones, a research proposal should address: (1) "Ultimately, to grow this fan base we want to identify how to market to them – what motivates them to attend an ... event?" and (2) "obtain a means to help assess our effectiveness in meeting strategic brand objectives regarding the consumer." That is, the research proposal should help to guide marketing strategies and tactics, and also develop measures to identify levels of success in achieving goals. In addition, research can be used to identify a "barrier profile," as Sones put it. Research could be used to identify marketing segments which show promise of becoming fans but who have not yet made that step.

Having worked from the research side on numerous projects, I can say that many clients are tempted to ask for everything because, after all, they really do want to market to everyone. But you can't do everything, neither from a research nor a marketing perspective. Clients who are able to identify priorities and maintain focus are more likely to benefit from research findings.

With respect to the LPGA, for example, fan avidity for golf fans is strongly related to participation. People who play golf are more likely to be golf fans. Approximately 80 percent of golfers are men. Should the LPGA market to male golfers? Are there segments of male golfers who might show promise?

EXERCISE

Writing a research RFP. Keeping in mind the end uses of research, write RFPs for sports properties that include (1) background (i.e., a situation analysis), (2) research objectives, and (3) research uses. That is: (1) Where is the organization at now?, (2) What do we want to know about current/potential fans?; and, (3) How would you use the findings? Choose two properties:

- Property with which you think you are familiar. Many sports marketing executives have personal experiences in the sports in which they work. They're fans themselves. The problem is that personal experiences might not be generalizable to larger populations. Examine your assumptions about what you think you know about one of your favorite sports or teams. How could you find out if you really know what you think you know?
- Property with which you are unfamiliar. Choose a sport or property with which you are not familiar. What would you need to know in order to market it? Which questions are most important?

THREE MAIN TAKEAWAYS

1   Sports academics should be more practice-oriented, and sports marketing practitioners should be more rigorous in their approach.
2   Sports marketers develop strategies and implement tactics to achieve marketing goals.
3   Data and measurement can be helpful in developing strategies and tactics, justifying sports marketing programs, and supporting sales efforts.

RECOMMENDED READING

Bednar, R. (2014). Level of accountability separates sports marketing by objectives. *Street & Smith's SportsBusiness Journal*, p. 15. www.sportsbusinessdaily.com/Journal/Issues/2014/04/28/ Opinion/From-the-Field-of-Marketing.aspx?hl=bednar&sc=0, accessed 5/20/2014. This article is a clear and succinct summary of how data can contribute to the effectiveness of "sports marketing by objectives." Bank of America was a long-time client of mine and I had the privilege of working with Ray Bednar on research studies which measured how Bank of America sponsorships contributed to corporate objectives. The approach Ray outlines in this article reflects a lot of what I had the good fortune to learn from the experience.

NOTES

1 Heylar, J. (2006). Failing effort: Are universities' sports-management programs a ticket to a great job? Not likely. *Wall Street Journal*, September 16: R5.
2 I was at that meeting. Dolich really did "let 'em have it" as the WSJ says.
3 Reibstein, D., Day, G., and Wind, J. (2009). Guest editorial: Is marketing academia losing its way? *Journal of Marketing*, 73(July): 1–3.
4 Mullin, B., Hardy, S., and Sutton, W. (2007). *Sport Marketing*. Champaign, IL: Human Kinetics.
5 Tapp, A. (2005). Why practitioners don't read our articles and what we should do about it. *The Marketing Review*, 5: 3–12.
6 Varadarajan, P. (2003). Musings on relevance and rigor of scholarly research in marketing. *Journal of the Academy of Marketing Science*, 31(4): 368–376.
7 12th Annual IEG/Performance Research Sponsorship Decision-Makers Survey. www.performanceresearch.com/2012-IEG-Study.pdf, accessed 1/7/2013.
8 Spoelstra, J. (1997). *Ice to the Eskimos*. New York: HarperBusiness.
9 O'Neil, S. and Kelly, M. (2012). Delivering exceptional experiences creates extraordinary fans. www.sportsbusinessdaily.com/Journal/Issues/2012/11/12/Opinion/From-the-Field-of-Fan-Satisfaction.aspx., accessed 9/10/2014.
10 Nagel, M. and Southall, R. (2011). *Introduction to Sport Management: Theory and Practice*. Dubuque, IA: Kendall Hunt, p. 11.
11 Lefton, T. (2010). White discusses UFC's global ambitions. www.sportsbusinessdaily.com/Journal/Issues/2010/06/20100614/SBJ-In-Depth/White-Discusses-Ufcs-Global-Ambitions.aspx, accessed 1/9/2013.
12 (2010). Michael Whan confident in LPGA's future despite challenges. www.sportsbusinessdaily.com/Daily/Issues/2010/02/Issue-109/Leagues-Governing-Bodies/Michael-Whan-Confident-In-Lpgas-Future-Despite-Challenges.aspx?hl=Golf&sc=0, accessed 1/9/2013.
13 (2010). Game changers: Beth Hirschhorn. http://m.sportsbusinessdaily.com/Journal/Issues/2012/10/08/Game-Changers/Beth-Hirschhorn.aspx, accessed 1/9/2013.
14 Barron, J., Ewing, B., and Waddell, G. (2000). The effects of high school athletic participation on education and labor market outcomes. *The Review of Economics and Statistics*, 82(3): 409–421.
15 Gould, D. (1998). Goal setting for peak performance. In Williams, J. (Ed.), *Applied Sport Psychology*. Mountain View, CA: Mayfield, pp. 182–192.
16 Mickle, T. (2007). He's bought the team; now Freeman is ready to sell seats. www.sportsbusinessdaily.com/Journal/Issues/2007/12/20071217/This-Weeks-News/Hes-Bought-The-Team-Now-Freeman-Is-Ready-To-Sell-Seats.aspx, accessed 1/9/2013.
17 Smith, M. (2011). PGA Tour Entertainment stepping up its game. www.sportsbusinessdaily.com/Journal/Issues/2011/05/30/Leagues-and-Governing-Bodies/PGA-Tour.aspx, accessed 1/9/2013.
18 Ordonez, L., Schweitzer, M. E., Galinsky, A., and Bazerman, M. (2009). Goals gone wild: How goals systematically harm individuals and organizations. *Academy of Management Perspectives*, 23(1): 6–16.
19 Lefton, T. (2012). USOC targets $100M in retail sales. http://m.sportsbusinessdaily.com/Journal/Issues/2012/07/23/Olympics/USOC-licensing.aspx, accessed 1/9/2013.
20 See Hill, T. and Westbrook, R. (1997). SWOT analysis: It's time for a product recall. *Long Range Planning*, 30(1): 46–52. The authors conduct a study about the use of SWOT analyses and find that a minority of organizations used them and among organizations which did, a small percentage used any of the results in practice.
21 Stone, S. (2013). Manchester United defend sponsorship strategy. *The Independent*, January 24. www.independent.co.uk/sport/football/premier-league/manchester-united-defend-sponsorship-strategy-8465182.html#, accessed 1/25/13.
22 Sports diplomacy. http://eca.state.gov/programs-initiatives/sports-diplomacy, accessed 1/25/2013.
23 What is sport and development? www.sportanddev.org/en/learnmore/what_is_sport_and_development/, accessed 1/25/2013.
24 (2012). 75 days out, Olympic executives talk London plans. www.sportsbusinessdaily.com/Journal/Issues/2012/05/14/Olympics/Olympic-roundtable.aspx, accessed 1/25/2013.
25 Kaplan, D. (2013). Can the NFL get to $25 billion? www.sportsbusinessdaily.com/Journal/Issues/2013/01/28/In-Depth/NFL-revenue.aspx?hl=nfl&sc=0, accessed 1/31/2013.
26 For a discussion about the history of the purchase funnel, see Barry, T. (1987). The development of the hierarchy of effects: An historical perspective. *Current Issues and Research in Advertising*, 10: 251–295.

27 Major League Soccer Job Board. http://mls.teamworkonline.com/teamwork/r.cfm?i=47233, accessed 8/9/2012.

28 Spanberg, E. (2012). Research explores the passions of fans. www.sportsbusinessdaily.com/Journal/Issues/2012/01/02/In-Depth/Fan-passion.aspx?hl=research&sc=0, accessed 2/4/2013.

29 Marketers want sponsorship and event metrics but lack necessary capabilities, ANA/IEG survey shows. www.ana.net/conten/show/id/582, accessed 1/23/2012.

30 DeGaris, L. (2008). Sport marketing consulting strategies and tactics: Bridging the academy and the practice. *Choregia: Sport Management International Journal*, 4(2): 11–20.

31 Kotler, P. and Armstrong, G. (2013). *Principles of Marketing*. Upper Saddle River, NJ: Pearson.

32 This is based on a research study I conducted for the Cleveland Indians while working for the Bonham Group in Denver.

33 Sones, Sharlene. Personal communication.

Chapter 2

Sports markets

CHAPTER OUTLINE

1 Chief revenue officer

2 Sources of revenue

3 Revenues by region

4 Consumer markets by sport

5 Business markets

6 Markets for sports properties

CHIEF REVENUE OFFICER

Chief Revenue Officer Job Description

The official organization representing retired professional basketball players from the NBA, ABA and Harlem Globetrotters for the past 20 years, seeks applications for the position of Chief Revenue Officer. *Candidates should possess a proven track record of revenue generation through sponsorships, events, licensing, fundraising and/or other monetizing opportunities....* Successful candidates must demonstrate an aggressive ability to sell/market, be a "doer" and be creative in identifying and landing revenue opportunities in support of member benefits/services.[1] (emphasis added)

The traditional "CMO" (chief marketing officer) is increasingly morphing into a "CRO" role (chief revenue officer). This job ad, CRO for the retired professional basketball players association, identifies the major areas of revenue generation in sports, except for media: sponsorships, events, licensing, fundraising, and "other." The "other" category is an area that is receiving special attention because, as the description indicates, it is important to be "creative" in identifying and landing new business.

During 2012, at least four NBA franchises created the position of chief revenue officer (CRO), joining six other NBA teams with similar positions in a departure from the traditional chief marketing officer (CMO) position. NBA teams are not alone. During the past decade many sports organizations have made the switch from CMO to CRO.

What is behind the switch from CMO to CRO? The shift is part of a broader business trend and not limited to sports. The change reflects some organizational changes in centralizing departments, such as ticket sales, luxury suite sales, and sponsorships. In particular, sales and marketing departments have tended to operate independently in their own "silos." The shift also represents a change in thinking with a greater emphasis on results and accountability, meaning rigorous measures of success.[2]

The CRO position also represents a greater recognition of the role of sales departments in sports organizations. "Sell or die" is a common mantra in the sports industry. Yet, it has taken a long time for sales executives to gain recognition and respect for a seat in the C-suite. The issue is not just that sales and marketing departments have operated independently, it is also that sales departments have been marginalized in many organizations.

The CRO can address some typical problems created by the sales and marketing divide.[3]

- *"Offerings and pricing developed without sales force input."* Salespeople are on the front lines of communication with clients. As such, they gain valuable feedback from prospects about benefits and pricing.
- *"Market and competitive intelligence collected my marketing that is not used by the sales force or top management."* As marketers can benefit from salespeople's input, so too can salespeople benefit from the marketing analysis.

Both sales and marketing units benefit from drawing upon the collective expertise and experience.

Beyond communication, sharing data and best practices between sales and marketing units highlights the growing emphasis on data and analytics in CRO positions. As a "C-level" executive, the CRO must possess the business acumen to gain buy-in for budgets and to demonstrate success.

CRO – American Airlines Center – Job Description

Responsible to provide leadership and direction in assessing and developing long-term revenue strategies, along with the creation and management of organizational structures to support those strategies, *based upon analytics, empirical data, and input from our team partners.*[4] (emphasis added)

Sources of revenue are important in determining priorities for sports organizations. Sports marketers need to understand where the money is coming from now, and where it might come from in the future.

Lastly, the CRO demonstrates an emphasis on results rather than process. The CRO must balance the long-term planning usually done in marketing departments with the short-term emphasis on monthly results. At the end of the day, to use a somewhat tired but still common-place marketing phrase, it is all about revenue. With more competition for limited resources, the pressure for revenue continues to grow. Even non-profit sports organizations must keep an eye toward revenue generation (but not profits) to ensure that their efforts are sustainable.

SOURCES OF REVENUE

While there are many sources of revenue for sports organizations, the major categories of revenue for the sports industry are:

Gate revenue. Gate revenue consists of ticket sales for live events, including premium seating such as luxury suites. Globally, gate revenue continues to constitute the highest percentage of revenue (32.6 percent, see Figure 2.1), confirming that at its core the sports industry is a live events business. In addition, live event attendance correlates strongly with other sports fan behaviors, such as media usage.

Growth opportunities for gate revenue are limited, however, because increases in ticket sales inventory require large investments in new or renovated facilities, which is both expensive and time-consuming. Not counting the effect of major events (e.g., Olympics and World Cup), PricewaterhouseCoopers (PWC) projected only a 2.5 percent annual increase in global gate revenues for the period 2011–2015, the lowest rate of change among the top four revenue categories.[5]

Sponsorships. Sponsors pay sports properties a fee in order to exploit the commercial potential of the property. Sponsorship is the second highest category of revenue, contributing

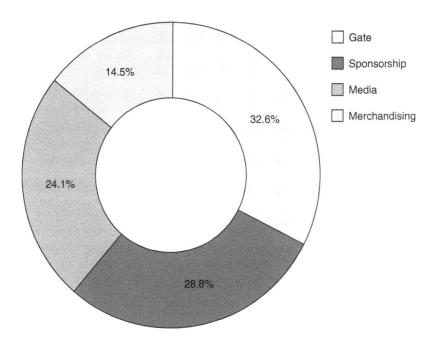

Figure 2.1 Global revenues by source (source: *Changing the Game: Outlook for the Global Sports Market to 2015,* PricewaterhouseCoopers).

28.8 percent of global sports revenue. PWC regards sponsorship as a "key engine" revenue growth, projecting a growth rate of 5.3 percent from 2011 to 2015. Many sports organizations look to sponsorship because there is still a huge upside for revenue while start-up costs are minimal, especially with the growth of digital technology. Contrary to the investments in infrastructure required to increase gate revenue, sponsorship inventory readily exists in the form of sports properties' trademarks and logos, with the main investment being one of creativity, not money.

While the total amount of sponsorship revenue is projected to increase at a strong rate, individual sports properties face an increasingly competitive environment. Many sports organizations are aware of sponsorship's growth potential and create more inventory, adding to an already crowded marketplace.

Media rights. Television, radio, and Internet broadcasters pay media rights fees for the right to broadcast sports events and related programming. Media rights accounts for 24.1 percent of the global sports market and is projected to continue to increase at a 3.8 percent annual rate until 2015. Many observers have been calling for a sports media rights "bubble" to burst for decades, but it has yet to happen.[6] To the contrary, the growing influence of digital media has placed a premium on live events. Television networks can use sports programming to drive viewers, especially male viewers, to other programming, and distributors can look to "must-have" live sports events to maintain the pay-for-television model.

Merchandising. Merchandising revenue is comprised of the sale of products licensed with sports logos and/or trademarks. Among the four main revenue sources, merchandising comprises the smallest contribution, at only 14.5 percent and the bulk of that coming from North America, which accounts for 71 percent of the total, according to PWC. PWC projects that merchandising revenue will grow at a 2.6 percent annual pace from 2011 to 2015.

With the growth of Internet-based retail and the expansion of sports media to international markets, merchandising and licensing create value for sports organizations beyond revenue. Merchandising and licensing, combined with expanded media distribution especially through digital channels, helps sports organizations to develop fan bases, which can then be monetized more effectively through sponsorship.

While gate revenue, sponsorships, media rights, and merchandising comprise the bulk of sports revenue, there are many other sources that are small when compared to the top four, but substantial nonetheless.

- *Fundraising*. Many sports organizations do not seek profits, but are primarily interested in sports development for beneficial social reasons, not revenue. For those organizations, philanthropy can be the primary source of revenue. In contrast to sponsorship, which is a commercial relationship, philanthropic donors do not expect a financial return on their investment. While many sales and marketing principles still apply to successful philanthropic fundraising, the benefits sought by donors are very different. Sports philanthropy can attract big dollars by tapping into the tremendously strong passion people have for sports.
- *Concessions*. Sports facility concessions have grown well beyond the traditional warm beer and cold hot dog. While a small source of revenue when compared to ticket sales,

concessions are an important part of the game experience and a reliable stream of revenue that has benefited from an increasingly professionalized approach.

- *Other.* The "other" category is becoming increasingly important to sports organizations that are facing stagnant revenue gains in an increasingly competitive environment. There is a constant need for sports marketers to "create new inventory" (find something new to sell) or to "monetize" existing inventory (make money from something you are already doing).

REVENUES BY REGION

Analyzing the sources of revenue among the regions of the globe helps sports marketers identify marketing opportunities and provides a relative basis for evaluating markets. For sports organizations that have been around for a long time, most domestic markets are "mature," meaning there is not a lot of growth opportunity. Companies across industry categories look to international markets for growth, and the sports industry is no different.

North America. North America is the largest region by revenue, comprising 41 percent of all global revenues in 2010, according to PWC. North America's influence is especially impressive given the comparatively small population relative to other regions, so sports revenue per capita is especially impressive. Gate revenues continue to comprise the highest percentage of revenue (31.4 percent, see Figure 2.1) but sponsorship is the fastest growing sector (6.1 percent).

In general, the sources of revenue are fairly evenly distributed in North America, with sports organizations not overly reliant on any one source of revenue in particular. Where the North American market really distinguishes itself from other regions, however, is in its ability to generate merchandising revenue relative to other regions. Nearly three-quarters

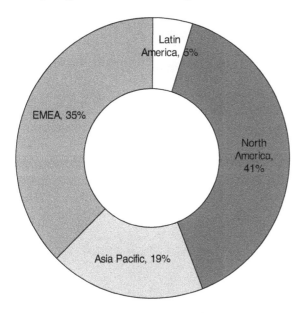

Figure 2.2 Global sports revenues by region (source: *Changing the Game: Outlook for the Global Sports Market to 2015,* PricewaterhouseCoopers).

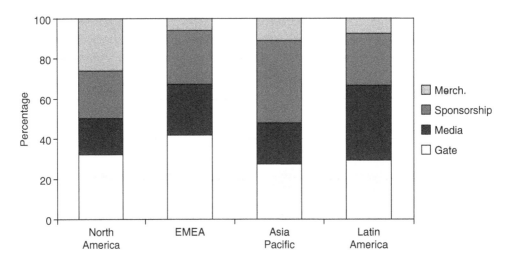

Figure 2.3 Revenue distribution by region (source: *Changing the Game: Outlook for the Global Sports Market to 2015,* PricewaterhouseCoopers).

(71 percent) of global merchandising revenues are in North America, providing other regions with both a goal and a template for marketing strategies.

EMEA. Europe, the Middle East, and Africa comprise the second largest region, according to PWC, with 35.3 percent of global revenue. EMEA is mostly a "mature" market with low growth rates expected, partly attributable to the region's reliance on gate revenue (38.6 percent) as its major source of revenue. With the EMEA, the Middle East and North Africa region is anticipated to grow more rapidly (6.8 percent).

Asia Pacific. Asia Pacific, buoyed by the tremendously large population, is currently the third largest region, comprising 19 percent of global revenues. Sponsorship comprises nearly half (43.2 percent) of sports revenues in the region, with sponsorship and media rights expected to continue to grow at a healthy pace (4.4 percent).

Unlike the impressive economic growth rates of many Asian countries, sports revenue is expected to grow at a relatively modest 3.9 percent, pointing out that developing sports markets is a long-term play requiring substantial investments in infrastructure. Sponsorship and media markets have developed rapidly in the region, but participation and live attendance require greater investments and take a longer time to see a return.

Latin America. Latin America is the smallest global region, accounting for only 4.9 percent of global sports revenue, though the region has gained a lot of attention with the awarding of both the 2016 Summer Olympic Games and the 2014 World Cup to Brazil. Media rights are the greatest source of revenue (38.3 percent).

CONSUMER MARKETS BY SPORT

Which sport has the most fans? That depends on how you measure "fans."

Ultimately, most sports marketers are primarily interested in a range of behaviors: buy tickets, consume media, and buy merchandise. Add to the equation that sports fan bases are complex: most individuals like more than one sport, and a simple, precise measurement becomes elusive.

One of the most common techniques to estimate fan-base size is to measure "interest" in specific sports because sports "interest" correlates strongly with the desired behaviors and is a much more parsimonious way to measure fan avidity. But that begs the question: How "interested" do you have to be in order to be a "fan"? For most syndicated research studies in sports, people must be "very," "somewhat," or "a little interested" to be considered fans, with "avid" fans defined as those who are "very interested."

Based on interest levels, sports interests in the US are dominated by football, baseball, and basketball. American sports interests, however, tend to be varied and extensive (see Table 2.1). Of course, "interest" does not necessarily translate into behaviors. According to Scarborough's definition of a "fan," for example, the NFL has about 25 percent more fans than MLB, but television ratings for the NFL, a key driver of revenue for the league, are much more than 25 percent higher than MLB television ratings.

In addition, on average, according to Rich Luker, the founder of the ESPN Sports Poll, Americans follow nine different sports as a fan.[7] So, "NBA fans" are highly likely to also follow the NFL, NCAA basketball, and NCAA football, with sizable percentages of NBA fans also following a wide range of other sports. Even "niche" sports can have substantial audiences, even if they are a small percentage of the overall population. The 3 percent of Americans interested in pro lacrosse constitute a potential audience of millions, though clearly not all fans "interested" in a sport will attend in person, follow in the media, or purchase merchandise.

Internationally, sports interest is more uniform. Soccer, "football" in most of the world, is the clear number one. According to a study conducted by SPORT+MARKT from 2001, more than two billion people worldwide are "interested" in soccer. As top leagues, domestic soccer leagues in England (Barclays Premier League) and Spain (La Liga) have gained international appeal because of the sport's widespread popularity. Outside of the World Cup and Summer Olympic Games, the UEFA Champions League European club championship in soccer attracts the greatest international interest.[8]

Other sports with notable international followings include: the NBA, primarily because of its popularity in the US and China; cricket, because of its position as the number one sport in India; and Formula 1 auto racing, which spans Europe and Asia.

In discussing international interest, of course two events stand out: the World Cup and the Summer Olympic Games. While both events are huge and can make a claim to be the biggest event worldwide based on different measures, the defining difference between the two is interest in the North American market, and the US in particular. As we have seen, North America accounts for almost half of all global revenues, in far greater proportion than the population. The Summer Olympic Games are tremendously popular in the US, exceeded only by the NFL, whereas interest in international soccer in the US is comparatively modest, though it is growing steadily.

Although soccer enjoys widespread international popularity (see Table 2.2), there are some notable exceptions in addition to the US. Australia boasts professional leagues for four different codes of football: Australian rules, rugby league, rugby union, and soccer. In South Asia (India, Pakistan, and Sri Lanka), with its massive 1 billion plus population, cricket reigns supreme, thereby putting up some impressive fan-base numbers.

Table 2.1 Sports interest in the US

Sports leagues	Total % (very, somewhat, or a little interested)
National Football League	62
Olympics	58
Major League Baseball	49
College Football	45
National Basketball Association	35
Gymnastics	34
Figure Skating	34
College Basketball	33
High School Sports	28
PGA Tour (men's golf)	27
NASCAR	25
National Hockey League	23
Horse Racing	20
College Baseball	19
Extreme/Action Sports	19
Pro Boxing	19
Women's Tennis	18
Men's Tennis	18
Major League Soccer	16
Ultimate Fighting Championship	16
Pro Bull Riding	15
Minor League Baseball	15
IndyCar Series	14
Pro Rodeo	13
NHRA Drag Racing	12
Monster Trucks	12
LPGA (women's golf)	12
European Soccer	12
Supercross/Motocross	12
WNBA	11
WWE (pro wrestling)	11
Formula 1 Racing	11
Arena/Indoor Football	11
AVP (pro beach volleyball)	9
College Hockey	9
Mexican Soccer	9
AMA Pro Racing (motorcycle/ATV)	8
Grand-Am Road Racing	8
Minor League Hockey	6
NBA Development League	5
Pro Lacrosse	3

Source: Scarborough Sports Marketing, 2011. Scarborough USA+ Study, Release 1 2011 (current six months).

Even within markets where soccer is the overwhelming number one choice, there are important variations among markets. In Germany, athletics is the second most preferred TV sport; in France, tennis; in Italy, Formula 1; and in Spain, basketball.[9] In addition, there are numerous "niche" sports which are not well-known but still enjoy sizable, loyal followings. Do an Internet search for Senegalese wrestling and take a look at how a traditional folk wrestling match can fill a soccer stadium with enthusiastic fans.

Table 2.2 Worldwide interest in soccer

Region	% interested/Number of fans
North America and Caribbean	25%/61 million
UK	49%/21 million
Europe (excluding UK)	50%/242 million
China	49%/331 million
India	49%/202 million
Central and South America	61%/237 million
Africa and Middle East	72%/531 million
Asia and Oceania (excluding China and India)	35%/453 million

Source: SPORT+MARKT Sponsoring 21+ May 2011.

While sports interest levels provide an idea of current and potential fans, the most meaningful measures of fan avidity for sports marketers are tied to revenue. With respect to revenue, not all fans are equal; some are more important than others. In particular, sports marketers are interested in the following fan behaviors:

- **Attendance.** More precisely, sports marketers are interested in long-term revenue from ticket sales. How many games do you attend? How long have you been coming to games? How much do you spend on tickets? In marketing terms, sports marketers are interested in the lifetime customer value.
- **Media usage.** Television rights fees are based on a network's ability to acquire subscription fees by gaining carriage by TV distributors, and selling advertising. Subscription fees are based on the perception of "must-have" programming, and advertising revenue is largely based on the number of viewers. Therefore, media usage by fans translates into revenue for sports organizations.
- **Merchandise purchase.** Purchasing licensed merchandise is an indication of fan involvement as well as a vital source of revenue. Wearing your team's colors is an indication of loyalty, and buying licensed merchandise contributes to the bottom line.

Fan behaviors tend to be related and incremental. Fans who attend live events watch more games on television and spend more money on licensed merchandise. Though the distribution varies by sport and behavior, a small percentage of fans are usually responsible for a larger percentage of fan behaviors. This trend holds across the major fan behaviors: a small percentage of sports media users comprise a high percentage of overall usage; a small percentage of attendees comprise a disproportionately high percentage of total attendance; and a small percentage of merchandise buyers comprise a high percentage of overall merchandise purchases. These "super" fans are a small but important subset of "avid fans" who are "very interested" in sports.

BUSINESS MARKETS

The rapid growth of the sports industry during recent decades has been fueled by the influx of corporate dollars into sports. Rapidly growing sponsorship rights fees, escalating media rights fees, and a rapid growth in corporate purchases of premium seating comprise the majority of sports revenues, so one could argue that the sports industry is in fact a business-to-business (B2B) industry. Most well-known consumer brands regardless of industry category are primarily business-to-business companies. Take Coke and Pepsi, two mega-brands for consumers. But consumers do not ever buy a can or bottle directly from either of those companies. Rather, Coke and Pepsi's "customers" are retailers and distributors.

The sports industry is no different with respect to the importance of business markets. Compared to consumer markets, business markets are smaller in number but much bigger in revenue. One individual consumer will not move the needle on Coke or Pepsi's bottom line, no matter how many soft drinks he or she consumes. A deal with Wal-Mart or another big retailer, however, could. Similarly, an individual fan will buy tickets to events but probably not a luxury suite, much less a sponsorship.

Nike, for example, is one of the world's biggest consumer brands, but the vast majority of the company's sales come from businesses, not directly from consumers. The vast majority (82 percent, see Figure 2.4) of Nike's revenues come from sales to wholesale customers. So while Nike might be a consumer brand, it is a business-to-business company.

Sports consumer markets still provide the foundation for sports business markets: companies buy into sports to gain access to sports fans. The *access* to sports fans, however, creates value because sports fans spend more money on "everything else" than they do on

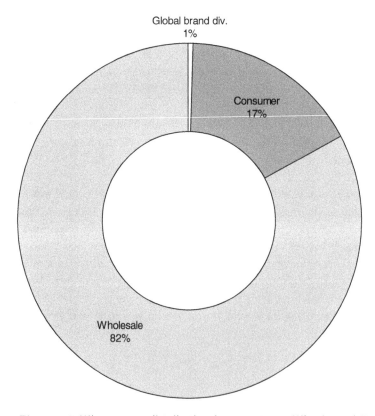

Figure 2.4 Nike revenue distribution (source: 2012 Nike Annual Report).

sports: television, cell phone, food, clothing, car, credit card, loans, etc. Total spending by sports fans is much greater than total spending on sports, and companies have found sports to be an effective vehicle in reaching fans.

Sports marketers must be sensitive to the needs of both consumer and business markets. Sports need to cater to consumers (fans) in order to build audiences, but also "monetize" those fan relationships by delivering access to business markets. It can be a difficult balance. One sports marketing veteran warns about the dangers of "catering to the corporate dollar":

> Take a look around the next time you are at a professional sports venue. Who has all the good seats, luxury suites, or club seats? It sure isn't the guy who has on the team jersey, cap, and crazy boxer shorts. It is the big shot CEO sitting with the corporate clients, eating shrimp cocktail and wining and dining the company's customers.[10]

What's the solution?

> More teams simply need to find a way to cater to both [corporations and fans]. The corporate dollar is important because their spending budgets are obviously a great deal higher than the individual's budget. However, teams need to build their fan bases with the average fan in mind – someone who will have an emotional attachment to the sport and team.[11]

For the sponsorship market, the importance of corporate dollars is clear. Sponsors are corporations seeking to gain access to sports fans in order to market their products and services. For media markets, the growing influence of sports programming on cable television and other "pay-TV" platforms has yielded a direct stream of revenue from consumers in addition to advertising revenue, though admittedly media rights "customers" are strictly business markets.

For gate revenue, the influence of corporate dollars is difficult to calculate precisely. According to informal estimates, about 60 percent of season ticket holders for "major league sports" in North America are corporate accounts. Revenue, however, is likely much higher as most premium seating and nearly all luxury suite holders are corporate accounts. Prestige Ticketing, a joint venture between Sodexo and the Mike Burton Group, bought the rights to set up hospitality at six venues for the London Olympics, with packages ranging in price from $795 to $12,000. According to Prestige Ticketing's CEO, 80 percent of the total $150 million revenue in tickets were bought by corporations, though no revenue percentage for corporate accounts was provided.[12]

In formulating their business objectives, sports marketers must be mindful of the distribution of revenue in their business model. In 2013, Forbes named Spanish soccer giant Real Madrid as the world's most valuable sports team. According to Deloitte's *Football Money League* report, Real Madrid enjoys a "balanced" revenue model (Figure 2.5) among matchday (25 percent of total revenue in 2010–2011), broadcast rights (39 percent), and "commercial" (combined sponsorship and merchandising: 36 percent).[13] Deloitte authors attribute Real Madrid's consistency as one of European soccer's top revenue producers to its balance

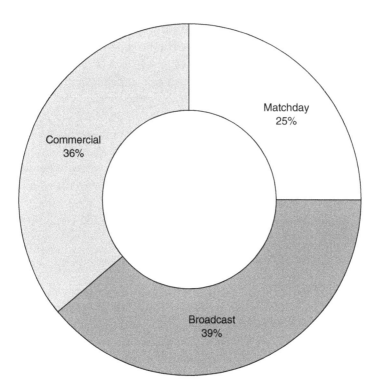

Figure 2.5 Real Madrid revenue model (source: *Deloitte Football Money League*).

of revenue sources, in particular because the club's current large share of broadcasting revenue is receiving increasing scrutiny by other Spanish clubs.

The balance of revenue for sports organizations is important because it can help set priorities and develop objectives. Real Madrid, for example, plans to expand and renovate its home stadium, the "Bernabeu," in order to accommodate more corporate hospitality on game day and increase gate revenue. According to Deloitte, Real Madrid also possesses more opportunities to monetize its huge fan base through commercial avenues. So, while balance of revenue is important, so too is the source of that revenue.

Understanding your customers is a basic starting point for all marketers. Knowing who your customers are is even more basic. Many sports organizations receive the bulk of their revenue from business sources but still think of themselves largely as consumer-based organizations (see Table 2.3). Professional golf, for example, receives almost all of its revenue from corporate sources through sponsorship or media rights. Even gate revenue for professional golf is often a majority of corporate hospitality given the limited inventory of event tickets. For large auto racing teams, winnings from races often make up about 10 percent of total revenues. The reliance on sponsorship for most auto racing teams makes week-to-week performance less important from a revenue standpoint. It also puts racing teams in the position of serving primarily as a marketing services company rather than being in the business of auto racing.

On the other end of the spectrum, boxing, martial arts, and professional wrestling all receive the vast majority of their revenues directly from consumers, particularly in

Table 2.3 Where does the money come from?

Estimated sources of revenue

					Consumer business
Boxing	Major League Soccer	MLB/NHL NBA NFL			Golf
UFC	Minor league baseball/ice hockey				Auto racing teams
Pro wrestling					

pay-per-view revenue. Other sports are more balanced in their distribution of revenue between consumer and business markets. The NFL's huge television contract and limited inventory of games attract more corporate dollars, whereas Major League Baseball's comparatively modest television contract and huge inventory of games slants revenue more towards consumers.

MARKETS FOR SPORTS PROPERTIES

Q. How do you make a small fortune?
A. *Start with a big fortune and buy a sports team.*

One of the main distinguishing aspects of sports as an industry is the composition of its ownership. While it is true that sports enjoys "consumers" who are more passionate about their brands than other industries – music and entertainment rival sports for passion – owners of professional sports teams are unique.

First, owners of professional sports teams almost always make their money in different industries and then buy a sports team. Second, from a purely financial perspective, owning a sports team is a shaky proposition at best. Here, business and consumer markets converge. If owning a sports does not make good business sense, why do good businessmen (and it is almost always men) spend big bucks to buy teams? Mostly, because they love the sport.

Most sports teams lose money. While working as a marketing consultant for a minor league sports organization in North America, an executive from the league commented about an owner who was complaining about losses, "How can you buy a sports team and not expect to lose money?" Former AOL executive and owner of the NHL's Washington Capitals Ted Leonsis calls owning a sports team a "labor of love."

During the NBA lockout in 2011, the league argued that 22 of 30 NBA teams lost money. While many observers felt that the league was posturing for the purposes of negotiating a more favorable collective bargaining agreement, other losses are better documented. According to UEFA's club licensing benchmark report, a rigorous financial analysis of European soccer clubs, total losses amounted to $2.28 billion in 2011.

Sports teams are not terrible investments, however. While most teams incur significant operating losses, most owners can recoup their losses when they sell as the market for sports teams has continued to be robust. According to JPMorgan's Sports Finance Group, the compound annual growth rate for the value of sports franchises in the "big four" North

35

American leagues (NFL, MLB, NBA, and NHL) were all in double digits, ranging from 11 percent for the NHL to 34 percent to the NFL.[14]

How do teams function in between incurring substantial operating losses and selling the team for a healthy profit? The owners write checks. Big checks. In 2011, 76 percent of the $2.28 billion in losses were "injected" into the balance sheets of European clubs. The NHL's Chicago Blackhawks have won two Stanley Cups in four years. And they lose money. *Crain's* estimates the Blackhawks lose between $10 million and $20 million per season.[15] The team's losses, according to Crain's, are "covered easily" by owner Rocky Wirtz's other business interests: "We're lucky enough to have a strong balance sheet, so we have the ability to bring money in from other businesses."

For many fans, there is an expectation that owners will write personal checks in order to make the club a winner. Even though most professional sports teams are private businesses – with notable exceptions such as Real Madrid and the Green Bay Packers who are owned by members/the public – most fans feel a sense of "ownership" toward their clubs. Somewhat ironically, then, UEFA's "Financial Fair Play" policy has been designed to increase the importance of revenue clubs generate by potentially punishing clubs that receive excessive "injections" from owners.

While the double-digit increases in sports franchise values do not seem to be ebbing, there is a movement to ensure the revenue sources of the sports industry are more stable than relying on the "love of the game" of wealthy oligarchs. While there is still a willingness on the part of tremendously wealthy individuals to open their checkbooks for sports purposes, there is a discernible movement toward relying more on sports markets, thereby giving sports marketing an increasing important role in the sports industry.

CASE: AS ROMA HOPES TO TRANSFORM ITS BUSINESS MODEL WITH A NEW STADIUM

How do you transform a business that has been operated the same way for nearly a hundred years? A good way to begin is to examine sources of revenue because revenue streams provide the parameters for marketing goals and strategies, but also opportunities for more radical transformations.

A Boston-based group of investors acquired Italian soccer team AS Roma in 2011, thereby creating the first for-profit team in Italy's top-flight league, Serie A. Some observers were excited about the prospect of importing an "American" business model to Italy. However, as the *SportsBusiness Journal* noted:

Running a "good business" in Italian soccer can be difficult. The goal of the 19 other Serie A clubs is to spend as much money as they take in. Ownership, in the European system, is a vague concept. The teams are run by clubs, normally with elected and temporary leadership. The concepts of profit and equity are much less definable than in the American commercial system. Franchise value relates more to a team's standing on the competitive "table" than in the marketplace. As a result, pleasing fans is more important than pleasing accountants, and clubs spend all available cash, and often more, on player personnel.[16]

In today's sports landscape, good business is linked strongly to competitive success because the strongest predictor of winning is player payroll, which means teams who can spend the most on players have the best chance at topping the table. During the past decade, Serie A has lost its standing as one of Europe's elite leagues, having lost a Champions League spot and fallen into Europe's second tier. While the match-fixing scandal in the middle of the decade certainly contributed to the slide, Serie A's revenue model is drastically different with respect to matchday revenue.

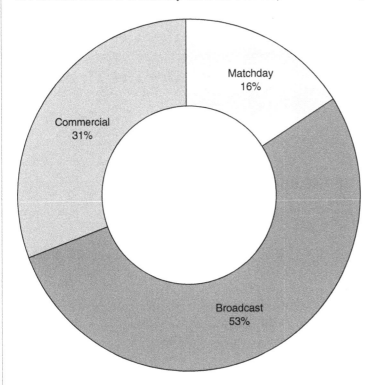

Figure 2.6 AS Roma revenue model (source: *Deloitte Football Money League*).

Serie A teams enjoy strong revenue from media rights, and respectable revenue from commercial sources, such as sponsorship and licensing. Matchday revenue for even the biggest revenue generators in Serie A, however, lags woefully behind the top teams in Europe. English club Arsenal, clearly benefiting from its new stadium, receives 42 percent of its revenue from matchday revenue (see Table 2.4). Matchday revenue for all of the Italian clubs in Deloitte's "money league" can be found at the bottom of the list, falling well behind English, Spanish, and German teams.

AS Roma has implemented programs to increase sponsorship and develop fans in Asia and the US, which can generate substantial but incremental revenue increases. It is the planned new stadium, however, that AS Roma's CEO calls "transformative"

Table 2.4 Matchday revenue as a percentage of total revenue

Team	Matchday percentage of total revenue
Arsenal	42
Hamburger SV	35
Chelsea	32
Real Madrid	30
Top 20 European club average	**25**
Olimpique de Marseille	18
Inter Milan	17
AS Roma	16
AC Milan	13
Juventus	8

revenue. In addition to increasing overall attendance, the new stadium plans include premium and "VIP" seating, which will also potentially increase the revenue per fan attending. If they are successful in building and packing the new stadium with fans, the strategy might propel AS Roma into Europe's top tier of clubs.

EXERCISE: BACK OF THE BUSINESS CARD BRIEF

Review sources of revenue and/or market research for a sports property (see "Recommended Reading" for some sources). Then, describe:

- **Current situation:** Create an overall summary statement about the current situation for the property. What is the business model? Where are the greatest revenue opportunities?
- **Target audience/s:** Who are current fans? Potential fans?
- **Marketing objectives:** Describe what the property is trying to achieve.
- **Back of the business card brief:** Identify the top priority and summarize in one sentence exactly what this marketing program should do.

THREE MAIN TAKEAWAYS

1   The majority of sports industry revenue comes from business markets.
2   Revenues sources vary greatly by sport and region.
3   The phenomenon of professional sports team owners also being fans creates a unique business model in which financial losses are often expected.

RECOMMENDED READING

Changing the Game: Outlook for the Global Sports Market to 2015, PricewaterhouseCoopers.
   This report provides an excellent summary of global sports revenues.

Deloitte Football Money League, Deloitte. This report analyzes revenue sources for the top 20 soccer clubs in the world.

Deadspin got a hold of financial statements for some Major League Baseball teams and posted them online. Usually confidential, the documents provide a rare insight into the inner works of MLB teams. Craggs, T. MLB confidential: The financial documents baseball doesn't want you to see. Posted on August 23, 2010. http://deadspin.com/5615096/mlb-confidential-the-financial-documents-baseball-doesnt-want-you-to-see-part-1, accessed 5/26/2014.

ESPN Sportspoll. A nationally representative poll that has been tracking sports interest for more than 20 years.

Scarborough Sports Marketing. Provides regional data for sports interests, and also includes brand preferences.

NOTES

1 www.workinsports.com/wisquickregapply.asp?idx=73716, accessed 7/26/2013.
2 Albright, P. (2012). The CEO's new secret weapon: The chief revenue officer. www.forbes.com/sites/cio-central/2012/03/13/the-ceos-new-secret-weapon-the-chief-revenue-officer/, accessed 5/1/2013.
3 Chief revenue officers: More dot-com hype, or sensible solution to the marketing and sales divide? www.itsma.com/news/chief-revenue-officers-more-dot-com-hype/, accessed 5/1/2013.
4 Chief revenue officer. http:/americanairlinescenter.teamworkonline.com/teamwork/r.cfm?i, accessed 5/1/2013.
5 *Changing the Game: Outlook for the Global Sports Market to 2015.* PWC, December 2011.
6 Ourand, J. (2013). Talk of rights bubble bursting is still strong – and still wrong. www.sportsbusinessdaily.com/Journal/Issues/2013/07/22/Media/Sports-Media.aspx, accessed 7/30/2013.
7 (2011). www.sportsbusinessdaily.com/Journal/Issues/2011/06/27/Research-and-Ratings/Up-Next.aspx, accessed 3/21/13.
8 Source: Sponsoring 2+ May 2011.
9 Source: Sponsoring 21+ 2007.
10 Washo, M. (2004). *Break into Sports Through Ticket Sales.* Rutherford, NJ: MMW Marketing LLC, p. 14.
11 Ibid, p. 16.
12 Mickle, T. (2012). Prestige ticket tops $150M for London Games' hospitality enterprise. www.sportsbusinessdaily.com/Global/Issues/2012/08/06/Olympics/Hospitality.aspx, accessed 8/6/2013.
13 Bosshart, A., Bridge, T., Hanson, C., Shaffer, A., Stenson C., and Thorpe, A. (2013). *Captains of Industry: Football Money League.* Manchester, UK: Deloitte.
14 Walden, R. (2010). The bottom line: What's behind the purchase price? www.sportsbusinessdaily.com/Journal/Issues/2010/10/20101018/Opinion/The-bottom-line.aspx?hl=what%27s%20behind%20the%20purchase%20price&sc=1, accessed 8/2/2013.
15 Ecker, D. (2013). Why the Blackhawks are losing (money). www.chicagobusiness.com/article/20130615/ISSUE01/306159983/why-the-blackhawks-are-losing-money, accessed 8/2/2013.
16 Genzale, J. (2014). The Roma revolution: US ownership group's aggressive approach revitalizes Italian club. www.sportsbusinessdaily.com/Journal/Issues/2014/01/13/Franchises/AS-Roma.aspx?hl=roma&sc=0, accessed 5/26/2014.

Chapter 3

Fan development

CHALLENGES TO SPORTS GROWTH

The sports industry has enjoyed rapid growth in recent decades. Yet, growth rates for both participation and fan interest have reached a plateau in recent years. While overall revenues have been stable and consistent, sports participation and fandom alike are becoming more and more elusive to the average citizen because of increased costs and declining public funding.

In some sense, the sports industry has become a victim of its own success. Demand to attend sports events has driven up ticket prices to the point that costs to attend a typical major league sports event is out of the reach of the average family. Sports attendees tend to be affluent because they are the ones who can afford to go to the games.

Similarly, interest in sports participation continues but has become more elusive with a decay in public infrastructure and decline in public funding. A recent report identified the following trends in youth sports:[1]

- *Slashed budgets.* The report documents how school districts and individual schools across the US have cut sports to reduce budgets.
- *Increased fees.* "Pay-to-play" systems are becoming increasingly common strategies to maintain programs in the face of budget cuts.

Table 3.1 Average age of viewers 2011

Event	Average age
The Masters (golf)	56.4
Indy 500 (auto racing)	55.4
World Series (baseball)	52.5
Daytona 500 (auto racing)	50.2
NCAA Men's Basketball Championship	47.0
Stanley Cup Final (ice hockey)	45.8
BCS Championship (college football)	45.3
Super Bowl	42.5
NBA Finals (basketball)	40.6
MLS Cup (soccer)	39.0
Winter X Games	34.0
Summer X Games	33.0

Source: SportsBusiness Daily.[1]

Note

1 Ourand, J., and Karp, A. (2012). Which sport can say: We are young. www.sportsbusinessdaily.com/ Journal/Issues/2012/03/19/Media/Sports-demos.aspx?hl=age%20event%20viewer%20ourand&sc=0, accessed 8/12/2013.

- *Cutting programs.* As budgets get cut, so do sports programs. Individual sports and entire sports programs have been cut or suspended in schools across the US.
- *Growing inequities.* The combination of budget cuts and fees to participate in sports affect communities that cannot afford to pay. In the face of cuts to public funding, parents in low-income families do not have the means to supplement their children's sports activities with private alternatives.

Older people across income segments were more likely to have benefited from publicly subsidized sports participation as children, which has long-term implications for sports involvement. In addition, people tend to be paid more money as they get older, so older people have higher incomes. Given the link between sports involvement and income, many sports are faced with old, and continually aging, fan bases. Table 3.1 shows the average ages for viewers of major sports property broadcasts in the US. Sports viewers are old and, for the most part, getting older. Viewers of the 1996 Summer Olympic games averaged 42.0 years of age; the figure for the 2008 games was 48.0.

THE FAN DEVELOPMENT PROCESS

Fan development goals

As I look at the [hockey] market, I see three different interests in the sport. Avids that have a tremendous consumption level – watch it, attend it, have the jersey autographed, the whole thing. You see casual fans, which is probably 60 percent, who are aware of the sport follow it sometimes, would watch it on TV

> if they came across it and if invited would attend games. Then you have no
> fans. I think the opportunity the NHL is looking for is to convert the casual
> fans to avids and the no fans to casuals. You want to do both those things
> without irritating or upsetting the avid fans.[2]
>
> Chief Marketing Officer, NHL

How do individuals become sports fans? How do they become bigger fans?

Sports marketers interested in developing new fans and increasing the "share of customer" operate on an underlying philosophy about how individuals become fans. While the image of some type of fan "escalator" is popular,[3] fan development is not a linear process across all behaviors and for all fans/sports. Does the comparatively young average age for viewers of the NBA Finals bode well for the future? That depends on whether the younger viewers still watch as they get older and do not outgrow the sport. Fans who grow up with a sport might not be able to attend games because of personal circumstances, such as starting a family, but might attend games more frequently after their kids get old enough.

In addition, the way people are involved with sports changes over the lifecourse. Youths who are highly involved in sports are more likely to spend time participating than watching on TV. Similarly, parents of children who are sports participants are not likely to have the time available to be season ticket holders because of the time requirements for their kids. While sports involvement trends across the lifecourse vary according to the specifics of sports and markets, as Rich Luker, founder of the ESPN Sports Poll, said, the path to being an avid sports fan is clear: "Know about it, play it, attend it, consume it in all its forms. All of these elements happen more powerfully when they are integrated with family/friend activity."[4]

Participation

There is a strong and consistent correlation between youth sports participation and fan avidity for that sport later in life. As the vice president of fan strategy and marketing for the NFL said:

> [The decline in youth sports] impacts our fan base. We have a strategic imperative
> of getting kids connected to the game at a young age. We know the correlation of
> kids playing the game and then becoming fans of the game. When you start to cut
> into the access to play sports and to play football, the prospect of that impacts our
> fan base over the long haul.[5]

According to NFL research, 75 percent of avid fans participated in football as a child, and avid fans are more likely to have played than casual fans.[6] Not all sports are widely available for youth participation. Auto racing fans, for example, tend to come to the sport later in life, after they start driving and become interested in cars.

The level and seriousness of sports participation is also a factor in how and why youth sports participants become fans later in life. In general, the more serious the participation, the more avid the fan. The level of competition reached is also related to the point of attachment fans have for sports. An athlete who plays college sports, for example, is more likely to be interested in the sport in general rather than a specific team, league, or player.

Of course, the end goal of youth sports participation is not simply to manufacture future fans, though that might be a strong consideration for professional sports leagues. Youth sports participation benefits the kids who play, their families, and society as a whole. According to a national study about youth sports, youth sports participation was linked with higher levels of family satisfaction, improved physical and emotional health, academic achievement, and children's overall quality of life.[7]

Sports comprise social and educational institutions in addition to an industry, which is one of sports' unique features and distinguishing characteristics. While most sports marketers tend to work on the industry side, many executives working in sports development in government or on behalf of non-governmental organizations are turning to marketing strategies and tactics to increase sports participation, often in partnership with corporate sponsors.

Socialization

Becoming involved in sports occurs in very specific social contexts and is enhanced by involvement with family and friends. Sport sociologist Jay Coakley defines this process as socialization: "an active process of learning and social development, which occurs as we interact with one another and become acquainted with the social world in which we live."[8] Rather than simply being passive learners, Coakley argues that individuals actively participate in the socialization into sports. While individual preferences are important, Coakley recognizes that there are influential agents of socialization, whom he calls "significant others."

The primary agents of socialization into sports involvement consist of both individuals and institutions, especially family, education, and the media.

- *Family*. Fathers, mothers, brothers, sisters, uncles, aunts, and cousins can all be very influential in introducing individuals to sports. While all family members can be influential, traditionally male, older family members exert the most influence, especially fathers. In addition, many women become involved in sports later in life through their male partners. As girls' sports participation has increased, and young girls grow up to adult women who have their own families, it will be interesting to see how this dynamic might change. Will we see women as more influential as agents of socialization into sports?
- *Education*.
  - Peers. Classmates and peers can exert strong influence on youths to become involved in sports. According to a national study, sports participation is linked to popularity at school: the more involved with sports, the more popular the kid.[9] Sports that are respected by peers become more attractive to kids looking to be popular with their classmates.
  - Coaches. Coaches can have a profound influence on sports involvement, both in introducing kids to become involved and discouraging them from further participation. In

one study, 18 percent of girls and 22 percent of boys who dropped out of sports identified not getting along with the coach as a reason for dropping out.[10]

- *Media*. The media can be a powerful influence on sports involvement, both as a participant and as a fan. After the Olympic Games, for example, sports participation increased in both England and the United States.[11] In addition to being a vital source of revenue for sports organizations, media strategies should consider the implications for fan development. According to the president of NBC Sports, "Leagues need broad exposure. They need exposure to the right audiences to grow their fan base and they need exposure in the right time periods."[12]

Motivations

Sports marketers tend to be occupied with day-to-day tactical concerns: how to spend their marketing dollars; where to place an ad; what to put in an e-mail; which benefits to emphasize to season ticket holders, etc. Yet, strategic thinking helps to inform tactical decisions, even if many sports marketers do not articulate explicitly the assumptions on which they base their programs. However, marketing programs benefit from a clearly articulated, cogent strategic vision about how and why individuals become involved in sports.

While external influences can be important in socializing individuals into sports, as Coakley argues people are active participants in the process so individual preferences are strong factors in sports involvement. Fan motivation has been a strong topic of interest among sports marketing academics for decades, yielding a robust literature about theories why fans become involved in sports. Researchers into fan motivations have identified the most common sports fan motives:[13]

- Entertainment: enjoyable pastime.
- Escape: diversion from everyday life.
- Aesthetics: artistic beauty and grace.
- Family: spend time with family.
- Group affiliation: spend time with others.
- Self-esteem: feel better about oneself.
- Eustress: enjoys the excitement and arousal of sports drama.

Octagon, one of the world's largest sports marketing agencies, developed Passion Drivers, a study of more than 40,000 sports fans that examines fan motivations. The purpose of the study is to provide clients with the "why" of sports fans, moving past demographic and behavioral profiles to create fan segments based on fan motivations. Results vary by sport. For NASCAR, Octagon identified four different fan segments, all of whom shared a similar psychographic profile. The NBA, in contrast, yielded four segments that profile evenly across the fan motivations in the study. The study's director concluded:

> That's great for NASCAR from a marketing perspective, because one size fits all. With the NBA, you have different groups of consumers who demographically may look similar, but in terms of emotional components and what is relevant, these are

very different relationships that each of them has with the sport. It becomes a challenge to know what message to market with, and you won't find the answer in the demographics.[14]

Research and investigation into fan motivations is particularly helpful in developing messaging strategies for sports marketers, though less useful in identifying targets for specific tactics. Identifying fans who are motivated by a "sense of belonging," for example, would be difficult. Including an appeal to a "sense of belonging" in marketing communications, on the other hand, is actionable.

Another unique aspect of sports fan behaviors as consumers is the deep level of identification fans have with sports brands. As loyal a following as a brand like Apple has among its fans, you would be hard pressed to find someone say, "*We're* coming out with a new i-Phone." Yet, sports fans commonly talk about their teams as if they are actually on it. Many researchers refer to the BIRGing phenomenon: basking in reflected glory, in which sports fans attach themselves to successful teams in order to attach themselves to that success. But then many perennial losers have substantial, loyal fan bases (see Chicago Cubs).

Duncan and Brummett argue that narcissism is a fundamental source of pleasure in sports fans enjoyment of televised sports.[15] Similar to BIRGing, fans project themselves into the

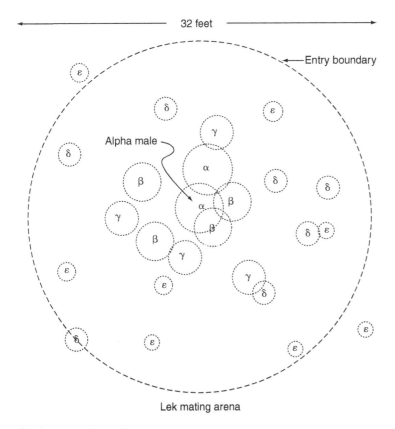

Figure 3.1 Lek mating arena.

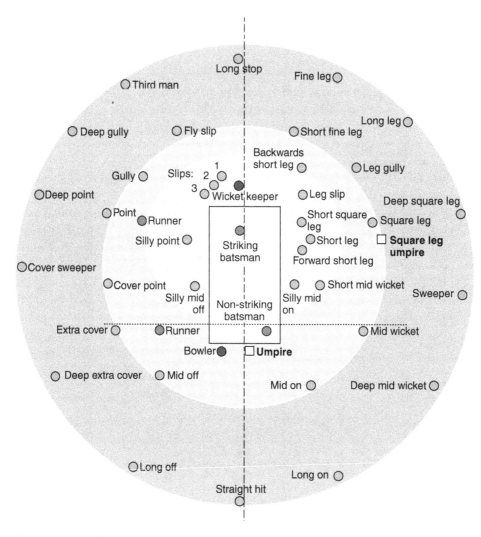

Figure 3.2 Cricket formation.

action on the field, identifying with athletes who are actually performing. A notable exception to this type of vicarious participation is Fantasy Sports in which fans project themselves into the position of general manager of a team, not a player.

On an anthropological or evolutionary psychology approach, other observers link sports fans to elemental animal behaviors:

> Fans of the San Diego Chargers football team are full of hate for fans of another California football team, the Oakland Raiders. They taunt each other, donning costumes to intimidate or humiliate the opposing team's fans. Some of the fans engage in ritual fight displays, not unlike those of aggressive birds such as the Noisy Miner.[16]

Sports have also been linked to group male displays to attract potential female mates called "leks." Visually, a diagram of a lek looks eerily similar to many sports competitions (see Figures 3.1 and 3.2).

Deep thinking about sports fans motivations and experiences can help sports marketers develop a strategic vision, especially with respect to messaging. In order to take action, however, those insights and strategies need to be leveraged into tactics. That is, fan development executives must leverage insights into what makes fans tick into what makes them buy tickets.

Fan Development Manager, Gold Coast, Australia

Job details

The Gold Coast Football Club (GCFC) is on the journey to become the most exciting Australian Rules Football Club in Australia. In 2011, they made their debut in the AFL and brought the excitement of live AFL football and a brand new state-of-the-art stadium experience to the Gold Coast Community.

To ensure continued success in our second AFL season and beyond, they are looking for a Fan Development Manager who will be *responsible for the acquisition and development of engaged fans* of the Gold Coast Suns.

The successful candidate will develop and implement strategy and have operational responsibility for *casual ticket sales* to maximize attendance at Metricon Stadium.

Reporting to the General Manager – Fan Development, you will work with a bold and fresh team to *identify new fans and turn casual fans into passionate fans in this exciting growth period for the football club. Your experience in loyalty marketing, CRM database segmentation, ticketing campaigns and creating fantastic consumer experiences* will make you a valued and dependable member of the Suns' team.[17] (emphases added)

As a new club without an existing fan base, the GCFC needs to acquire and develop new fans.

Casual ticket sales are an effective technique for getting new fans in the pipeline. A positive first experience is a strong predictor of future attendance and loyalty. Therefore, creating "fantastic consumer experiences" is a priority.

The Club identifies CRM database segmentation and loyalty marketing as strategies to develop fans from casual to loyal supporters. What kind of loyalty programs would you implement?

FAN DEVELOPMENT STRATEGIES AND TACTICS

Fan development usually entails some combination of growing existing fans or developing new fans either with an existing product or a new or modified product. In a standard marketing growth matrix (see Table 3.2), fan development executives are most often concerned with market development, developing new fans with the existing product. Considering that most sports have been around for a long time, where will new fans come from? As with

Table 3.2 Growth matrix

	Existing fans	New fans
Existing product	Market penetration	Market development
New product	Product development	Diversification

most marketing efforts, sports marketers often first look to demographic and geographic markets, mostly because of their size, growth potential, and competitive environment.

Youth markets

Youth markets tend to be the most common targets for fan development programs because they hold the largest and most likely potential for future fans, especially among sports participants. The relationship between youth and sports participation in fan development programs is so closely intertwined that "youth marketing" and "grassroots marketing" are often conflated to mean pretty much the same thing. Professional sports leagues and elite level sports organizations have a strong interest in promoting sports participation, partly because it is the right thing to do for social reasons but also because it is good business. The level of investment, however, varies greatly.

For many sports organizations, promoting the sport to youth is the top priority. The president of the International Ski Federation says that his biggest challenge, "is to promote skiing as a whole. We have huge campaigns, such as 'Bring Children to the Snow,' and many more that target the youth with the intention to bring the youth to the sport."[18] The challenge for fan development is especially acute in sports that have barriers to participation.

Sports without a broad base of participation, such as tennis, need to pay particular attention to developing participants in order to maintain long-term stability. As the chief marketing officer of the United States Tennis Association says of the biggest challenge in her position:

> Making sure everyone in the tennis industry understands 10 and Under Tennis has to have a long-term focus. In order to really change the game and drive participation, we need to stay at this for years to come.... What I'm most excited about is we've actually created departments that are solely focused on 10 and Under Tennis.[19]

Although still comparatively small in number, recognition of the importance of fan development has led to an increase in job openings for fan development executives, both at the league and team levels.

Because sports participation is broadly seen as a social good, many private sports organizations seek to lobby for increased government spending or forge public-private partnerships to encourage sports participation. In 2000, the NFL commissioner and executive director of the NFL Players Association co-authored an op-ed in a trade journal lobbying for support of the Conservation and Reinvestment Act (CARA), which would have used funding from oil and gas leases to fund recreational projects, including football fields.[20] As the authors recognized, "Tens of thousands of fields for football and other sports, as well as other youth sports facilities, exist today because the federal government made a commitment to recreation 35 years ago." Unfortunately, government funding is no longer that far sighted.

Consequently, sports organizations are left to pick up the slack. Often, the onus of fan development initiatives has fallen on non-profit, non-governmental organizations, though it should be noted here that the NFL has non-profit status at the league level, though all NFL teams are for-profit business. In contrast to the small percentage of the NFL's total revenue devoted to football participation, the England and Wales Cricket Board (ECB) announced a commitment of a £96 million investment in community cricket over a four-year period, a significant portion of which is incurred to enthuse participation.[21]

To be fair to the NFL, youth participation can be complicated in heavy contact sports. Youth participation in mixed martial arts and boxing, for example, is constrained by concerns about the physical violence these sports entail. Ice hockey can be prohibitively expensive because of equipment costs and facility requirements. Sports organizations facing these challenges can modify their products in order to be able to get youths involved while reducing costs and/or physical risks. The NFL has responded by promoting flag football in its youth programs. Similarly, the Rugby Football Union (RFU) has created a development strategy that includes touch and tag rugby in an effort to increase participation numbers (see Head of Rugby Growth box below).

Head of Rugby Growth

Job details

The world's third largest sporting event will see all eyes on the Rugby World Cup 2015 in England. This is a once in a lifetime opportunity for rugby union and the tournament will significantly expand and develop the sport across the nation, creating a lasting legacy. There could be no more exciting time to join rugby union's governing body in England as the Head of Rugby Growth.

> Hosting a major event in a home country is often used as a catalyst for fan development. The World Cup in the US in 1994, for example, provided the foundation for Major League Soccer a short time after.

It will be your responsibility to harness this opportunity, providing the strong leadership and strategic direction for the RFU's work to grow the breadth and depth of the game. *You will ensure that fun forms of rugby like touch and tag feature alongside the first XV's and are integrated into the Union's plans. With overall responsibility for increasing the numbers playing rugby on a regular basis,* you will maximise existing opportunities while developing innovative solutions to address identified challenges. With a particular focus on helping RFU member clubs to grow the game, you will identify and form partnerships with appropriate external organisations to support this work.[22] (emphasis added)

> As a full-contact collision sport, rugby officials have adapted rules to get more kids involved, similar to the NFL's efforts around flag football. The foundation of the strategy is the link between participation and all-around growth of the

> sport. At the same time, RFU officials need to be cognizant of developing elite level players – hosting a tournament is less effective if the home team is eliminated quickly. Therefore, RFU executives sought a candidate who could increase participation at all levels.

Participation and attendance are cornerstones of long-term sports devotion. Sports marketers want young people to play their sports, and they also want them to attend events. Aggressive ticket pricing is a common strategy to attract youth. In the German Bundesliga (pro soccer), cheap tickets are a "social policy." According to Bayern Munich's chief executive, "German stadia are always full because we implement a social policy to keep our tickets affordable to the poor, being as low as €7 with Bayern."[23] While Bayern's ticket policy is based on income, younger people tend to have lower incomes so low ticket prices can be an effective tool in attracting younger fans. Arsenal in Barclays Premier League instituted a £10 "teenagers-only" section, setting aside 800–1000 seats in the section, an estimated £400,000 per year investment in developing future fans.[24]

While teams struggling at the gate might look to youth markets to pack the stands, successful teams should keep an eye out for the future. Many successful teams set aside tickets for youth groups even when they sell out regularly, knowing that current fans will need to be replaced with new fans at some point. MLB teams often schedule weekday games during the day in the summer. Attendance is usually lower than a similar night game but they are able to attract youth groups in huge numbers, often providing young people with an opportunity to attend a game.

Female markets

Most sports fan bases fall along a traditional 60/40 male/female split. A heavy male audience like drag racing might skew 70/30 in favor of men while more gender equal sports like MLB might be 50/50. Even for heavily skewed male audiences, a substantial number of fans are women, even if they are outnumbered by male fans. Appealing to female sports fans is especially important for women's professional sports.

Sports that traditionally skew towards men can grow their fan bases by appealing to women. Sometimes women are targeted through children, with the idea that youth participants will bring Mom to the sport, then Mom can develop an interest independently of the kids. Or, women can be introduced to a sport through a male partner and the relationship with sport can outlast the romantic relationship. Workshops for women are a common strategy, with the idea being that if women understood football's rules and strategies better, for example, it would deepen their interest in the sport.

It works the other way, too. The vast majority of golfers are men, about 80 percent. For the LPGA, then, if they are looking to convert golfers into LPGA fans, the biggest opportunity is with men. The LPGA is faced with the challenge of either persuading male golfers/golf fans to follow the LPGA, or to try to convince women with little to no interest in golf to follow the sport. Which do you think is more likely?

The WNBA targets both youth and female audiences with a "Dads and Daughters" promotion across the league. The program leverages the fact that fathers are the most common

WNBA Daughters and their Dads

I love what Dads and Daughters means to the WNBA. When I was younger and growing up and even through high school, my dad spent many, many hours in the gym with me mostly rebounding. That is something special that we shared with each other. The bond that the WNBA fosters between father and daughter is a special thing. My dad has been great. He has been there for me every step of the way. I've had to make some tough decisions in my life, like where to attend college, but neither one of my parents ever pressure me, but they always encouraged me to follow my heart and promised to support me no matter what I did.[25]

Kendra Wecker, San Antonio Silver Stars

socializing agent into sports. The program draws on the deep emotional connections that many girls experience with their Dads through sports.

Hispanic markets

Hispanic markets have attracted the attention of sports marketers in North America because, like youth markets, they offer a lot of growth potential. In fact, there is a big crossover between Hispanic and youth markets as Hispanics tend to be younger than the average American and the Hispanic population is projected to grow rapidly.

Marketing to Hispanics, however, is a challenge because there is no unified "Hispanic market." Hispanics may share a common language, though even with language there is continuum of Spanish or English dominance. Some Hispanics speak only Spanish, other a combination of Spanish and English ("Spanglish"), and others mostly English but are proficient in Spanish. Culturally, however, Hispanics are diverse. In most of the US, the majority of Hispanics are of Mexican descent. Hispanics in Miami, however, are most likely to be Cuban. And sports interests vary depending on country of origin.

Sports that have not been traditionally associated with diverse audiences, such as NASCAR, have placed an emphasis on reaching out to Hispanic markets. According to NASCAR's vice president of public affairs and multicultural development, "Over the next five years, we want to index more closely to the Hispanic share of the US population. We know that's not going to happen overnight."[26] NASCAR and its associated racetracks have invested in staffing Hispanic marketing efforts (see Manager of Hispanic Marketing box below). The common thread to these efforts is Spanish-language marketing communications, though as the job description indicates, the "Hispanic market" is not a unified whole. Rather, markets need to be identified under the broader Hispanic market umbrella.

In many large US markets, Hispanics have already become "mainstream." MLB's Los Angeles Angels, for example, look for strategies and tactics that will play across Hispanic and non-Hispanic markets because Los Angeles' population is more than half Hispanic.[28] But even sports properties that enjoy an ethnically diverse fan base pay special attention to the Hispanic market. According to the NBA's senior director of US Hispanic marketing, "We

Manager of Hispanic Marketing – Homestead Miami Speedway

ESSENTIAL DUTIES & RESPONSIBILITIES

- Developing short and long term marketing plans for the Hispanic community.
- Oversee creation of Spanish-language collateral including posters, ticket brochures, postcards, etc.
- Creating and executing a strategy to connect with Hispanic population via large-scale events, neighborhood programs, special interest programs, community-based organizations, appearances, clinics, etc.
- Creating and administering the delivery of brand-specific e-newsletters to Hispanic community.
- Determining target Hispanic markets and choosing the proper media to reach them.
- Creating Hispanic Fan Development strategies throughout the calendar year.
- Participating and networking within the Hispanic community and industry.

QUALIFICATIONS
- Ability to read, listen and communicate effectively in English and Spanish, both verbally and in writing.[27]

Spanish-speaking sports marketing executives are in demand in the US because Hispanics are a sizable and rapidly growing demographic.

In many organizations, Hispanic marketing managers serve as "the" Spanish-speaking contact, with duties ranging from translating materials to developing relationships in the local community. Consequently, a broad range of skills is required. In this position, job responsibilities are fairly representative of the entire marketing process with the addition of Spanish language proficiency.

understand that the Hispanic market is growing and we need to continue to engage it."[29] While the percentage of Hispanic NBA fans is close to the percentage of Hispanics in the US population (about 15 percent of NBA fans are Hispanic), the NBA launched its first major Hispanic marketing effort during the 2009–2010 season because that demographic will become increasingly important as it comprises a greater percentage of the population.

Geographic markets

In developing new markets for fans, sports organizations also look to geographic areas: new cities, regions, and countries.

During the past decade, there has been a huge realignment of schools in college athletics conferences. The Atlantic Coast Conference got the ball rolling by adding Virginia Tech,

Boston College, and Miami in 2003. Since then, there has been a ripple effect of conferences expanding and recruiting members from different conferences. The impetus for this movement has been conferences' desire to expand their geographic footprint in order to generate more television revenue. For the ACC, for example, Boston was not a great college sports town, as there are successful and popular professional sports franchises there (Patriots, Red Sox, Bruins). But Boston is a major media market with a big population, which made adding the school as a member attractive.

When the NHL looked at their strategy in the 1990s, they sought to expand to markets with high population density. Although the league never consciously adopted a "Southern strategy," most of the expansion teams were located in the Sunbelt. That is simply a function of population shifts in the United States. Population is growing rapidly in the Sunbelt states and flat or declining in the Midwest and Northeast. Many cities in the Midwest that have long traditions of professional sports struggle to keep pace with rapidly growing markets in other parts of the country.

The biggest opportunities for developing fans in new geographic markets is with international markets. For sports that are mature in their native markets, their growth potential is limited. The NFL is already the most popular sport in the United States. How much bigger can it get there?

One of the most cost-effective ways to enter international markets is through media. Seeking to leverage their Asian stars, the LPGA sought to develop more fans in Korea, China, and Japan.[30] In contrast to hosting tournaments in those regions, which can incur costs, placing content in media in those markets can turn a profit because the content is already produced. The LPGA's vice president of television and emerging media said, "There is some financial upside, but it's much more about growing the fan base and planting the seeds in these countries, especially China."

Brazil, Russia, India, and China are often referred to as the "BRICs," a group of target markets poised to grow in economic influence because of their populations and economic growth. So it should not be surprising that these markets have recently or are scheduled to host sport's biggest global events: the Summer Olympic Games and the World Cup.

FIFA in particular has been ahead of the curve in developing new markets. Since North America represents close to half of the world's sports market by revenue, it was not a surprise that FIFA awarded a World Cup to the United States in 1994, which helped to launch the professional league in the country and grow the sport. Although North America is a cluttered sports market, even the sixth or seventh most popular sport can generate substantial revenue. Noticing rapid growth for sports markets in the Middle East, FIFA is set to develop that market as well.

Using events and grassroots marketing to increase participation are costlier than placing media but more effective, so the relative costs and the potential benefits need to be weighed closely. The NFL closed down NFL Europe because it lost too much money, but came back to London with pre-season, then regular season games. European teams tour North America and Asia in the off-season but there has yet to be an added game to the European schedule. In some cases, however, organizations are willing to incur losses because the market potential is so big. The Euroleague, Europe's professional basketball league, staged its Final Four in London, despite the lack of basketball tradition in the UK. Because the Euroleague hopes to expand to the UK, the Euroleague CEO says, "For us, the UK is part of our 'target.' We need the ambition to have all countries having a presence in the Euroleague. It is not just a promotion or a slogan, it is pure reality."[31]

CASE: WHO HAS THE BEST FANS?

Who has the best fans? It might be a popular topic among bar patrons over a pint but it is a serious question for sports marketers as well. In designing a fan development strategy, sports marketers must keep in mind what kind of fans they want to develop. What are the desired attitudes, feelings, and behaviors? From a business perspective, which fans are most profitable? Which fans align with the overall business strategy?

A study[32] conducted by Turnkey Intelligence and Toluna on behalf of *SportsBusiness Daily Global* compared NFL fans living in the US and Barclay's Premier League (BPL) fans living in the UK. Results of the research prompted Bernie Mullin, veteran sports marketer and self-professed Evertonian, to say that he has had to "bite his lip" when he hears US fans talk about being passionate. But hold on, Bernie.

First, let's look at the methods of the study. Sample sizes were 300 each, which is big enough to yield reliable comparisons, but they were not randomly drawn from the national populations. In order to qualify for the survey, participants needed to be "very interested" in the NFL or BPL/nPower League Championship and have a favorite team in the respective league. Participants were also required, however, to be self-described "very avid supporter" or "strong supporter" for their favorite team. There is a problem in nomenclature. "Supporter" is not a term used by US fans. "Die-hard fan," sure. So, one of the things the study might be measuring is what it means to be a "supporter" to US fans.

The results of the study are far from conclusive. According to the study, BPL fans attend more games and NFL fans watch more on television. Makes sense. BPL teams play more games (38 regular season plus international competitions). NFL games are more widely available because most are on broadcast television. BPL fans spend more time following their team than NFL fans, but NFL fans spend more time following the league. The study also found that NFL fans were more likely to encourage others to watch games on TV, and BPL fans were more likely to encourage others to attend team away games. So, the NFL is more TV-based and the BPL is more attendance-based. That is a difference, but which is better?

NFL fans will watch games even when their favorite team is not playing. BPL fans will not. Bigger ratings mean a bigger television contract. On the other hand, BPL team "supporters" might require less marketing investment to maintain their loyalty. As the importance of media rights revenue continues to grow for the BPL, and as the league continues to grow outside Great Britain, BPL executives might take a page from the NFL playbook in building more television-based "supporters." Conversely, facing an aging fan base and increased attendance challenges, the NFL might look to develop more team-based die-hard fans.

So, who are the best fans?

EXERCISE: SPORTS TALK

Most readers of this book are probably used to talking sports with others. Often, sports fans tend to congregate with fans with similar interests. This assignment, however, invites you to speak with fans of sports that you personally don't like. Hate golf? Find a golf fan and learn about the connection. How do golf fans get started? What do they like about it? Think soccer will "never" become "big" in the US? Find a soccer fan and ask what it's all about. In your conversations, see if you can identify themes discussed in this chapter.

THREE MAIN TAKEAWAYS

1   The sports industry faces significant financial challenges to further widespread growth.
2   Fan involvement is based on playing, attending, and consuming sports across all media forms, and accelerated in social environments.
3   Sports properties are in constant search of new markets to grow their fan bases, especially youth, ethnic, and geographic markets.

NOTES

1   Up2Us (n.d.). *Going Going Gone: The Decline of Youth Sports*. New York: Up2Us.
2   Bernstein, A. (2006). Ex-beer exec targets same demo for NHL. www.sportsbusinessdaily.com/Journal/Issues/2006/04/20060410/This-Weeks-News/Ex-Beer-Exec-Targets-Same-Demo-For-NHL.aspx?hl=ex-beer%20exec%20targets&sc=0, accessed 8/6/2013.
3   Mullin, B., Hardy, S., and Sutton, W. (2007). *Sport Marketing*. Champaign, IL: Human Kinetics.
4   Luker, R. (2013). What is your sports property doing to build, keep its fan base? www.sportsbusinessdaily.com/Journal/Issues/2013/07/22/Research-and-Ratings/Up-Next.aspx?hl=luker&sc=0, accessed 8/6/2013.
5   King, B. (2010). High school sports running on empty. www.sportsbusinessdaily.com/Journal/Issues/2010/08/20100802/SBJ-In-Depth/High-School-Sports-Running-On-Empty.aspx, accessed 5/9/2013.
6   Show, J. (2009). Leagues aim to build next generation of fans. www.sportsbusinessdaily.com/Journal/Issues/2009/08/20090817/SBJ-In-Depth/Leagues-Aim-To-Build-Next-Generation-Of-Fans.aspx?hl=leagues%20aim%20to%20build%20next%20generation&sc=0, accessed 8/6/2013.
7   Sabo, D. and Veliz, P. (2008). *Go Out and Play: Youth Sports in America*. East Meadow, NY: Women's Sports Foundation.
8   Coakley, J. (2004). *Sports in Society: Issues and Controversies*. Boston: McGraw Hill Higher Education, p. 98.
9   Sabo and Veliz. *Go Out and Play*.
10 Ibid.
11 Gibson, O. (2012). Britain's Olympic success leads to record boost in sport participation. www.theguardian.com/sport/2012/dec/06/olympic-record-boost-sport-participation, accessed 8/7/2013; (2012). Summer Games usually leads to boost in participation in Olympic sports. www.sportsbusinessdaily.com/Daily/Issues/2012/08/02/Research-and-Ratings/SGMA-Olympics.aspx?hl=summer%20games%20usually%20leads%20to%20boost&sc=1, accessed 8/2/2012.
12 Ourand, J. (2009). Big deals, bigger questions. www.sportsbusinessdaily.com/Journal/Issues/2009/11/20091109/SBJ-In-Depth/Big-Deals-Bigger-Questions.aspx?hl=big%20deals%2C%20bigger%20questions%20&sc=1, accessed 8/6/2013.
13 Wann, D., Melnick, M., Russell, G., and Pease, D. (2001). *Sport Fans: The Psychology and Social Impact of Spectators*. New York: Routledge.
14 King, B. (2010). What makes fans crazy about sports? www.sportsbusinessdaily.com/Journal/Issues/2010/04/20100419/SBJ-In-Depth/What-Makes-Fans-Crazy-About-Sports.aspx?hl=what%20makes%20fans%20crazy%20about%20sports&sc=1, accessed 4/9/2013.

15 Duncan, M. and Brummett, B. (1989). Types and sources of spectating pleasure in televised sports. *Sociology of Sport Journal*, 6: 195–211.
16 Churchland, P. (2013). *Touching a Nerve: The Self as Brain*. New York: W.W. Norton and Co., Inc. www.scientificamerican.com/article.cfm?id=touching-a-nerve-exploring-the-implications-of-the-self-as-brain-part-2, accessed 8/12/2013.
17 Fan Development Manager. http://sportsrecruitment.com/jobs/details/370/fan-development-manager, accessed 11/17/2011.
18 (2012). FIS president Gian Franco Kasper talks about Sochi, safety concerns and sponsorships. www.sports-businessdaily.com/Global/Issues/2012/10/26/Leagues-and-Governing-Bodies/QA-Kasper.aspx?hl=fis%20president&sc=0, accessed 1/9/2013.
19 (2012). Hunt's love for marketing takes her to CMO position at USTA. www.sportsbusinessdaily.com/Journal/Issues/2012/02/13/People-and-Pop-Culture/Spotlight.aspx?hl=hunt%27s%20love%20for%20marketing&sc=1, accessed 1/9/2013.
20 Upshaw, G. and Tagliabue, P. (2000). Kids need a place to play. www.sportsbusinessdaily.com/Journal/Issues/2000/09/20000925/No-Topic-Name/Kids-Need-A-Place-To-Play.aspx?hl=kids%20need%20a%20place%20to%20play&sc=1, accessed 5/10/2013.
21 ECB Annual Report 2012.
22 Head of Rugby Growth. http://sportsrecruitment.com/jobs/details/346/head-of-rugby-growth, accessed 11/17/2011.
23 (2012). Bayern chief urges Serie A to follow Bundesliga's example. www.goal.com/en-gh/news/4630/soccerex/2012/10/08/3434530/bayern-chief-urges-serie-a-to-follow-bundesligas-example, accessed 8/15/2013.
24 Bennetts, J. (2013). Exclusive: Arsenal's £10 ticket for teen fans. www.standard.co.uk/sport/football/exclusive-arsenals-10-ticket-for-teen-fans-8580084.html, accessed 8/15/2013.
25 WNBA Daughters and Their Dads. www.wnba.com/features/ddplayerquotes07.html, accessed 8/13/2013.
26 Mickle, T. (2011). NASCAR, tracks appeal to Hispanics. www.sportsbusinessdaily.com/Journal/Issues/2011/08/29/Marketing-and-Sponsorship/NASCAR-Hispanics.aspx?hl=nascar%2C%20tracks%20appeal%20to%20hispanics&sc=0, accessed 8/13/2013.
27 Manager of Hispanic Marketing – Homestead Miami Speedway. http://iscmotorsports.teamworkonline.com/teamwork/r.cfm?i=43681, accessed 8/9/2012.
28 King, B. (2013). Angels seek messaging that will play across both the Hispanic and general markets. www.sportsbusinessdaily.com/Journal/Issues/2013/06/24/In-Depth/Los-Angeles-Angels.aspx?hl=angels%20seek%20messaging&sc=0, accessed 8/13/2013.
29 Lombardo, J. (2009). New NBA campaign is first major Hispanic effort. www.sportsbusinessdaily.com/Journal/Issues/2009/10/20091019/This-Weeks-News/New-NBA-Campaign-Is-First-Major-Hispanic-Effort.aspx?hl=new%20nba%20campaign&sc=1, accessed 8/13/2013.
30 Smith, M. (2011). LPGA adds TV deal, launches websites in Asia. www.sportsbusinessdaily.com/Journal/Issues/2011/12/05/Media/LPGAweb.aspx?hl=lpga%20adds%20tv%20deal&sc=1, accessed 8/6/2013.
31 (2013). Despite low attendance for Final Four in London, Euroleague seeks UK expansion. www.sports-businessdaily.com/Global/Issues/2013/05/13/Events-and-Attractions/Euroleague-Final-4.aspx, accessed 5/13/2013.
32 Broughton, D. (2013). Survey: EPL fans more passionate about their teams than NFL counterparts. www.sportsbusinessdaily.com/Global/Issues/2013/03/11/International-Football/Fan-Survey.aspx, accessed 5/3/2013.

Chapter 4

Brand management

Nike brand marketing

> As a member of this team, you'll help communicate one of the most recognized brands in the world. You'll drive our mission of connecting with consumers through a variety of channels by working with Digital Marketing, Sports Marketing, Event Marketing, Regional Marketing and our Field Reps. Help us tell stories our consumers want to be a part of and always think big.[1]

Brand management is often seen as a form of storytelling, as indicated by Nike's description of its brand marketing department on its corporate website. What do you see as Nike's story? How would you tell it? How big can you think?

Figuring out who you want to reach and what you want to say are the cornerstones of marketing strategy. In marketing terms, we would say that marketers define target market segments and develop brand positioning. Marketers need to communicate a value proposition or unique selling proposition to customers. That is, marketers need to tell customers why they should buy a product or use a service relative to competing options.

"Brands" can mean two things. First, a brand is the visual representation of a company, product, or service. In a tangible sense, brands consists of logos, trademarks, and packaging. But brands are also made up of perceptions, which can be tremendously valuable. For huge sports brands like Nike, adidas, ESPN, Sky Sports, Gatorade, IMG, and EA Sports, the primary source of value for the companies lies in the name, not physical assets like buildings and equipment. That is, there is "equity" in the brand.

Brand equity is a term used to describe the value of the brand, but is not limited to financial value even though equity is a financial term. But brands can also build equity in perceptions and attitudes. Strong brands have high levels of awareness, clearly defined attributes, and attract favorable attitudes. In simple terms, sports audiences need to know who you are, know what you stand for, and like you. Marketers should seek to craft brand strategies that are clear, consistent, and compelling.

In sports, many brands are mature. Sports, leagues, and teams have often been around for a hundred years or more. Like universities, it is hard to differentiate a particular sports property because many sports and teams share common attributes. Take a look at university websites and see how many feature "excellence." Similarly, look at sports teams' websites and see how often they mention pride, passion, and tradition.

Director Marketing Programs/Brands NY Knicks

Job description

> This position is *responsible for increasing target consumer awareness of the Knicks brand via development of TV spots, OOH [out-of-home] advertising, print and other marketing platforms*. In this capacity, the Director will also direct and oversee the activity of the teams internal A&D [Advertising & Design] group. The Director will also serve as the lead, working closely with the SVP Marketing, for the programming, look and feel, data analysis/insight generation, and growth of all of the Knicks digital/social media platforms, including KnicksNow.com, nyknicks.com, Facebook, and Twitter...[2] (emphases added)

While relationship marketing and Customer Relationship Management (CRM) are dominant paradigms in sports marketing, traditional media still plays an active role, particularly in generating awareness. The job description also highlights the importance of integrating traditional media with digital assets, that is integrating paid and owned media so that a clear, consistent message is communicated.

In the case of mature sports brands, those brands must be managed to maintain consistency. For iconic brands like the NFL's Green Bay Packers, sports marketers must ensure that no communications are "un-Packer-like." For brands that have yet to be established, whether because they are new or because they are weak, marketers must first establish an identity.

BRAND IDENTITY

One of the attributes of iconic brands is that they are immediately recognizable in all of their forms. No matter where you are in the world, you can recognize a Coca-Cola bottle no matter what the language. That is no accident. Coca-Cola's guide just for the Coke Zero brand is 146 pages long, and Coca-Cola has more than 500 brands. For consumer brands, a rigorous, systematic approach to establishing and managing the visual keys of a brand's identity is common. That has not been the case in sports:

> When package-goods marketers migrate to sports properties, the most dramatic difference they find is the seat-of-the-pants marketing endemic to sports. Marketing institutions like Procter & Gamble won't even consider changing packaging colors from Pantone 179 to 180, an almost imperceptibly darker shade of red, without six months of study.[3]

Style elements such as colors, fonts, and image sizes must be uniform in order to create a consistent appearance across different formats.

The passion that fans have for sports is a double-edged sword when it comes to branding. Because there is so much equity in sports, sports brands are more resistant to inconsistencies than typical consumer product categories. One shade of Pantone is likely not going to make much of a difference to a die-hard Miami Heat fan, as it might to someone buying laundry detergent. To further complicate the matter, ownership changes and the whims of executives can come into play. For example, team colors have been traditionally red but the new team owner likes blue as a color, so the new team color is blue. However, recognizing the value that their brands possess, sports marketers have taken a more rigorous and systematic approach to branding in recent years. In 2005, the NFL hired a brand consultant to conduct a comprehensive study of the NFL's brand and develop a brand style guide.

In sports, there are numerous brand "touchpoints," ways that fans can come in contact with the brand, both from the property itself and from sponsors and licensees that develop merchandise (see Senior Manager, Quality Control box below). In order to develop a cogent brand identity, those different elements need to be integrated along a defined set of visual keys. As the NFL's vice president and executive creative director says: "We had a lot of pieces to be unified. We have a lot of opportunities to communicate with fans through our own media and through our partners – we just want to make sure it's consistent."[4] After cable TV provider Comcast purchased NBC Universal, there was a need to align Comcast's

---

Senior Manager, Quality Control – National Hockey League

DUTIES AND RESPONSIBILITIES: Review and approve QC submissions (products, packaging, promotions, catalogues, print advertising, internet web sites and sales offerings). Review submissions for compliance with contract, quality of goods, execution of logos and trademarks, execution of colors, NHL policies, player related issues and trademark compliance and other trademark issues and applications (including trademark clearances and restrictions).[6]

Quality control for licensed products is an important component of brand management. Brand identity must be recognizable across a wide variety of formats, from beer mugs to t-shirts.

regional sports networks with the parent network. The SVP, creative services and brand integration for NBC Sports Regional Networks said, "The job was more complicated than simply adding a peacock to network logos." The rebranding involved set design and graphics, with the executive concluding, "The biggest challenge was tying all of these logos into one and make it a cohesive brand."[5]

Creating a brand identity also entails defining the desired core attributes of the brand, what the physical attributes are designed to communicate. Brand identities must be clear and consistent, but they also must be compelling. In the NFL's brand study, consultants defined the core brand equities as: integrity, excellence, community, teamwork, innovation, and tradition.[7] In response to the gloomy economy during the economic recession, the CMO of the NHL's Washington Capitals said, "What we are selling is hope, passion, community and escape. In today's economy, those are all more important than ever."[8]

The key to making a brand identity compelling is to match the attributes to the desires of the target audience. For that reason, many sports organizations adopt a targeted brand strategy that emphasizes different attributes to different audiences, rather than a comprehensive approach. Even many mega-brands that have clear, consistent, and compelling brand messages to a wide swath of consumers would differentiate between consumer and business markets, for example.

SPORTS BRANDS

One of the biggest challenges for sports marketers in developing and managing strong brands is the variety of sources for brand identities.

Country. Soccer is a popular sport world-wide and fans consume soccer in a variety of ways regardless of the World Cup or other international competitions. But how often does curling attract a national audience outside of the Winter Olympic Games? For sports strong brands or big fan bases, nationalism and patriotism can be a valuable source of brand equity.

There are more US residents who feel patriotic toward their country, for example, than there are fans of women's golf. To tap into these sentiments, the LPGA Tour created the International Crown, a global match-play tournament featuring eight countries. As one observer stated:

> The reality is that women's golf has limited windows to attract the so-called "average" sports spectator/viewer in the United States. A team event that involves the concepts of national pride and patriotism? Well, as hokey and contrived as that can sometimes seem, it's definitely a hook. One that women's golf needs.[9]

State/City. Many sports teams tap into hometown loyalty or access brand equities from their host cities. While some teams are branded by region (New England Patriots) or state (Minnesota Vikings), most sports teams tap into the brand equity of hometown loyalty to cities. Two MLB teams recently rebranded from their state to cities, Los Angeles Angels and Miami Marlins. In both cases, the cities have reputations as hip, modern, stylish cities, brand attributes that the teams hope to tap into. Anaheim, the city where the Angels actually play, is much less sexy than LA.

Logo changes and rebranding tend to attract a lot of controversy, not just for sports teams. Iconic retailer the Gap's rebranded logo lasted all of about a week. When the Florida Marlins sought to rebrand to the Miami Marlins, their brand consultant recommended that "Miami" be placed on the front of the uniforms instead of "Marlins."

Sport. Sports themselves have brand attributes, both good ones that they can leverage to their advantage and bad ones that they need to address. For years, the UFC has attempted to counter the notion that mixed martial arts competitions are equivalent to "human cockfighting" while retaining the edgy, "ultimate" image. Tennis can be seen as a "country club" sport, appropriate for elites but not for mass participation.

Where many sports seek to modify existing images, "extreme," "action," or "alternative" sports was created as a new brand, largely as a creation of ESPN when it launched the X Games. While skateboarding and BMX biking had been in existence for quite a long time, they were more likely to be regarded as recreational activities than a cogent sports brand. The branding initiatives have been a huge success, as evidenced by the inclusion of these sports in the Olympic Games. Critics might argue that including action sports events in the Olympic Games is pandering to a youth audience, but there is also a branding issue: sports can be labeled as "old" and "out-of-touch."

League. In North America, most professional sports leagues are the only game in town and therefore become somewhat synonymous with their sports. Leagues develop brands and identities independent from the sport in general. The NFL shield, for example, is widely recognizable as different from USA Football's logo.

Leagues also have identifiable brand identities, which are often related to the characteristics of their audiences. The NBA indexes high in fan interest among African-Americans and has an "urban" image. In contrast, NASCAR, which indexes low in fan interest among African-Americans, is more likely to be identified as a "redneck" sport. Actor Ashton Kutcher, after being the honorary starter at NASCAR's Daytona 500, said: "This is like one of the greatest redneck sports there is. I mean redneck in a good way; I'm a redneck."[10] In contrast, in reaction to country music stars performing during the halftime of the NBA's All-Star game, former NBA player Charles Barkley said: "I just hope whoever put the halftime together, they're getting their resume ready. This is a hip-hop weekend. This ain't no NASCAR race."[11] In an effort to appeal to broader audiences, but also to counter the leagues' images, both the NBA and NASCAR try to move toward the middle on the "country" and "urban" continuum.

One of the challenges for less-established sports and leagues is to build strong brands that can stand on their own. Soccer in the United States is well-established as a participatory sport. On the professional level, 19.4 million viewers watched the US Men's National team play Ghana in the 2010 World Cup (14.9 million on ABC and 4.5 million on Spanish-language Univision).[12] Those 19.4 million fans, however, do not translate into fans of Major League Soccer. The challenge for Major League Soccer is to convert "soccer snobs," fans who will watch the World Cup and follow international teams, into fans of MLS.

Team. Building strong brands for teams is important because they are a strong predictor of season ticket holder loyalty. Winning helps, but is not the only answer. A big part of the New York Yankees brand is the 27 World Series victories, but an equal part of the Chicago Cubs brand is the lack of World Series victories. Team brands are also influenced by owners, facilities (arenas and stadiums), and players.

For successful, well-established teams, the major issue in branding is simply maintaining consistency. The Yankees do not want to do anything "un-Yankee-like." The Yankees certainly would not change their iconic logo. For less successful teams, or for new teams, building new brands requires identifying your core attributes and representing those attributes in a tangible brand identity.

Players. Michael Jordan was a basketball player. He is also a brand. In fact, Nike has a separate web page for "the Jordan Brand" (http://nikeinc.com/jordan-brand). The "Jordan Brand" has even exceeded Michael Jordan himself as Blake Griffin is a featured player in the brand. Sports celebrities – athletes, coaches, television personalities, etc. – have become more deliberate in how they manage their public perception with an eye toward monetizing their "personal brands." Athletes now receive more comprehensive training than just "media training," or how to give an interview – they are coached in improvisation and communications (see Improvisation & Communications Coach box below).

"Players" can also be a brand in the collective sense. The NHL, for example, has enjoyed strong team brands, especially among the older, more established clubs. But it has traditionally lacked the star power that the NBA enjoys with its numerous celebrity players. After the 2004–2005 season NHL lockout, the league saw an opportunity to feature and promote NHL players. An Anheuser-Busch executive said, "The players are regular guys, and a lot of our customers can relate to that."[13]

NHL players face the same challenge as NFL players: they wear helmets so fans cannot see their faces while they play. Therefore, fans are less likely to associate a face with the action on the field. Neil Pilson, a former CBS Sports president, added, "Athletes are the story, so a chance to get players to take off their helmets has to be good for hockey. Hockey players are perceived as warriors, guys who play through pain and injury. That's the mystique."[14]

Improvisation & Communications Coach – IMG Academies[15]

Position responsibilities

- Develop and document instructional curriculum for secondary and post-secondary student athletes and professional athletes in the areas of personal and group dynamics, communication, self-awareness and intra/interpersonal skills.
- Deliver curriculum in a highly interactive, enjoyable, experiential, and dynamic fashion, including role-play, games, mock events, and demonstrations.

Knowledge, skills and ability

- Bachelor's degree or equivalent in Education, Theater, and/or Fine Arts.
- Experience delivering improvisation, performing arts, communication skills, self-improvement, or motivational programs.
- Dynamic, engaging personality with excellent written and verbal communication skills.

One of the biggest challenges for managing brands in sports is trying to differentiate your brand. The NFL's core equities – integrity, excellence, community, teamwork, innovation and tradition[16] – can be applied to a number of brands, whether sports related or not. Where sports brands differ from other consumer brands is in their ability as a social connector in bringing fans together. The NFL recognized that other sports properties functioned as social connectors, too, so they revised their brand positioning statement as: "The premier sports and entertainment brand that brings people together, connecting them socially and emotionally like no other." Sports as a social connector is what sports marketers mean when they talk about the "brand experience" for their properties. "Image" is a useful concept, but limited to an individual's perceptions about the property. That is important, but for most fans sports is an intensely social and emotional experience. So, for many sports properties, the most important source of brand associations are the fans themselves.

Fans. A sport's fans and/or participants contribute a lot to the tone and feel of the sport. Action sports participants tend to be young with an edgy style. So, action sports' brand image is "young" and "edgy." Fan loyalty for certain teams can become a big part of the team's brand. Pittsburgh Steelers fans are famous for their willingness to travel to away games (Steelers fans take over the City when the team is in the Super Bowl). The MLS's Seattle Sounders are strongly identified with having the "best fans" in the US, though that claim is hotly disputed by rival Portland Timbers fans.

Sports marketing executives outside North America tend to concede that they are "about five years behind" the North American market. While it is true that the North American market enjoys the highest revenue, North American sports marketing executives would do well to take a page from the way Europeans and Australians brand their "fans." Most professional sports teams in North America have some kind of "fan club," often targeted at children. European and Australian leagues have "clubs," not teams, and "members," not fans. In rare cases, such as Spanish soccer giants Real Madrid and Barcelona, the teams are actually still owned by their members.

Structurally, "membership" programs and "fan clubs" tend to be very similar with respect to the benefits they offer to fans and members. The major exception in the way North America sports treat their stakeholders is in big-time college athletics, where "booster" clubs offer a strong sense of membership with the organization. It should not be surprising, then, that college sports tend to enjoy much greater repeat purchases for season ticket holders.

The underlying principle is the recognition that fans are an important part of the club. Part of the issue is simply branding: calling your best customers members instead of fans. Some organizations have institutionalized the sentiment. The MLS's Seattle Sounders, for example, give fans a vote in player personnel decisions, like hiring a general manager and making player trades/signings.

BRAND EXPERIENCES

Brands are not simply ideas that exist in people's minds. Most people have some kind of idea about what Coca-Cola is. But Coca-Cola is more than an idea; it is a physical product that is consumed in very specific social circumstances. "Brand experiences" are not just ideas, they are feelings and sensations associated with using a product or service. In sports, the "experience" is the product, so brand managers in sports must pay close attention to how their products and services are experienced, not just how they are perceived.

Sports fans are not just consumers of sports products; they are the product. In college sports, for example, a big part of the experience for older ticket buyers is watching the youthful exuberance of the students in attendance. Therefore, sports marketers are taking a more deliberate approach to how they can craft sports experiences.

For spectator sports, there has been an increasingly blurred line between sports and entertainment. Over the past few decades, sports teams, especially those in North America, have added more non-sports entertainment to sports events in an effort to attract attendees beyond the core sports fan, while attempting to avoid alienating the core fan who is there primarily for the sport. There is a wide variety along the sports–entertainment continuum, and sports marketers are constantly trying to find the right mix.

Director of Entertainment – Erie SeaWolves Baseball Team (Erie, PA)

Responsibilities:

- "Create, plan and implement entertainment segments from 'gates open' until the last fan exits.
- Rehearse all skits and contests with each entertainment staff member.
- Oversee all entertainment department functions: audio, scripts, mascots, field staff and hosts.
- Develop Master Entertainment (skits, contests, etc.) book and Game Scripts for each home game.
- Plan, create, rehearse and implement entertainment inning breaks...
- Complete & update Master Entertainment Calendar (First Pitch, National Anthem, Honor Guard, etc.)"[17]

Minor league baseball teams tend to set the curve for game entertainment. With less equity in players and teams, minor league sports tend to focus on the sport and game entertainment. Often with little media, fan involvement in game entertainment also provides valuable sponsorship inventory.

As this job description notes, professional sports games have highly detailed scripts so that there is very little 'dead time.' The challenge is to balance entertainment for attendees who are not interested in the sport with potential distractions for more traditional sports fans.

Minor league baseball tends to integrate a lot of entertainment into its game presentations because it is difficult to market a team with unknown players who probably will not be there long. One minor league executive said, "We put in-game entertainment up there as almost as important as the game itself."[18] Commenting on a promotion in which dogs were admitted free with a paying owner, another minor league executive said, "Anything to get people in the building."

Other game experiences have traditionally been more pristine. It is unlikely that golf tournaments will add music or entertainment on the greens anytime soon (though the US

Tennis Association has experimented with encouraging more vocal fans). Chicago Cubs games have historically been very conservative when it comes to entertainment – the only music was provided by an organist. After seeing a decline in attendance related to a down economy and poor on-field performances, however, the Cubs "upgraded" the music with more modern, taped music, and more stats on the LED board.[19]

While European and Australian clubs might set the curve in encouraging fan identification through their membership programs, North America clearly sets the bar for game entertainment. Premier League fans rate the pre-match and halftime entertainment as poor.[20] Many European soccer teams have adopted "American-style" entertainment options – Italian team Napoli added NFL-style cheerleaders to their games – but run the risk of alienating "purists" who are there for the game and provide enough "entertainment" themselves through chants and singing.

Outrageous, unrelated entertainment can attract new visitors to an event, but it can also alienate attendees who are there primarily for the game: "They'll say, 'Cut the crap, it's too much.' And sometimes we're guilty of doing too much, but it's better than holding back."[21] In contrast, the NBA's Orlando Magic recently cut back the amount of music during games, with the goal "to have a little more of a balance and focus a little bit more on the game while the ball is in play."[22] Striking the appropriate balance means keeping in mind the audience members you are trying to appeal to: "One timeout there may be something for the basketball purists, while the next timeout we may feature a funny mascot video – that way there is something for everyone at our games."[23]

Sports marketers also try to influence the overall tone and feel of their events. They want attendees to be engaged (so that they will return), without going overboard. They want excitement, but no profanity or violence. That is a delicate line to walk. Many teams in North America are adding branded fan sections in an effort to increase the energy during games. The NHL's LA Kings created a "soccer-style" supporter section, called the "Royal Army," with the Kings COO reasoning:

> We thought that [MLS] fans are very similar to NHL fans when it comes to passion, so why couldn't that concept work if we brought it to hockey. We see this as a chance to create electricity in the Staples Center and help the club create a tight fan community.[24]

We are the Royal Army, The LA Kings Supporters Group

At home or away, we cheer the WHOLE game. The Royal Army was created by the fans, for the fans. We are loud and proud. We stand, chant, cheer and support our LA Kings to the fullest. Our goal is to unite Kings fans everywhere, and help create the best atmosphere for our beloved Kings and cheer them on, win or lose.[25]

MERCHANDISING AND LICENSING

Product Associate Men's Running Apparel, Nike

Job description

> As our Global Product Associate for Men's Running Apparel, you will be responsible for collecting product, consumer and competitive trends in the key global markets for the Category. You will be responsible for understanding consumer needs and conducting analysis of the current business. You will contribute to drafting line plans and participate in all facets of the product creation process and work with direction to meet key deliverables...

Qualifications
- General understanding of product construction and consumer trends
- Creativity and passion for product
- Retail experience and acumen a plus
- Connection to the Running consumer a plus[26]

Note that this position for Nike starts with an understanding of consumers. In fact, retail experience and a connection to running are merely "pluses." Understanding product construction and consumer trends are the requirement, along with personal qualities of creativity and passion. This is a fairly common phenomenon in sports marketing, in which marketing is more important than sports.

It is important to keep in mind that brands are not built or managed just for their own sake, but to drive revenue. For the most part, brands are effective to the extent that they can be "monetized." In-game entertainment is designed to increase gate receipts. Nike is a tremendously strong consumer brand, but the company's focus on growth and innovation requires a steady stream of new products that are both consistent with Nike's brand and drive sales at the retail level.

While Nike might be most famous for its basketball shoes in North America (where it enjoys a huge share of the market), revenues from its running category are nearly double basketball globally. In order to maintain and grow revenues, Nike must develop running products that runners will purchase at retail locations. It should not be surprising then, that in looking for a Men's Running Apparel Product Associate, Nike sought a candidate with retail acumen and a connection to the "Running consumer."

Sports equipment and apparel companies, such as Nike and adidas, leverage their brands to drive product sales at retail. Revenues for other sports brands are more diversified in their sources of revenue. For teams, leagues, and players, merchandise can be a source of revenue, but it can also be a brand strategy. "Merchandising" tends to indicate a strategy in which retail sales are the primary goal. In "licensing," increasing merchandise revenues is often subordinated to growing the brand in order to increase other revenues, such as ticket sales. While brand building is an important marketing function, it is most effectively done with a purpose in mind. By licensing their logos and trademarks to merchandisers, sports properties can provide more and better products to their fans.

Senior Manager Licensing & Merchandising, New York Road Runners

About the department

To manage and optimize all merchandising, licensing and retail initiatives for the New York Road Runner's. *A critical objective for the Licensing & Merchandising Department is to transition the organization from using "merchandising" as a business strategy to "licensing" NYRR's rights in order to enhance and grow the brand.*

About the position

The purpose of the position is to lead the organizational transition from the current business approach to a new approach of "outsourcing" all of our merchandising functions through a licensing strategy. At the highest level, the successful candidate will be charged with developing and executing a long-term licensing plan to develop NYRR properties through *brand enhancing, cohesive merchandising activities.*[27] (emphasis added)

According to this job ad, the NYRR sought to enhance their brand more effectively by outsourcing their merchandising functions. Licensing their brand to merchandisers would allow greater exposure and variety, while potentially taking advantage of licensing partner's expertise. What do you think the licensing priorities for the NYRR should be? How can the NYRR enhance its brand through a licensing strategy? How would you balance brand management and the need to generate revenue?

The NFL and NFL Players Association signed a sponsorship and licensing agreement that, for the first time, gave team sponsors group player rights (using six or more players in advertising or promotions). The NFL's senior vice president of business affairs said, "[This structure] will facilitate sponsorship activation, more players will be used in advertising and promotion, and it will be done in a more authentic way by combining the assets of the clubs and the league."[28] While merchandising revenues for the NFL are substantial, they are a fraction of sponsorship and media revenues, so it is not surprising that the licensing deal was designed to deliver more value to local sponsors.

Ticket sales and fan engagement are also a strong consideration in many licensing decisions. In the NBA, teams are allowed to have seven different uniforms. For the NBA's Miami Heat, the marketing division determines when the team wears the different uniforms. The Heat's chief marketer said, "We look at the schedule strategically and look for a group of games where we can have impact at home."[29] Cultural uniforms, such as the Heat's "Noche Latina" (Latin Night) jersey can help build a brand to a targeted audience while also increasing ticket sales for the event.

While licensing strategies aimed at ticket sales, sponsorship, and advertising revenues can take precedence, revenue from licensed merchandise can be substantial on its own, especially in North America. For minor league sports, merchandise sales can be an important source of revenue because they typically lack large media audiences and the sponsorship and advertising revenues that come along with that.

In the minor leagues, many teams are named and logos developed with the goal of leveraging the brands into merchandise sales. Names like the Sand Gnats, Isotopes, Iron Pigs, Sea Dogs, and Blue Wahoos (all minor league baseball teams) lend themselves to the development of licensed merchandise. While the names might not attract corporate sponsors, they are popular with kids who play baseball: "About 45 percent of our royalties come from the Little League program," said the merchandise manager of the Class A Wisconsin Timber Rattlers.[30]

Smaller properties have benefited greatly from increases in online sales, allowing small properties such as minor league teams to sell products outside their region. But properties of all size have benefited from the increase in the size, quality, and sophistication of retail at events. Event attendees are more likely to be avid fans of the property, and therefore more likely to spend and spend more on licensed merchandise.

Sports-related licensed merchandise comes in and out of style. During boom years for licensed sports products, typically the number of licensees increases. But as more companies develop licensed sports products, product quality can be compromised. For that reason, there has been a trend toward fewer, higher quality licensed products.

While the lure of merchandise revenues is attractive, sports marketers must stay true to the brand. Sometimes brand extensions – using the brand for an unrelated product – work, and sometimes they do not. Barclays Premier League team Everton developed a new crest because the old one had become "increasingly difficult to reproduce in the digital age." Team officials consulted their retail partners, Kitbag and Nike, on the switch. Supporters of the team, however, were unhappy, with 16,000 fans signing a protest petition within two days of the new crest's launch. As one supporter stated, "This will not only be an embarrassing crest to represent the club but it will also make the club lose money on merchandise, due to no one wanting to buy any merchandise with that awful crest printed on it."[31]

CASE: JORDAN OR JAMES?

Pele or Messi? Lara or Tendulkar? Jordan or James? Debates about the best on-the-field players are popular with sports fans precisely because they cannot be answered. How would a 26-year-old Michael Jordan match up with a 26-year-old LeBron James? We shall never know. While Michael Jordan at 50 cannot match up with LeBron James in his prime, Jordan is decidedly the better marketing asset, even years after his playing days have ended.

As Henry Schafer, Executive Vice President of the Q Scores Company said to me in a personal communication:

Overall, Michael Jordan has consistently been perceived as the most appealing sports personality during most of his active playing days and through today as a retired athlete. He appears to handle any miscues during his career very well with the public, as his appeal has remained very strong over the years. On the other hand, LeBron James took a significant public image hit in 2010–2011 for the ESPN fiasco, primarily due to the way he handled it. He is currently recovering in the past year or so, but it clearly slowed his gradual rise to a more iconic status with the general public and sports fans alike. In sum, for athletes, winning is not everything when it comes to the strength of consumer appeal and image – much of an athlete's marketability is tied to how he/she deals with the public on and off the court, so to speak, and with respect to miscues or social indiscretions, how quickly a response is issued to the public and the quality of the response is a key factor.

Q-scores measure awareness and favorability for celebrities and are a common research tool to identify potential celebrity endorsers for marketing campaigns. As the data in Table 4.1 show, despite being retired, in 2013 Michael Jordan continues to enjoy higher awareness among both the general US population (78%) and sports fans (87%) than James (65% and 83%, respectively).

Not only is Jordan more well-known, he is more well-liked even among younger sports fans. As Tables 4.2 and 4.3 show, 12–17-year-old male fans liked Jordan more and disliked James more in each year during the period 2010–2013. James is somewhat of a polarizing figure with negative scores nearing, and in some years exceeding, positive scores. If you were James' agent, what would you suggest? James looks on track to match Jordan's performance on the court. Can he match it off the court?

EXERCISE

Like many sports teams, the Indiana Pacers have started special seating sections in an effort to develop avid fan communities. Honoring players Roy Hibbert (Area 55) and Paul George and George Hills (G2 Zone), the Pacers website describes the sections thusly:

> Area 55 and the G2 Zone are the loudest sections in Bankers Life Fieldhouse. Area 55 is filled with 55 wild and crazy Pacers fans selected by Roy Hibbert himself. The remaining seats in the section are comprised of friends and family of those winning members. Every offseason, Roy invites all Pacers fans to submit their application online or in-person. Of those submissions, 110 fans make it to the final auditions in Bankers Life Fieldhouse with 55 winning season tickets in his exclusive section.[32]

Applicants submit a brief video online in order to apply for the program. Your assignment is to use your understanding of fan development and sports brands to create a winning video. If you like, you can invent your own section for your favorite sport or team and create a video application.

Table 4.1 Jordan and James Q-scores

Michael Jordan						LeBron James					
Performer Q studies: general population 6 years and older			Sports Q studies: sports fans 12 years to 64 years old			Performer Q studies: general population 6 years and older			Sports Q studies: sports fans 12 years to 64 years old		
Year	Awareness	Q-score	Year	Awareness	Q-score	Year	Awareness	Q-score	Year	Awareness	Q-score
	%	%		%	%		%	%		%	%
1985	37	27	1990	83	42	2004	43	16	2003	47	17
1986	42	27	1993	91	47	2005	43	18	2004	64	25
1987	47	33	1994	95	53	2006	46	24	2005	67	26
1988	55	37	1995	95	55	2007	49	19	2006	67	27
1989	65	42	1996	92	50	2008	52	21	2007	70	25
1990	75	42	1997	93	53	2009	56	22	2008	72	26
1991	81	42	1998	90	61	2010	60	24	2009	74	31
1992	86	37	1999	92	61	2011	60	17	2010	78	34
1993	79	36	2000	92	57	2012	65	16	2011	75	16
1994	89	34	2001	90	57	2013	65	17	2012	84	19
1995	89	38	2002	90	52				2013	83	25
1996	83	38	2003	91	51						
1997	91	43	2004	91	49						
1998	86	42	2005	92	49						
1999	91	42	2006	88	50						
2000	83	39	2007	90	55						
2001	73	40	2008	89	53						
2002	82	35	2009	85	50						
2003	85	35	2010	89	51						
2004	84	31	2011	85	47						
2005	84	34	2012	89	43						
2006	80	34	2013	87	46						
2007	75	33									
2008	82	33									
2009	79	36									
2010	76	33									
2011	80	36									
2012	83	30									
2013	78	27									
Sports Personality Average	30	14		44	16		30	14		44	16

Source: The Q scores company.

Notes
General population data based on nationally representative samples of 1800 respondents for each performer Q study.
Sports fan data based on nationally representative samples of 2000 respondents for each sports Q study.

Table 4.2 Michael Jordan sports Q demographic profile

	2010 Positive Q-score %	2011 Positive Q-score %	2012 Positive Q-score %	2013 Positive Q-score %	2010 Negative Q-score %	2011 Negative Q-score %	2012 Negative Q-score %	2013 Negative Q-score %
Total males (12–64)…	53	51	47	50	12	14	8	7
12–17 years…	58	57	65	51	9	11	7	8
18–34 years…	67	59	45	55	13	12	9	5
35–49 years…	44	40	39	45	10	16	11	9
50–64 years…	40	52	56	51	14	13	2	6
18–49 years…	56	49	42	50	12	14	10	7
25–54 years…	51	51	45	47	12	15	9	8
18–64 years…	52	50	45	50	12	14	8	7

Table 4.3 LeBron James sports Q demographic profile

	2010	2011	2012	2013	2010	2011	2012	2013
	Positive Q-score %	Positive Q-score %	Positive Q-score %	Positive Q-score %	Negative Q-score %	Negative Q-score %	Negative Q-score %	Negative Q-score %
Total males (12–64)…	38	17	22	27	19	35	27	20
12–17 years…	44	49	40	19	11	16	14	22
18–34 years…	44	19	20	29	18	30	31	24
35–49 years…	31	6	20	24	20	46	27	17
50–64 years…	35	16	20	31	22	33	28	19
18–49 years…	38	12	20	26	19	38	29	19
25–54 years…	33	13	20	24	18	39	30	23
18–64 years…	37	13	20	28	19	37	29	20

THREE MAIN TAKEAWAYS

1 Strong sports brands are clear, consistent, and compelling.
2 Sports brands derive their identities from a variety of sources, including the sport, the league, teams, players, coaches, and fan communities.
3 Licensing and merchandising strategies must balance the needs to enhance brand image and generate revenue.

NOTES

1 http://nikeinc.com/pages/career-areas, accessed 8/19/2013.
2 http://newyork.jobing.com/philips-arena/ny-knicks-director-marketing-programsbrands, accessed 5/27/2014.
3 Lefton, T. (2005). Study helps NFL unify branding efforts. www.sportsbusinessdaily.com/Journal/Issues/2005/09/20050905/SBJ-In-Depth/Study-Helps-NFL-Unify-Branding-Efforts.aspx?hl=study%20helps%20nfl&sc=1, accessed 8/17/2013.
4 Ibid.
5 Ourand, J. (2012). Game changers: April Carty-Sipp. www.sportsbusinessdaily.com/Journal/Issues/2012/10/08/Game-Changers/April-Carty-Sipp.aspx?hl=april%20carty-sipp&sc=0, accessed 1/9/2013.
6 Senior Manager, Quality Control. http://hockeyjobs.nhl.com/teamwork/jobs/jobs.cfm/Sales-and-Marketing, accessed 5/16/2013.
7 Lefton. Study helps NFL unify branding efforts.
8 Lefton, T. (2009). Even on analytics' home court, gut feeling has its fans. www.sportsbusinessdaily.com/Journal/Issues/2009/03/20090316/Marketingsponsorship/Even-On-Analytics-Home-Court-Gut-Feeling-Has-Its-Fans.aspx?hl=merchandise%20sales&sc=1, accessed 8/19/2013.
9 Voepel, M. (2013). Time is right for LPGA's new global event. http://espn.go.com/espnw/news-commentary/article/8878626/espnw-lpga-new-event-invites-world, accessed 8/19/2013.
10 (2005). Open up the doors to different kinds of fans. www.sportsbusinessdaily.com/Journal/Issues/2005/02/20050228/Opinion/Open-Up-The-Doors-To-Different-Kinds-Of-Fans.aspx?hl=open%20up%20the%20doors&sc=1, accessed 8/17/2013.
11 Ibid.
12 Sandomir, R. (2010). World Cup ratings certify a TV winner. www.nytimes.com/2010/06/29/sports/soccer/29sandomir.html, accessed 8/21/2013.
13 Kreda, A. (2006). All about the players. www.sportsbusinessdaily.com/Journal/Issues/2006/10/20061002/SBJ-In-Depth/All-About-The-Players.aspx?hl=all%20about%20the%20players&sc=1, accessed 8/17/2013.
14 Ibid.
15 Improvisation & Communications Coach. http://imgworld.teamworkonline.com/teamwork/jobs/jobs.cfm/Marketing, accessed 7/4/2012.
16 Lefton. Study helps NFL unify branding efforts.
17 Director of Entertainment – Erie SeaWolves Baseball Team. http://mandalay.teamworkonline.com/teamwork/r.cfm?i=49401, accessed 1/7/2013.
18 Andelman, B. (2007). Minors bank on entertainment options. www.sportsbusinessdaily.com/Journal/Issues/2007/04/20070423/SBJ-In-Depth/Minors-Bank-On-Entertainment-Options.aspx?hl=minors%20bank%20on%20entertainment&sc=1, accessed 8/21/2013.
19 Sullivan, P. (2013). Fresh marketing coming to the Cubs. http://articles.chicagotribune.com/2013–02–19/sports/ct-spt-0220-cubs-spring-training-chicago–20130220_1_cubs-gary-pressy-jeff-samardzija,accessed 8/17/2013.
20 Downer, J., Munby, R., and Stone, J. (2003). *The F.A. Premier League National Fan Survey Research Report: 2002/03 Season*. The Football Association Premier League Limited.
21 Andelman. Minors bank on entertainment options.
22 Cooper, W. (2009). Quiet down: Magic cut back in-game music to focus on action. www.sportsbusinessdaily.com/Daily/Issues/2009/03/Issue-122/Franchises/Quiet-Down-Magic-Cut-Back-In-Game-Music-To-Focus-On-Action.aspx?hl=magic%20cut%20back%20in-game%20music&sc=0, accessed 8/21/2013.

23 Baucom, R. (2011). Team execs share their in-game approach. www.sportsbusinessdaily.com/Journal/Issues/2011/02/20110207/In-Depth/Fan-team-execs.aspx?hl=team%20execs%20share&sc=1, accessed 2/4/2013.

24 Dreier, F. (2011). LA Kings eye soccer-style support section. www.sportsbusinessdaily.com/Journal/Issues/2011/07/11/Franchises/Kings.aspx?hl=kings%20eye%20soccer-style&sc=0, accessed 8/6/2013.

25 http://kings.nhl.com/club/page.htm?id=69961, accessed 8/26/2013.

26 http://jobs.nike.com/oregon/merchandising-%EF%B9%A0-product-management/jobid4068228-product-associate-men%27s-running-apparel-jobs, accessed 8/19/2013.

27 www.micasportslink.com/jobs/show-jobs/247/Senior-Manager-Licensing--Merchandising-/New-York/New-York-City/191/Brand-Management/, accessed 6/21/2013.

28 Kaplan, D. (2011). Big changes in new NFL-NFLPA licensing deal. www.sportsbusinessdaily.com/Journal/Issues/2011/08/22/Leagues-and-Governing-Bodies/NFL-licensing.aspx?hl=big%20changes%20in%20new%20nfl-nflpa%20licensing%20deal&sc=0, accessed 5/13/2013.

29 Mickle, T. (2013). Business, and luck, drive NBA color choices. www.sportsbusinessdaily.com/Journal/Issues/2013/08/19/Franchises/Uniforms-NBA.aspx, accessed 8/10/2014.

30 Broughton, D. (2011). Increases at ballpark retail space help MiLB teams boost merchandise sales 12 percent. www.sportsbusinessdaily.com/Journal/Issues/2011/05/16/Marketing-and-Sponsorship/MiLB-merch.aspx?hl=increases%20at%20ballpark%20retail%20space&sc=1, accessed 8/19/2013.

31 Hunter, A. (2013). Everton fans up in arms about club's redesigned crest. www.theguardian.com/football/2013/may/27/everton-fans-clubs-redesigned-crest, accessed 5/28/2013.

32 www.pacersarea55.com/about/, accessed 5/26/2014.

Part II
Gate revenue

Chapter 5

Gate revenue marketing mix

There is a big difference between a sports fan and a ticket buyer. Not all sports fans buy tickets to events. In fact, in a given year, most do not. In my research on NASCAR fans, I have found that about half of all self-described "fans" had never been to a race, and about a quarter had been to a race that year. Since auto races are geographically dispersed and can accommodate huge numbers of fans, a relatively high percentage of fans have the opportunity to attend a race.

For professional teams based in a local area, the percentage of "fans" who attend games can be even smaller. For NFL teams, ticket inventory is limited, most games sell out, and there is a high percentage of season ticket holders who attend multiple games. That means that there is overall a small number of people attending games, even if the fan base in the area is very large.

NHL and NBA teams typically play in arenas that hold about 20,000 fans. In order to fill the arena to capacity on a regular basis, teams would likely need to sell approximately 75 percent of their tickets before the season begins, equivalent to 16,000 season ticket equivalents (combined full season and partial season tickets). If the average number of tickets per season ticket account is 2.5, then the number of season ticket accounts would be 6000. Factor in shared season tickets and partial plans and that number can increase to 9000 season ticket buyers. Assuming the remaining inventory of tickets are bought by single game purchasers buying an average of two tickets per game and two games per season, that means an additional 41,000 ticket buyers.

That means that an NHL or NBA team can consistently sell out their building, attracting more than 800,000 in attendance per year, with approximately 50,000 ticket buyers. You

Table 5.1 Number of ticket buyers needed for consistent sell-outs

Arena capacity	20,000
75% full-time season ticket equivalents	20,000 * 0.75 = 16,000
Number of FTE season ticket accounts (2.5 tickets per account)	16,000/2.5 = 6000
Number of season ticket buyers, including shared tickets and partial season tickets	**9000**
Total single game tickets	4000 * 41 = 164,000
Single game ticket buyers (avg. two tickets per buyer/two games per season)	164,000/2/2 = **41,000**
Total ticket buyers	**50,000**

can play around with the numbers for games attended and number of tickets per purchase to arrive at a higher figure, but even at double the number of estimated ticket buyers, the percentage of ticket buyers in markets for professional teams in North America is small relative to the population, which averages about 5 million residents for NBA and NHL markets.

Ticket buyers do not equal attendees. Corporations that own season tickets, for example, are likely to invite different clients to games. For consumers, fans take spouses, partners, family members, and friends to games as guests. There are many attendees who are not ticket buyers, and who may not even be fans of the team.

For gate revenue, some customers are more important than others. Season ticket holders account for a large percentage of attendance for teams that consistently draw well (see Table 5.1). Add in premium seating, such as luxury suites and club seats, and season ticket holders account for a higher percentage of gate revenue than the average fan sitting in the stands. While many sports teams and events enjoy a broad base of interest, the point here is that ticket buyers tend to be a more tightly defined market segment. Therefore, sports marketers seeking to increase gate revenue have eschewed traditional mass marketing techniques in favor of more targeted efforts customized to reach segments of ticket buyers.

RELATIONSHIP MARKETING AND CRM

Relationship marketing has become the dominant paradigm for sports marketers looking to sell tickets and increase gate revenue because of the targeted marketing segment of ticket buyers and the high costs of tickets for many teams. In relationship marketing, the focus tends to be on customer satisfaction and retention than on just making the sale. In sports, fans already identify with teams on an intensely emotional basis, so there is an expectation of a strong relationship and close, direct contact.

Personalized, direct approaches to ticket sales have been popular for decades. In *How to Sell the Last Seat in the House*, a workbook first published by Jon Spoelstra in 1991 and the first-of-its-kind book focused exclusively on sports ticket sales,[1] Spoelstra recommended that ticket sales executives "personally tell each of your fans on a one-to-one basis" about ticket packages. In a subsequent book targeted at a wider audience, Spoelstra argued that the quickest way to jump-start sales for any business is: "You personally ask each of your present customers on a one-to-one basis to buy some more."[2]

Among the promotional tools available to marketers – advertising, public relations, sales promotions, direct marketing, and personal selling – personal selling is the preferred, and most effective, option, especially for an organization's bigger customers. Ticket sales representatives tend to constitute the greatest number of employees for any division of professional sports teams, and are probably the most likely point of entry for job candidates seeking to work in sports. For that reason, personal selling will be examined in much greater detail in the next two chapters of the book. Other marketing promotions, however, continue to contribute to ticket sales, especially direct marketing, and especially digital and e-mail direct marketing, and especially for single game promotions.

Database and Analytics Coordinator – New Orleans Hornets

Key responsibilities:

- Creating customer segments within ticketing database for use in sales and marketing efforts, with forethought about who is receiving and what is the purpose of the message.
- Assigning campaigns to sales reps in CRM system, monitoring progress. As with many job descriptions for sports marketers, this one emphasizes data analysis.
- Assist with database management and maintenance, including ongoing data cleansing, importing new data into CRM, ARCHTICS and tracking database statistics...
- Grow comfortable with existing CRM reports and brainstorm new data views to monitor sales processes and identify areas for improvement.
- Create targeted lists in Ticketmaster Mail Manager for e-mail communication.
- Create weekly reports tracking e-mail statistics and e-revenue generated, in particular single game promotions...

Minimum requirements:

- Basic knowledge of relational databases
- Working knowledge of Microsoft CRM[3]

Database and analytics positions are a new phenomenon but growing rapidly among professional sports teams.

One of the major functions of CRM is to support the ticket sales staff, helping to score leads and establish priorities so that salespeople make the most of their time. ARCHTICS is a sales management software system which is linked to Ticketmaster.

E-mail marketing is by now an almost universally used tactic. Evaluating effectiveness of e-mail marketing efforts, however, is still in the early stages.

The Chicago Bulls, for example, developed a lead generation program that produced a database of 800,000 fans. The team used a variety of techniques to sell ticket packages: television, radio, newspaper, billboards, bus tails, a team website, e-marketing, direct mail, and inside sales. However, it was the staff of 22 ticket sales representatives that has proven to be the most effective ticketing marketing option for the Bulls, according to the Bulls VP of ticket sales.[4] Ticket sales representatives often have proven to be the most effective ticket sales marketing technique, and therefore often represent the greatest number of staff members in the marketing (or revenue) department.

Building a quality customer database

In order to contact present customers, it is necessary to have contact information for each of them. Therefore, the foundation of direct marketing approaches is a quality customer database, often referred to as a CRM system (customer relationship management). Acquiring customer contact information has been a long-standing marketing principle, since the days of "fish bowls" in restaurants. Some restaurants still do it. They place a fish bowl on the counter and invite customers to drop a business card in it for the chance to win a free meal. It is a very cheap and effective technique for acquiring contact info for current customers. Of course, advancements in digital technology have led to a variety of techniques for acquiring, storing, and analyzing data about customers across a variety of "brand touchpoints" with sports organizations.

CRM Database and Research Manager – The Detroit Lions

Summary

The CRM Database & Research Manager will oversee all of the Lions' data assets including the support and programming of a DBM/CRM, data capture, paperless ticket technologies, e-mail marketing, SMS marketing, and marketing research technologies...

Essential duties and responsibilities:

Work with Ticketmaster, Maingate, Levy, NFL and other data providers in regard to system and data integration[5] (emphasis added)

This job description lists typical sources for teams: ticketing software, merchandising (Maingate), concessions (Levy), league databases, and other data providers. Many teams buy e-mail lists for targeted campaigns from established providers.

Integrating data. Information for customer databases can come from a variety of sources, both internal and external to the organization. For example, the Detroit Lions sought a CRM Manager who could integrate data from Ticketmaster (ticketing), Maingate (merchandise), Levy (concessions), and the NFL (website usage), in addition to insights gained from market research. The challenge for CRM managers is to integrate the data in a way that marketers can use, which is no easy task. Often, data are integrated into a single database, such as Microsoft CRM, but also distributed to other databases for use by another department. For example, ACT!, Salesforce.com, and Archtics continue to be popular among sales departments.

- **Tickets.** Almost all teams and events have some type of automated ticketing system, with Ticketmaster being the most popular. Automated ticketing systems allow organizations to collect information about how often fans buy tickets, when, which nights, how many tickets, where they sit, etc. Even something simple, like number of games attended for season ticket holders, can be extremely important and useful. Season ticket holders are less likely to renew their tickets if they are not attending enough games. For a 36-game minor league ice hockey league, the sweet spot for renewal was about 27 games according to research I've done. If a season ticket account is not on track to attend enough games, the organization can reach out to help ensure those tickets are put to use, increasing the odds for renewal.
- **Merchandise.** Fans buy merchandise from a variety of channels: on-site at events, online for an organization's website, online but from a different website, and/or from a brick-and-mortar retailer.
- **Concessions.** In addition to providing a source of incremental revenue, data from concessions can help organizations understand fan experiences, especially when linked to repeat attendance. Insights from concession usage, for example, have helped teams develop successful "all-inclusive" ticket packages in which (often unlimited) concessions are included. Fans who spend a lot of money on concessions might feel like the total cost is prohibitive but buy more tickets and attend more events with the all-inclusive option.
- **League.** Keeping in mind that many fans do not live near their favorite teams or have the opportunity to attend events, league databases can be a valuable source of acquiring fan contacts, especially for marketing merchandise.
- **External lists.** Internally generated contact lists are the most effective because they tend to consist of individuals who have expressed some interest in the sports property, either through a purchase or website visit. However, contact lists are available for purchase from external providers with both general consumer expertise, such as Axciom or Experian, or specialized sports expertise, such as provided by Full House Entertainment Database Marketing.

With payment card technologies and automated ticketing systems, it is fairly easy to acquire data about customers who make a purchase, but not all attendees purchase a ticket. For personal season tickets, many accounts are shared. There is only one name on the account, but there are many "holders." For corporate season ticket holders, there is one account but attendees can be comprised of many employees and/or clients. For group sales, there is one "group leader" but several attendees. In addition, some attendees still do pay cash for tickets.

Acquiring names and contact info for non-purchasing attendees requires some ingenuity and creativity, often in the form of some kind of promotion. For shared season ticket holders, for example, a team can invite more than one person on the account to register to receive a media guide for the season. My personal favorite promotion that acquires names comes from minor league ice hockey. During the game, fans are invited to sign up to receive a foam puck, which they throw to a target placed on the ice during intermission. Closest to the target wins a prize. People who sign up are likely to provide accurate contact information because they will want to collect the prize if they win. Plus, watching hundreds of foam pucks fly through the air is fun. As an added feature, sponsors can be involved to provide the prize, such as a flat-screen TV, providing the sponsor with a qualified lead list, too (fans signing up are interested in the prize but most won't win it).

Analytics. One of the primary uses of CRM systems is to become more efficient with marketing efforts. Sports organizations collect and have access to huge amounts of data about their current and potential customers. That data needs to be analyzed in a way that yields actionable insights. Perhaps influenced by the popularity of "Moneyball" and an increased emphasis on "analytics" for on-field performance, many sports teams have created positions specializing in data analytics.

Manager of Analytics – Tampa Bay Buccaneers

The Manager of Analytics will be responsible for:

- Analyzing existing customer information from various data sources to improve segmentation, profitability
- Determining the results of our marketing efforts in terms of response, sales and ROI...
- Predicting and understanding fan behavior and patterns through metric and statistical analyses.[6]

The main goals for a candidate in this position would be evaluation (determining the results) and strategy (predicting and understanding fan behavior).

Scoring with RFM. One of the main goals of analytics is to "score" customers based on likelihood to purchase. External providers, such as Turnkey's *Prospector*, can help sports organizations rank the potential of future customers. Internally, analytics managers can draw upon increasingly user-friendly software to aid in analysis, such as IBM's Predictive Analytics.

The strongest predictors of future purchasing are recency, frequency, and monetary amounts. How long ago did the customer buy? How often does the customer buy? And how much does the customer spend? Single-ticket buyers are most likely to respond to offers sent after they have recently attended an event, when it is still fresh in their minds. Season ticket holders are more likely to renew their season tickets if they have bought them in three consecutive years. After three consecutive years, retention rates tend to increase greatly for season ticket renewal. Monetary amount is a strong predictor of future monetary amounts. By analyzing recency, frequency, and monetary amounts, analytics managers can "score" the value of customers in the database.

What databases don't tell you. Corporations have long ago merged customer analytics with traditional market research to form "customer insights" departments. Few professional sports properties have a market research tradition, either in employing market research professionals with the organization or in establishing budget lines for market research. For many sports teams, the market research function has been assigned to analytics managers who may or may not have any market research skills or experience. That is a loss for sports properties.

Customer databases can tell you a lot about the *who*, *what*, *when*, and how *much*. But not the *why*. For example, executives from a professional soccer team notice that many season ticket holders attend only 2–3 games per season out of a 16-game schedule but renew their tickets year after year. And this segment tended to skew towards more expensive club seats than standard season tickets. Market research finds that the number one reason season ticket holders renew is "to support the success of the sport in the US." While a positive relationship between games attended and renewal rates generally holds true, there were significant exceptions for this valuable segment of season ticket holders.

While insights from market research can be integrated into insights from database analytics, the actual data itself cannot. In market research, participant anonymity and confidentiality is extremely important in obtaining valid responses. People will not provide open and honest answers to questions if they think someone will try to sell them something based on the results. "Surveys" that are not confidential, where responses are linked to individuals, are unethical from a research perspective. Overuse of these types of promotional surveys can also be confused with valid market research, lowering response rates among fans for confidential surveys. While insights from database analytics and market research can and should be integrated, results and techniques must remain separate in order to retain credibility for market research.

Segmenting ticket buyers. The two main categories of ticket buyers are:

1 *Business*. Businesses buy tickets for business reasons, although personal tastes are often still a factor in business-related ticket sales. Many business executives are sports fans, which helps to provide an intuitive understanding of how tickets can be used for client entertainment. Sometimes, businesses use tickets to boost employee morale or provide incentives for employee performance.
2 *Personal*. Sports fans can be segmented by:
   a **Usage.** This is perhaps the most meaningful way to segment fans. Fans who spend the most are the most valuable.
   b **Demographics.** Fan segments can be identified by family status and ethnicity.
   c **Benefits.** What fans get out of attending events can cross usage levels and demographic categories. For example, fans who respond to a "dollar beer night" promotion can comprise a segment motivated by cheap beer.

Data analytics and market research can help inform ticket sales strategies and identify potential targets, but sports marketers must develop marketing tactics to implement those strategies. That means developing strategically informed products, promotions, distribution, and pricing.

TICKET PACKAGES

Not all fans are interested in a full season ticket. For MLB, for example, that means an 81-game commitment of home games not counting potential play-off games. That is a lifestyle choice. For the Barclays Premier League teams, 19 home games plus League and Cup competitions, plus potential European competitions, as well as attending feasible away games. Again, that is a sizable commitment and not for everyone.

Most sports organizations understand that fans want more choices than a full season ticket or single-game packages. For that reason, most sports organizations offer some form of "full menu marketing," or a variety of ticket packages designed to meet the needs of their targets.

Season tickets. Full season tickets are the lifeblood of sports franchises. In crafting season ticket package benefits, it is important to understand not only what fans are looking for but, more importantly, what they are willing to pay for. Team merchandise, for example, might be appealing to season ticket holders but not influence renewal rates, especially for businesses accounts. While season ticket packages should be customized for specific circumstances, the most common benefits include:

- **Location.** Seat location is the most valuable asset in ticket sales, regardless of whether the account is for business or personal reasons.
- **Discounts.** Price discounts for volume purchases across industry categories are a common, and often appealing, benefit. That applies to sports settings as well.
- **Access and priority.** Season ticket holders are important to sports organizations, so they should be made to feel that way. Season ticket holders do, in fact, comprise a special club. The Chicago Bulls provide a number of benefits to season ticket holders, which combine to let them know that they are special (see Table 5.2). Most of the

Table 5.2 Chicago Bulls season ticket benefits

- A substantial saving of at least $5 to $100 per ticket from single-game prices.
- The right to purchase the same seats for every home playoff game.
- ClickTix, an online management system: email your tickets for free.
- NBATickets.com: sell your tickets above face value to other fans.
- Annual mailing of premium items given away at the gates.
- Special "Backstage Tours" of the United Center and the locker room.
- Complimentary subscription to BasketBull Magazine.
- A free copy of the official team Yearbook.
- Presales to buy extra tickets before the general public.
- The chance to participate in on-court contests.
- Opportunity to buy tickets to selected United Center events.
- A "VIP Card" for a 10% discount at the team store (Bull Market).
- Access to reserved tables at the Budweiser Select Brew Pub and Carvery.
- Season ticket upgrade window to improve seat locations on game nights.
- First priority at annual seat improvements.
- Invitations to special events like "An Evening with the Chicago Bulls."
- A VIP email address for questions and requests.
- Five-color, foil-stamped, collectible souvenir style tickets.
- Opportunity to purchase Ketel One Club membership.
- Opportunity to purchase priority parking.

benefits are "valuable," but do not cost the team anything. Other than discounts, most of the benefits are priority for purchases or access to existing inventory.

Partial season tickets. "We understand not everyone can make it to all 50 Sioux City Explorers home games," according to the minor league baseball team's website. "With that in mind, we've created a series of Partial Season Ticket Packages designed to maximize fun and flexibility."[7] There is a wide variety of partial season ticket packages available. While all packages are customized to match the team's objectives with customer benefits, some typical features include:

- *Number of games.* Caution should be exercised in not encouraging fans to attend fewer games. Most teams offer reduced attendance packages in the 10–15-game range, depending on demand. Teams with poor attendance might consider five-game packages. Sports such as football sometimes have three-game packages, again depending on demand.
- *Opponents.* Teams can use a roster of desirable opponents to create attractive packages. It is not advisable to leverage "attractive" opponents in order to sell unattractive games because fans can become resentful at having to buy tickets they do not want in order to gain access to games that they want to attend.
- *Flex packs.* For teams with a lot of inventory, "flex packs" offer fans full flexibility in the number of games and tickets per game they purchase. Rather than being locked into specific dates with a specific number of tickets, flex packs allow fans to redeem vouchers at their convenience. A 20-ticket flex pack, for example, could allow a fan to use one ticket for 20 games, 20 tickets for one game, or any combination in between.
- *Weekend.* Weeknight games can be a challenge for families with children or for people who do not live close to the facility. Therefore, many teams create weekend packages to accommodate fans' busy schedules.
- *Promotional.* Fireworks and give-aways can be popular attractions for ticket buyers, and leveraged into a multi-game package. Minor league baseball's Brooklyn Cyclones, for example, offer a "Day at the Beach Plan," which includes five weekend games, each with an exclusive special beach themed giveaway (e.g., beach bag, pail and shovel, etc.).

Group tickets. The main feature of group tickets is usually the price discount. Businesses or community groups that buy in volume receive tickets at a reduced price. Many teams are adding new innovative features to group packages, including:

- *Performance opportunities.* Youth dance and cheerleading groups, school bands, and youth sports groups are often interested in performing in front of large crowds in a "big-league" environment. A dance school with 50 students is likely to come with another 100 adults and 50 siblings, resulting in 200 tickets sold primarily for the opportunity for the dancers to perform at halftime of a game.
- *Access.* Behind-the-scenes access can be a great bonding experience for groups. Being able to watch players up close during warm-ups, lining the halls for player entrances – these types of experiences can be especially thrilling for young fans.

PROMOTIONS MIX

While personal selling is the dominant marketing promotion in the ticket sales promotions mix, other communication options can be integrated into the sales effort. While ticket packages are best-served by salespeople, it is not cost-effective for ticket salespeople to sell single-game tickets. Single-game tickets are important not only as a source of revenue, but also to get future season ticket holders into the pipeline. For non-team sports that do not have league schedules, such as auto racing, tennis, and golf, single-game ticket purchases comprise the majority of ticket purchases.

Public relations

Public relations is often best used to build brands, but the sports information arm of PR is very important to single-game ticket sales. Fans need to know when and where events are being held. Ensuring that schedules and game times are distributed and published by news outlets is vital to single-game ticket sales.

Director of Advertising and Promotions – National Hot Rod Association (NHRA)

Essential functions

- Work with NHRA National Event track management to develop advertising and promotion campaigns that drive attendance.
- Oversee and assist the development, approval and execution of event media plans for partner tracks. For NHRA-owned facilities, oversee media buying agency development and execution of media plans.
- Oversee development and execution of TV, Radio, digital, direct and print event creative. Includes approval of creative concepts, assisting and writing and editing advertising material, securing voice talent, etc...
- Provide ongoing evaluation of ROI for event promotion programs and provide analysis and reporting to improve performance for NHRA, tracks and sponsors."[8]

Sports properties with seasonal events, such as auto races and tennis and golf tournaments, typically do not have full-time sales staffs. While advertising is most frequently used to achieve "upper funnel" objectives, such as awareness and liking, these events use advertising to sell tickets.

Advertising

Similar to PR, advertising is often used to build brands and influence attitudes. With increased accountability for marketing budgets, many sports organizations are demanding a more direct ROI from advertising expenditures. Communicating a "theme" for a team's

Table 5.3 Radio behaviors for non-attending Galaxy fans

Radio format	Percent of target	Index
Mexican Regional	32	175
Rhythmic Contemporary	26	144
Spanish Contemporary	22	162
Alternative	14	103
Classic Hits	13	105

Source: Scarborough.[9]

season, for example, might lead to some enthusiasm, but does it sell tickets? For the NHRA, for example, advertising and promotion campaigns must demonstrate a ROI in driving attendance (see Director of Advertising and Promotions box above).

Direct response advertising provides a way to track the return on advertising efforts. An ad can contain a promotional code, which links the ad to the purchase. In digital environments, the link is easier to establish. Advertising for ticket sales is most often used to generate awareness of a promotional offer.

After deciding the content of the advertisement, sports marketers must decide where to place it. Syndicated research services, such as Scarborough, are especially useful in identifying media strategies. Fans who watch or listen to a team but do not attend games are prime targets for single-game ticket sales. In Table 5.3, the radio listening habits of Los Angeles residents who watch or listen to MLS's Los Angeles Galaxy games but did not attend are profiled. Nearly a third (32 percent) of these non-attending fans listen to Mexican Regional radio, yielding an index of 175, meaning non-attending fans are 75 percent more likely to listen to that radio format. Similar analyses can be performed for print and TV preferences and behaviors, assisting in more efficient media placement for single-game advertising efforts.

Sales promotions

What industry execs are saying . . .

> What has become clear over the past decade is that if you are not a team that sells out every game, the answer to the question "Does merchandise move the needle on attendance?" . . . is unequivocally "Yes."[10]
>
> CEO, BDA (merchandise provider for MLB)

Given limited marketing budgets, sports marketing programs are coming under more scrutiny for how well they achieve their goals. Premium merchandise can be expensive. If a team is giving away bobbleheads or sending jerseys to season ticket holders, it is important to understand if that affects sales.

Premium give-aways and themed events are popular methods to increase attendance among single-game buyers (see Table 5.4). But even when attendance increases because of a gameday promotion, is it worth it financially?

Table 5.4 Top gameday promotions in MLB

Category	Number of games
Ticket discounts	265
Fireworks	195
Concession discount	169
Run the bases	145
Autographs	129
Festival	121
Family Day	118
Cultural celebration	91
Charitable causes	82

Bobbleheads are a popular gameday give-away in MLB and demonstrate increases in attendance. But units costs for each bobblehead range from $2.50 to $4.50 for a customized bobblehead, and teams will give away 10,000–40,000 units depending on the team and player. On the low end, that means a team needs $25,000–$180,000 in *incremental* ticket sales just to cover the costs of the bobbleheads, not including any advertising costs associated with promoting the game.

A common way to help defray the costs of these promotions is to involve sponsors. According to one industry exec, "Red Sox partners are far and away the most likely of any MLB club to buy custom-made premium items. They have about 100 sponsors putting their company logo on Red Sox product."[11] T-shirts and caps remain the favorites for promotional giveaways and also represent opportunities for sponsors to get involved. Teams get more sponsorship inventory to sell and sponsors are afforded a way to engage fans, provided the fans do not feel that the sponsors are an unwanted intrusion into the merchandise. How a sponsor's logo is integrated into a premium item, and how fans define "tasteful" in a particular circumstance, is important to the success of the promotion.

Determining promotional effectiveness. Price discounts remain the most popular sales promotion across sports. By traditional definition, sales promotions are short-term incentives to buy, though the sub-discipline has come to mean a lot more than that in current practice. Are price discounts worth it? Do fans buy tickets they would not otherwise buy? Or, are marketers cannibalizing their own profits by sending discount offers to fans who would buy tickets anyway?

The equation is complicated when considering the lifetime value of an acquired fan. Among fans who respond to a promotion to attend an event for the first time, what percentage attend a second time? What is the conversion rate to long-time fans, season ticket holders, etc.? Short-term sales and profits must be balanced with fan development considerations.

Digital technology provides sports marketers with the capacity to design field experiments that measure the effects of promotions. The NBA's Golden State Warriors, for example, run experiments on offers they send to its 200,000-person e-mail list. Executives "break [the list] into chunks, testing different times, different subject lines and different links in the body of the message to gauge what brings the quickest response."[12] It is also important in these research designs to include a control group. An equal number of fans on the list should receive no e-mail at all because it could be that managers get better at finding fans who will buy tickets, but not because of the e-mails or offers.

PRICING

Advances in digital technology combined with automated ticketing systems have supplied sports marketers with tons of data about ticket pricing. The key to pricing efficiently is to understand the value that sports organizations deliver to ticket buyers. As with merchandising and licensing, there has been a trend toward fewer, more expensive tickets. Fans might complain about spiraling tickets costs, but they continue to pay.

Rigorous analyses of pricing and ticket sales data have yielded the following trends in pricing:

1 **Tiered.** The difference has grown between front row seats and seats in the "nosebleeds" far away from the action. MLB's New York Mets tickets, for example, range from $15 to $455. Tiered pricing reflects the emotional attachment avid fans have for the team – they will pay the high prices to be close to the action. In contrast, there are many teams who cannot fill their facilities even when they give tickets away for free, but have thousands of core fans who will pay top dollar for good seats.

2 **Variable.** Not all games are the same, so not all ticket prices should be the same. While ticket prices used to be set in stone for most teams, now most teams divide the schedule into different levels of demand, and price accordingly. Popular opponents, heated rivalries, and premium dates can all accommodate premium prices.

3 **Dynamic.** The popularity of secondary ticket markets, such as StubHub, has added a dynamic component to ticket prices. In addition to secondary ticket markets, ticket sellers themselves are beginning to use more dynamic pricing, adapting to late season conditions. Marketers can understand demand for games and help determine future pricing by looking at what fans actually paid for tickets.

4 **Discounts.** The "d" word is usually avoided when it comes to pricing because it can devalue a product. If a fan is accustomed to free tickets, why would he or she ever buy one? Discounts can be used effectively to spur demand for low-demand events. Again, advances in ticketing technology, data storage, and data analysis can help marketers adjust prices to more accurately reflect fan interest and increase profits.

CASE: WOMEN'S PROFESSIONAL SOCCER: CUSTOMERS, MEMBERS, FANS, OR GENDER EQUITY ADVOCATES? (ALL OF THE ABOVE)

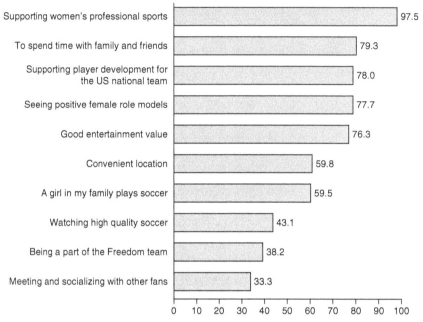

Figure 5.1 How important are the following reasons in your decision to attend Washington Freedom games? Percent agree. (source: *Washington Freedom Web-based Research Report* (2009). Sponsorship Research & Strategy, CO Springs).

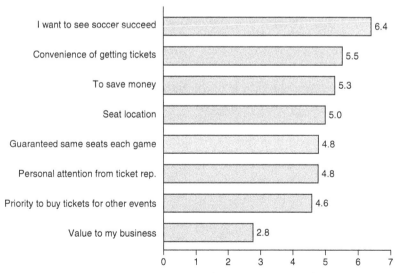

Figure 5.2 Average importance for purchasing a season ticket plan versus individual game tickets. 0 means "not at all important"; 10 means "extremely important" (source: *Washington Freedom Web-based Research Report* (2009). Sponsorship Research & Strategy, CO Springs).

Women's professional soccer in the US faces a double whammy: neither soccer nor women's professional team sports have been well-established in the marketplace. Both women's professional sports and the sport of soccer in the US are underdogs in the sports landscape. While many sports teams stress the entertainment value of their events or the opportunity to show loyalty to a team, women's professional soccer provides an opportunity to show support both for women's sports and soccer. In that respect, buying tickets can be a form of social activism in solidarity for gender equity.

According to a survey of 471 fans of a women's professional soccer team, supporting women's sports is by far the number one reason fans attend games (see Figure 5.1). Watching soccer and supporting the team were comparatively minor factors in fans attending games. Supporting players for the national team was equivalent to more common motivations of entertainment value and social time with friends and family.

In sports outside North America, which have rich traditions as clubs, fans tend to think of themselves as members. In the US, the most avid fans of college sports teams are "boosters" with an official designation (and ranking) within athletic department. For fans of women's professional soccer, buying a season ticket is primarily an act of support. Contrary to typical season ticket holder (STH) "benefits," women's pro soccer STHs' primary motivation in buying a season ticket instead of individual tickets was because they want to see soccer succeed (Figure 5.2). They are supporters not only of the league, team, and players, but for the sport as a whole.

Fans of men's professional soccer in the US are also strong supporters of growing the sport in the country. According to research I have done with Major League Soccer teams, "supporting soccer in the US" is a strong motivation for season ticket and club seat. In discussing this phenomenon with a high-level soccer executive, he noted that he consistently found a cohort of club seat holders who attend only a few games a year but renew every year, which puzzled him. But the desire to see the sport grow fits – club seat holders are supporters of the sport of soccer who see the MLS as a key component to the growth of the sport.

Advocates and supporters for women's professional sports and the growth of soccer in the US present an unusual opportunity for sports marketers. The traditional model of treating fans as consumers, however, does not apply to these situations. The primary benefit for these fans is the opportunity to contribute to the causes of women's sports and/or soccer, rather than seat location, parking, concessions, or merchandise.

EXERCISE

Table 5.5 Washington Freedom demographics

Demographics	
Category	Total
Female	58.1
Married	61.2
Average age	40.9
Average income	$103,000
College degree	81.9
Caucasian	86.8

Fans of women's professional soccer in the US are more likely to be female, much more likely to be college educated, and highly affluent. In short, it is an extremely attractive demographic. Review the data in the case study for this chapter about motivations for women's professional soccer season ticket holders to renew. Then, create ticket and/or membership packages for women's pro soccer "boosters" whose primary motivation for buying is the opportunity to support women's sports.

- Create new inventory for these segments
- Identify the primary benefits of packages
- Discuss pricing

THREE MAIN TAKEAWAYS

1   Sports marketers attempt to build meaningful relationships with fans on a personal basis.
2   Effective ticket packages are based on an understanding of fan desires and experiences.
3   Sports marketers must integrate the different elements in the promotion mix in order to create a clear, consistent, and compelling message.

NOTES

1   Spoelstra, J. (1994). *How to Sell the Last Seat in the House.* Portland, OR: SRO Partners.
2   Spoelstra, J. (1997). *Ice to the Eskimos.* New York: Harper Business.
3   Database and Analytics Coordinator – New Orleans Hornets (New Orleans, LA). http://nbateamjobs.teamworkonline.com/teamwork/r.cfm?i=51654, accessed 2/4/2013.
4   Migala, D. (2006). Anything but small. http://migalareport.com/MuchAdoAboutMiniPlans, accessed 9/2/2013.
5   CRM Database and Research Manager – The Detroit Lions (Detroit, MI). http://footballjobs.teamworkonline.com/teamwork/r.cfm?i=50854, accessed 1/7/2013.
6   Manager of Analytics – Tampa Bay Buccaneers (Tampa, FL). http://footballjobs.teamworkonline.com/teamwork/r.cfm?i=50541, accessed 1/7/2013.
7   Sioux City Explorers Partial Season Tickets.
8   http://nhra.teamworkonline.com/teamwork/jobs/jobs.cfm/Sales-and-Marketing, accessed 11/17/2011.

9 www.scarboroughsportsmarketing.com/dia_conduct_media.php, accessed 2/27/2013.
10 Broughton, D. (2011). How best to use the bait? www.sportsbusinessdaily.com/Journal/Issues/2011/10/17/In-Depth/Lead-story.aspx?hl=How%20best%20to%20use%20the%20bait%3F%, accessed 9/8/2014.
11 Ibid.
12 (2013). Warriors show keen usage of data research in refining ticket sales process. www.sportsbusinessdaily.com/Daily/Issues/2013/02/07/Franchises/Warriors.aspx?hl=warriors%20show%20keen&sc=0, accessed 5/3/2013.

Chapter 6

Consumer ticket sales

WHY TICKET SALES?

While the reputation of ticket sales as a profession has come a long way over recent decades, biases remain. Ticket salespeople are sleazy, aggressive, work in a boiler room, it's only an entry-level job. So, why ticket sales?

For one reason, gate receipts remain the largest source of revenue for the sports industry. One of the reasons behind the rapid growth in the sports industry over recent decades has been an increasingly professional approach to ticket sales. The old model of printing up the schedule and opening the box office window is pretty much obsolete. Even US college athletics departments, which tend to lag behind the industry in business practices, have taken a professional approach to ticket sales. So, the first answer to the question of "Why ticket sales?" is that it is important. In fact, for many professional sports leagues, the majority of gate revenues pass through the front office, meaning without professional ticket sales, there is no team or league.

The second answer to the question follows from the first and is perhaps more relevant to readers of this book. As sports organizations have recognized the importance of ticket sales as a revenue source, they have put more resources behind ticket sales departments. That means ticket sales is where the jobs are, especially entry-level jobs. For someone looking to break into the sports business, ticket sales remains the most likely option. Once working in the organization, the opportunities are endless.

After *Jerry Maguire* came out, there seems to have been an increase in the number of students who wanted to be "sports agents." I would explain that "sports agents" really work in athlete representation, which meant selling their client as an endorser to potential sponsors. Since *Moneyball*, the pendulum seems to have swung from sports agent to general manager. Instead of admonishing students with the dream, I now share a story of a law school grad who took a job with an NBA team in inside sales and after being promoted to sales manager started doing some salary cap work for the team in addition to his sales duties. I think at some point that he will be a GM in the NBA. So, inside sales to GM, it could happen. The more likely avenues for career advancement from ticket sales remain in sales – tickets, sponsorship, media, etc. – but many salespeople leverage initial jobs in the industry to work in community relations, PR, marketing, or event management. The best chance to get your foot in the door, however, is with ticket sales.

According to industry veteran and ticket sales innovator Jon Spoelstra, many sports teams continue to under-staff ticket sales.[1] Many sports teams, however, have developed a "sales-oriented culture" and respond to declines in attendance with increases in ticket sales staff. A recently hired chief executive for the NBA's Philadelphia 76ers summed it up this way:

> The biggest challenge is ramping up sales staff. We are coming off a disappointing season [34–48 on the court; 16,717 fans a game, below the leaguewide average] and have a lot of inventory to sell. We have a low season-ticket base, and instead of cowering in a corner, we are quadrupling down with full-time ticket sellers.[2]

Unlike branding and advertising efforts, the financial case for hiring salespeople is direct and clear. Spoelstra argues that trained salespeople cost 20 percent of a sale and untrained salespeople cost 50 percent, but that 50 percent of something is better than nothing.[3] Factoring in the influence on current ticket purchases on future ticket purchases – putting more fans in the pipeline – further supports the case for increasing ticket staff.

Employing a staff of professional ticket sellers is now very well established in North America, partly out of necessity. While some sports benefit from the luxury of long traditions of fan following and solid history of event attendance, other sports had to build from the ground up. Major League Soccer, for example, now averages close to 20,000 tickets sold per game, and it has been estimated that 80 percent of those tickets sold pass through the front office. In short, without professional ticket sellers, there is no MLS. Professional ticket sales is gaining traction as a marketing technique in other markets as well, partly because of the influence of US-based owners buying teams abroad and partly because the US attracts international attention because of its size.

STRUCTURING TICKET SALES DEPARTMENTS

Marketers often distinguish between "product-based" marketing and "consumer-focused" marketing. In a product orientation, the mode is to produce and sell. A consumer orientation begins with the customer, not the product. While a growing number of ticket sales departments are structured based on customers, the majority still sell by product.

By product

A product-based ticket sales department assigns representatives to specific ticket products: premium account executive, season ticket account executive, group sales account executive, etc. The problem with beginning with the product rather than the customer is that very different customers can buy the same product. A season ticket buyer might be a company using tickets for client entertainment or a long-time fan who attends every game personally.

By method

Many sports organizations in North America have a staff of "inside sales reps" (See Inside Sales Representative – Pittsburgh Pirates box below) who might sell a variety of different ticket products but primarily via telephone. Inside sales staffs help to provide a training ground for full-time account executives while providing teams with a staff to contact what is often huge volumes of single-game ticket buyers.

For some teams, inside sales is a "sink or swim" proposition. Inside sales representatives are given a chance to prove themselves worthy of a full-time position. In addition, with the growing use and sophistication of CRM systems, many teams have a huge database of contacts in need of being contacted. As the Pirates ad indicates, most inside sales reps will make an average of 100 calls per day, most often from lists provided by the team.

Inside Sales Representative – Pittsburgh Pirates (Pittsburgh, PA)

Job summary

This position requires participation in a nine month career growth-oriented sports sales development program. This is an entry level position focused on selling full season tickets, partial plans, group tickets and all of our premium products including club seats and suites via the telephone (outbound and inbound) and face to face meetings at PNC Park and out of office appointments. This program provides extensive training and teaches sales skills and fundamentals as well as presentation skills. The intent of the program is to expand the employee's ability to a level that will merit consideration for a promotion to a full time sales position.

Responsibilities

- Make a minimum of 100 outbound sales calls daily from provided lists to individual buyers, businesses, churches, schools, canceled plans as well as referrals."[4]

Inside sales is the most common way for entry-level candidates to break into the sports industry.

The job consists primarily of smilin' and dialin', so phone skills can be a big asset.

The level of training varies across teams and leagues, but there is a discernible trend toward sports properties providing more and better sales training for entry-level candidates. Since sports is a sales-based business, it is great preparation for the future.

For inside sales, lists are often provided. Without prospecting responsibilities, inside sales reps can bang out one hundred calls a day or more.

By customer

The approach taken in this book is customer-focused, which is also being adopted by some teams as a sales management structure. The NBA's Indiana Pacers, for example, recently restructured their ticket sales staff into "Corporate" and "Consumer" sales. The premise is that there is a huge difference between personal and business ticket buyers. Therefore, this chapter will discuss ticket sales to consumers for personal use, and the next chapter will discuss ticket sales to companies for business use.

SALES ELEMENTS

"Consultative selling" is the dominant paradigm in sales. Although terms such as "consultative," "solutions," and "partnership" tend to get overused, the underlying principle of consultative selling is a consumer focus. Rather than simply communicate the features of a product (e.g., price discount for season tickets), consultative selling involves identifying the needs of the prospective customer and then providing a solution. In this sense, good salespeople are effective problem-solvers.

The emphasis on consultative selling and problem-solving is consistent with the long-term goal of sales: to develop and maintain strong relationships. The most valuable customers in sports have long-term committed relationships with sports organizations. Selling people something they do not want might be profitable in the short term but burning customers is a quick way to go out of business in sports. As we have seen in the previous chapter, most sports organizations rely heavily on a relatively small number of very important customers. Those relationships are vital to long-term success and must be nurtured.

Regardless of the product, most salespeople follow a process with similar steps. Like the marketing funnel, there are numerous versions of the steps of the sales process, the most common of which includes seven steps. Some models include as many as ten steps. Many of those steps, however, can be collapsed into four main categories:

- **Prospecting:** Determine who you will contact.
- **Needs analysis:** Find out what they are looking for.
- **Presentation:** Make a recommendation.
- **Closing:** Ask for the business.

Prospecting

In consumer sales, lists of previous ticket buyers – the most likely future ticket buyers – often are provided by the organization. Frequently, the primary responsibility of inside sales staffs is to contact single-game buyers to sell partial season tickets. Account executives selling group tickets must be more industrious and creative when developing contact lists for community groups.

Internal lists

Single-game buyers. Most sports organizations collect contact information through automated ticket systems, such as Ticketmaster. Most automated ticketing systems can be linked to sales contact databases, such as Salesforce.com or ACT!. Ticketmaster has a proprietary system called Archtics, which is very popular in the sports industry because of the dominance of Ticketmaster as a ticketing system.

The main goal in contacting current customers is to move fans along the "conveyor belt."[5] Sales staff contact single-game buyers to offer partial season tickets; partial season ticket holders to offer full; and full season ticket holders to renew for bigger packages. In addition to storing contact information, most CRM systems based on ticket sales provide basic product usage information, such as:

- Games attended (when, how many)
- Account history (years as a ticket buyer)
- Communications history (previous sales calls)
- Customer contacts (promotional participation, website registration, etc.)

Season ticket holders. One of the fastest ways to decrease gate receipts is to have season ticket holders not renew. It takes a long time to "grow" a season ticket holder but a short time to lose one. While sales departments had traditionally been divided into "hunters" and "farmers" – hunters who sell and farmers who service – the recognition of the importance of season ticket holder retention has blurred that line. As a veteran ticket sales trainer said about the hunter/farmer distinction:

> we're not making that distinction anymore. I'm seeing service staffs that are being staffed by people who are superb at relationship building, they can connect. But they're also superb sales people. They upsell, they handle it, and they acquire referrals for new business.[6]

Job titles, such as account executive or account manager, support the view that selling and servicing are equally important roles, as opposed to "ticket sales representative," which might suggest an emphasis on sales over service.

In my research with dozens of professional sports teams, I have found a consistent positive relationship between increased intent to renew a season ticket and simply knowing an account representative's name. Furthermore, strong relationships can lead to "upselling" opportunities, from season ticket to premium seating, and from personal use to business use. Keep in mind that many season ticket holders are affluent and therefore likely to be decision makers at work.

Referrals. Existing ticket buyers can provide valuable referrals. Season ticket accounts for personal use are often shared, yet there is only one name associated with the account formally. Sales staff can obtain contact info for all of the account users in order to develop and maintain relationships. Similarly, single-game buyers often attend with others who do not personally pay for the tickets but are fans and attend. Promotional offers, such as media kits and other team merchandise, can be used as incentives to obtain contact info from referrals.

Season ticket sales events have become a popular technique in leveraging the fan interest of existing customers.[7] "Influencer parties" in which team executives host an event at a current season ticket holder's home have become increasingly popular as a way to leverage the passion of a team's biggest fans within their social circles. Fans invite friends and business associates to a party, usually hosted at the fans' homes, where team executives can gather contact info for referrals.

Groups. Group sales has become an increasingly important source of revenue and fan development for many sports organizations. Group sales help to generate attendance by selling at least 20 tickets at a time, though many group packages are much greater. Five groups of 200, for example, can really move the needle on attendance figures. Perhaps more importantly, group sales are more resistant to team performance.

Teams in markets without a big corporate base can have difficulty in generating season ticket accounts. Likewise with teams that have had poor record on the field of play. While being a fan of the team can be a big factor in motivating a group leader; and many groups are based on youth participation for the sport, the action on the field of play is almost incidental to many groups' attendance.

Prospecting for group sales involves a lot more creativity than simply following up on leads provided by an existing database. Since prospects need not be related to the team or sport, the pool of prospects can be huge. Table 6.1 lists some categories for group sales prospecting, but there are lots of options even within those categories. Take K-12 schools: that can mean elementary or high school; clubs or groups within the high school, etc. High school bands, for example, often seek opportunities to perform in public. Performing in front of thousands of fans in a professional arena can be a thrill. Since many high school bands have 100 members or more, plus parents and other siblings, a group event for a high school band can generate 300–500 ticket sales for a game. For social services, membership organizations, and other group categories, a sports event provides a fundraising opportunity in addition to a chance for members to get together in a social setting.

Needs analysis

The stereotype of a good salesperson is someone who is a "good talker," but in consultative selling it is listening skills that are more important. The old adage that people have one mouth and two ears is a common phrase meant to show that salespeople should listen twice as much as they speak.

Table 6.1 Consumer group sales categories

A *Social Services*

- Youth Organizations & Centers
- Non-Profit Organizations/Social Service
- Child Care Service (Day Care)

B *Membership Organizations*

- Churches/Religious Organizations
- Business Associations
- Professional Membership Organizations
- Labor Unions
- Civic, Social & Fraternal Organizations
- Political Organizations

C *Education*

- Schools (K-12)
- Colleges & Universities
- Libraries

D *Other Group Categories*

- Parks & Recreation Departments
- Camps
- Tours – Operators & Promoters
- Sports Clubs
- Private Golf Courses (Country Clubs)
- Bars, Night Clubs, Cocktail Lounges
- Bowling Centers
- Marinas
- Health Clubs
- Nursing, Personal Care, Residential Care (Retirement Homes)
- Dance Instruction/Gymnastic Instruction/Martial Arts Instruction
- Special Event & Wedding Planners
- Police Departments/Fire Departments
- Military Organizations[1]

Source: Full House Entertainment Database Marketing.

Note
1 www.fillthehouse.com/services_group.php, accessed 8/30/2013.

Establish rapport

In speaking with consumer ticket buyers, it is important to remember that they are fans. Sports fans love to talk about sports and love to talk about their teams. They do not want to be sold a product. Gaining valid information from a prospect requires that the prospect speak freely and openly. Sales calls should be conversational in tone. Effective salespeople are good at establishing a positive rapport that engenders trust, which can be accomplished through showing empathy and having a genuine interest and appreciation for the prospect's needs and wants. Making a good first impression is extremely important, so a strong introduction is vital. Keeping in mind that most calls will go to voice-mail, it is also important to be prepared with a message that will generate interest.

Sample introduction:

> Hi [prospect name] this is [your name] with the [team]. I'm really glad you answered today because we're reaching out to our best fans with some exciting deals on seats today.

Sample voice-mail:

> [Prospect name], we are calling our best fans to share some great deals on seats. I'm [name] with the [team], please call me at . . .

Fact finding

Salespeople need to understand prospect needs and wants before they can make an effective proposal. While it is important to be conversational in tone, salespeople must also gather information. And while CRM databases can do a good job of tracking fan behaviors, they do not provide much information about fan experiences and motivations to attend. Fact finding questions for individual fans typically include:

- Behaviors:
    - How many games do you go to?
    - Who do you come with?
    - Where do you sit?

- Motivations:
    - Who is your favorite player?
    - What do you enjoy most about games?

Groups are often motivated by other factors. In group sales, it is first necessary to identify the group leader or leaders, the contacts who will help organize the event, distribute the information, collect the money, and plan the event. Account executives are instrumental to this process. Group leaders can be motivated by being fans themselves: they want to organize the outing because they want to attend the game. Many groups simply seek a social outing, but some groups are motivated by a fundraising opportunity in which a portion of ticket sales goes to the group.

Presentation

If a salesperson conducts a thorough needs analysis, then the sales pitch should consist of simply restating the prospect's needs and wants in the form of benefits, and matching the ticket package to the prospects desires.

- *You say you like to attend games as an escape? Well, this ticket package consisting of weekend games will allow you to unhook from the week.*

101

- *You say that going to games is great family time? Our family package offers kid-friendly dates and start times.*
- *You say that you like to attend exciting games? Our 11-game packages feature the team's hottest rivalries.*

The list of fan motivations in Chapter 3 can provide a more comprehensive list of potential benefits for consumer ticket buyers:

- Entertainment: enjoyable pastime.
- Escape: diversion from everyday life.
- Aesthetics: artistic beauty and grace.
- Family: spend time with family.
- Group affiliation: spend time with others.
- Self-esteem: feel better about oneself.
- Eustress: enjoys the excitement and arousal of sports drama.

It is then important to link those motivations to specific ticket product offerings in the presentation.

Closing

If the needs analysis is accurate and the presentation of benefits meets prospect needs, then closing should consist simply of asking for the business. Few sales, however, are that simple. "Trial closes," in which a salesperson floats an idea to gauge prospect interest, are helpful in analyzing needs. Questions such as, "How does that sound?" or "What do you think?" can help to tease out underlying objections. Pauses in the conversation and moments of silence can allow a prospect to think through some potential issues. Remember, salespeople deal with the product all day, day-in and day-out, whereas prospects get only a matter of seconds to weight the product and alternatives.

Prospect objections must be identified before they can be resolved. Objections must be probed:

How do you mean?
I'm not sure I understand, can you explain a little more?

. . . and clarified:

So, what you're saying is . . .
If I understand correctly, you're saying . . .

Countering objections straight away can come across as argumentative or aggressive. Salespeople should validate the concern:

I understand how you can feel that way.
A lot of my customers have that concern.

And then propose a solution. Of course, it is important that ticket packages are structured so that they can provide solutions:

> I understand that you're concerned about the time commitment for season tickets, but our flex-pack allows you to choose the games you want to attend. How does that sound?
>
> I understand that you're concerned about the expense, but last season you ended up paying extra to attend play-off games. This package gives you priority access for play-off tickets. What do you think?
>
> I understand that you think a lot of the tickets will go to waste, but our season ticket exchange website allows you to sell any unused tickets. How would that address the problem?

"Always be closing" is a popular sales mantra. Closing involves much more than simply asking for the sale. Customers rarely buy on the first contact. Therefore, it is also important to set intermediate objectives:

- *When should I follow up?*
- *How would you like to come down to the facility to check out the seats?*

Customer relationships are built over time.

Service and retention

Relationships must also be maintained. In order to grow accounts and move fans along the "conveyor belt," sports organizations must deliver on promised benefits. Many teams, for example, set aside promotional items on game nights for season ticket holders so that STHs do not have to stand in line and are guaranteed of receiving the item before they run out. Why damage a relationship with an account worth thousands over a t-shirt or bobblehead?

Servicing the account also provides additional closing opportunities. Determining whether a prospect is a hot lead for an upgrade to more expensive seats requires asking.

> How interested are you in upgrading your seats?

While the sales process is divided into "steps" for conceptual purposes, in practice many of these functions are integrated. Strong customer relationships require good communication to determine needs, present benefits, and close on sales, while maintaining positive personal relationships.

What industry execs are saying...

> "To be successful in ticket sales, one must be on an endless pursuit of relationships."[8]
>
> Nick Sakiewicz, former GM, NY/NJ Metrostars

Relationship building has become the dominant paradigm in sales. Relationships in sports marketing settings are particularly important because sales are rarely made on the first call. For B2B relationships, sales cycles easily can exceed a year.

CASE: TICKET SALES SUCCESS

Ticket sales veteran Mark Washo wrote a book entitled *Break Into Sports Through Ticket Sales*,[9] which provides candidates interested in working in the sports industry with a detailed road map about how to do it. In the book, Washo identifies 15 tips for success in ticket sales:

1 *"Recognize that ticket sales is a volume business requiring you to be on an endless pursuit of relationships."* One of the reasons former athletes can make a smooth transition to sales is that, as in sports, in sales you get out of it what you put into it. Sales people who work harder tend to be more successful.

2 *"There are things you can control and things you cannot."* You can control the number of calls you make. You cannot control players' behavior in nightclubs.

3 *"Referrals, referrals, and more referrals!"* Building professional networks is associated with business success in general. In sales, maximizing your time means prospecting efficiently. Referrals are the most effective source of qualified leads.

4 *"Ask for and get testimonial letters from your clients."* Client testimonials can be a cost-effective method of providing support for assertions of benefits.

5 *"Renewal business is critical to long-term sales success."* Season ticket holder retention is a primary goal for many sports organizations.

6 *"Mix it up."* Experiment with different contact methods. Phone call followed by an e-mail or direct mail piece, or e-mail followed by phone call.

7 *"Stay organized because ticket sales is a unique industry where you actually create work for yourself over time."* Building more new relationships means having more current relationships to maintain.

8 *"The very best sales professionals maximize what is called 'prime time selling'. "* Early mornings and early evenings are when people tend to be at their desks and not in meetings. There are certain times of the day where salespeople really need to turn the jets on.

9 *"Don't quit; stay persistent and stay consistent."* This is another area where former athletes can draw upon experience from sports. In sports, players go through peaks and valleys in form and performance. In sales, it is important to stay focused on the process and not get obsessed with outcomes.

10 *"Keep the pipeline full and don't bank on 'that one big sale'. "* According to Washo, many inexperienced sales reps lose focus in anticipation of big sales and then are crushed if that sales evaporates, which they often do.

11 *"Don't sound like a cheesy or canned salesperson and don't 'show up and throw up'. "* Hiring managers greatly appreciate entry-level salespeople who have the confidence to be themselves. Although it is important to convey passion for the product, being overeager can be alienating.

12 *"Attend networking events."* This is good advice for anyone in any career, but especially crucial for salespeople.

13 *"Develop a plan, implement your plan, and set goals."* Washo suggests starting a sales plan with the question: "How much money do you want to make in the

upcoming calendar year?" Then, work backwards from there to identify more specific short-term goals and strategies.

14 *"Build on your strengths, and strengthen your weaknesses."* Some people are comfortable being outgoing and gregarious; others are more introverted but hardworking. If your strength is an outgoing personality, you can build on that. If your weakness is discipline and organization, likewise that can be addressed.

15 *"Last but not least, have fun and remember you are selling entertainment."* One of the major benefits of selling sports is that most sports salespeople have a genuine belief in the product. That personal passion can be leveraged into professional success.

EXERCISE: SALES ROLE PLAYS

Role play. Sales role plays can be based on various levels of script preparation. Some sales people, especially beginners, find detailed scripts helpful. In sports consumer sales, however, prepared scripts can inhibit building rapport. In many sports organizations, sales people are required to perform role plays in front of the entire group. However, smaller groups can be formed to provide more preparation. Groups of two can exchange roles of salesperson and prospect, or a third can be added to provide an observer role.

Ultimately, the goal would be for two students to complete a full role play in front of the entire class. However, comprehensive sales scripts can fill entire notebooks. Therefore, it is often helpful to break down a sales call into its component parts. For example, the sales call can be divided into:

1 *Building rapport.* This is one of the few areas in the sports business in which "talking sports" is part of the job. If the prospect is a fan, as most consumer prospects are, he or she will likely want to talk about the team, league, or sport in general, which is a great way to build rapport. Here's a simple rapport exercise: have students line up in two lines and introduce themselves to each other briefly. Kind of like a receiving line for a wedding.

2 *Needs analysis.* This is where a ticket sales executive asks questions to understand which ticket package is most suitable for the prospect. Interview each other about favorite sports, desires, and behaviors.

3 *Presentation and closing.* After building rapport and understanding needs, ticket sales executives must present the benefits of the ticket package and ask for the business. After learning about other people's sports interest, try to come up with some solutions to their problems. Practice making a recommendation and asking for a sale.

THREE MAIN TAKEAWAYS

1 Ticket sales is the most common way to break into the sports business.
2 Sales is about understanding and helping to solve problems.
3 Sales is a relationship-based discipline; successful salespeople are in constant pursuit of relationships.

105

RECOMMENDED READING

Spoelstra, J. (1997). *Ice to the Eskimos*. New York: HarperCollins. This book is a sports marketing class, even though Spoelstra claims it's not a sports marketing book. Even better, try to get a hold of a copy of Spoelstra's 1990 workbook: *How To Sell The Last Seat In The House*. Originally self-published by SRO Partners, Inc., it's probably one of the most photocopied books around.

Washo, M. (2004). *Break into Sports through Ticket Sales*. Rutherford, NJ: MMW Marketing LLC. If you're serious about wanting to work in sports, buy this book, read it, and do what it says. I can almost guarantee you'll get a job in sports.

NOTES

1 Spoelstra, J. (201). A three-step strategy to sell out a stadium, absent a superstar. www.sportsbusinessdaily. com/Journal/Issues/2010/12/20101206/From-The-Field-Of/Athree-Step-Strategy-To-Sell-Out-A-Stadium-Absent-A-Superstar.aspx, accessed 9/16/2013.
2 Lombardo, J. (2013). Sixers quadruple sales staff, add to executive ranks. www.sportsbusinessdaily.com/Journal/Issues/2013/09/16/Franchises/Sixers.aspx?hl=sixers%20quadruple&sc=0, accessed 9/16/2013.
3 Spoelstra. A three-step strategy.
4 http://baseballjobs.teamworkonline.com/teamwork/r.cfm?i=58334, accessed 9/16/2013/.
5 Washo, M. (2013). The ticket sales process. In Reese, J. (Ed.), *Ticket Operations and Sales Management in Sport*. Morgantown: West Virginia University.
6 (2013). Developing sales talent, part 4: How to determine hunters or farmers. www.sportsbusinessdaily. com/SB-Blogs/On-The-Ground/2013/04/Part-4-Developing-Sales-Talent.aspx, accessed 9/16/2013.
7 (2007). Top NBA execs discuss state of the League as season tips off. www.sportsbusinessdaily.com/Daily/Issues/2007/10/Issue-36/NBA-Season-Preview/Top-NBA-Execs-Discuss-State-Of-The-League-As-Season-Tips-Off.aspx?hl=top%20nba%20execs%20discuss%20state&sc=1, accessed 9/20/2013.
8 Washo, M. (2004). *Break Into Sports Through Ticket Sales*. Rutherford, NJ: MMW Marketing LLC.
9 Ibid.

Chapter 7

Corporate ticket sales

Businesses use sports tickets primarily for business reasons, both marketing and managerial. The primary business goals of tickets to sports events are to build and maintain relationships with potential and existing clients. Nearly all premium seating (e.g., luxury suites and club seats) and the majority of season tickets for North American major league sports are corporate owned and used for client entertainment. Using tickets for managerial purposes in the form of employee rewards and/or incentives, often in the form of group tickets, is a secondary function both in terms of corporate priorities and gate revenue.

Luxury suites and premium seating has come under fire as a frivolous indulgence of corporate "fat cats," especially in the wake of slow economies. Yet, corporate ticket sales remains a dominant force in the sport industry's gate revenue. The boom in facilities construction in the US since the 1990s has been motivated primarily by the need for increased premium seating capacity. Although less important in other international markets, Scotland's bid to host group stage matches for UEFA's 2020 European Championships does not meet UEFA's requirements for "fatcat seats,"[1] that is the 80 hospitality boxes with 10 seats outside.

Using sports to entertain clients has been a long-standing business technique. As one salesperson put it: "The common denominator in our business would be the golf outing. And the advantage of that is that you have somebody's undivided attention for about four hours."[2] While the golf course has a reputation as a traditional site where deals are made, the practice of tapping into sports passion to build and maintain business relationships has been extended to spectator sports in a big way.

As the use of sports tickets for client entertainment and corporate hospitality has grown, so has the accountability required to demonstrate business benefits.

> In the early days, I reckon people knew inherently that they should invite certain clients and prospects to events and as a casual consequence of that they built relationships – at times. Nowadays the approach is far more accountable, in that they are looking strategically as to what they can achieve and when they need to form relationships. They are looking at outcomes.[3]
>
> VP, Meetings & Events Australia

Luxury suites, club seats, and season tickets are increasingly likely to be viewed as business investments by the companies that buy them, not personal indulgences for the company's executives. Accordingly, sports properties are taking an increasingly business-like approach in selling tickets to corporations.

As is somewhat common, however, the sports industry lags behind other industries in research and measurement. According to a 2011 survey of premium seating directors for sports properties in North America, 87 percent said their clients do not use a measurable return-on-investment (ROI) system.[4] Among the 13 percent who do, the ROI system is based in Microsoft Excel. While many B2B marketers employ White Papers as a technique for initiating contact and strengthening business relationships, "best practices" guides for client entertainment are virtually non-existent in the sport industry, despite the importance of client entertainment to gate revenues.

While business-owned sports tickets are used primarily for business reasons – or at least business goals are the stated reasons – there is a strong personal element in corporate ticket sales. In my research experience, the majority of corporate account holders are also fans of the sport or team that their companies are buying into. There are always emotional and personal factors involved in sales despite efforts and rigorous processes designed to minimize the human element. But many corporate ticket sales accounts holders are themselves fans. By relying on fan avidity for the sports to make sales, sports properties miss out on larger markets for whom sports events could be a good business decision.

Like most B2B sales, corporate ticket sales relies on derived demand: businesses buy tickets because their clients want to attend the events. A corporate ticket buyer might not be a fan, but his or her customers could be. In this respect, sports properties can expand their pool of prospects greatly by providing more support for corporate tickets as a business investment and rely less on personal interest in the sport.

At the end of the proverbial day, however, personal and business often converge. People like to buy from people they like. Strong personal relationships contribute to feelings of trust, which are very strong drivers of sales.

THE BUSINESS CASE FOR CLIENT ENTERTAINMENT

While client entertainment clearly mixes business and personal elements in practice, business purchases most often must be justified on business grounds. That is, businesses leverage personal interests in order to attain business goals. While client entertainment can be used as a marketing function, it is most often targeted at the bottom of the marketing funnel.

In particular, tickets to sports events are assets for sales people to increase sales effectiveness, especially for B2B sales. Sales people can use tickets to sports events to help develop prospects, conduct needs analysis, increase presentation effectiveness, and close sales. Overall, sports tickets help businesses build and maintain relationships with current and prospective clients.

Marketing through client entertainment

Although client entertainment is usually targeted at sales goals, it can also be used to build brands. As one salesperson said:

> In a lot of cases you do get involved in social outings, a golf outing, a day at the races, and I think it is important to support the company as a brand. A lot of the time we forget that [COMPANY] is a brand that *we have to market as well and we have to sell*. And through these corporate events you can build a certain image and a certain profile.[5] (emphasis added)

While the comparatively small number of tickets relative to media audiences make sports tickets an inefficient vehicle to reach consumer audiences, it can make a lot of sense for business markets.

For example, a luxury suite for a basketball or ice hockey team might accommodate 20 prospects spread out over 40 or so games, totaling 800 potential prospects. For many industry categories, that number could represent the entire pool of prospects in a market, in which case sports tickets could be an efficient vehicle to reach the audience. As sports tickets build not only awareness but positive attitudes toward the brand (liking), client entertainment can be an effective brand building technique in addition to being efficient.

Selling through client entertainment

The most common business use of sports tickets is to provide salespeople with an asset to make their efforts more effective.

Prospecting. Sports tickets can establish contact with clients who would not otherwise respond. Indianapolis, for example, recently hosted a Super Bowl. The Super Bowl is "mardi gras" for Corporate America, with most of the country's top executives in town for the event. Indianapolis is not a huge market (26th in size among US media markets) and not a popular tourist destination outside of huge events. It would be difficult, if not impossible, to attract high-level corporate executives to Indianapolis under normal circumstances. But they came for the Super Bowl. While the process is clear for mega-events, such as the Super Bowl, the principle holds true for lesser sports properties as well.

One of the biggest challenges salespeople face is navigating clients' "buying centers." In B2B sales, many people often are involved in the decision-making process, including informal influences. Entertaining clients in relaxed settings can facilitate obtaining more honest and open communication to help identify the ultimate decision maker and learn who else will be influencing the decision.

Helping potential clients prospect for leads is an area in which sports marketers could be much more proactive. Most sports properties selling corporate tickets themselves have access to databases of local businesses in addition to a sales staff available to make calls. As most corporate ticket buyers are small businesses themselves, not having the capacity to invite and host prospects at games is a big barrier to purchase. If sports properties were to view themselves as selling marketing services instead of a sports product, as they are in this case, they could create programs in which their inside sales staff "sells" free tickets to business executives in specified industry categories and retention staff "concierge" corporate guests, in effect making corporate ticket sales a "turnkey" marketing service.

Needs analysis. The day-to-day demands to develop business tactics can cause people to lose sight of strategic considerations. As noted earlier, one of the challenges sports marketing executives face is maintaining focus. As one salesperson said: "Day to day, when you are just reacting to the immediate requirements, you don't have time to think about the long-term requirements that they might have. So social occasions allow us an open forum for that kind of discussion."[6] Having the opportunity to speak with clients in a relaxed setting can yield more and better information about their businesses.

Client entertainment also provides salespeople with an opportunity to learn more about their clients on a personal basis, so that personal relationships can be strengthened. Strong personal relationships and personal attention can be valuable in supporting business relationships, especially in establishing trust.

Presentation. One of the main strategic considerations in how to entertain clients is figuring out the balance between the business and the personal. Most often, clients attending a sports event are there for the event, not to receive a pitch. Pushing business topics could be alienating. As one salesperson said: "I would see it as probably the most important thing to get them to relax and to open up, and to create a nice environment that is conducive to us presenting to them later on."[7] While sports events are not a great opportunity to make a pitch, they can be valuable tools in warming up clients to a formal pitch at a later time. Spending time with clients in a social setting can help to establish a non-adversarial rapport, as noted by the following salesperson:

> There was one guy, . . . he was there ready to tear us to strips. . . . And we brought them out for dinner and we said to ourselves the one thing we would do would be not a single word about business. And that's what we did. . . . And it broke the ice with him, because he had come, he had met us twice and neither time had he talked business, both times had been all about having a bit of a laugh. And we had now gone from a situation where we would have sat with him and if we had negotiated first thing he would have been prepared to go hammer and tong. And it was more easygoing, the negotiation was more easygoing, more relaxed, and we came to an agreement.[8]

Closing. The primary business value of strong personal relationships is their role in increasing sales to new clients and retaining existing clients. Client entertainment helps in both areas. As the salesperson below noted, a relaxed environment can help handle objections to a sale, especially emotional objections:

> A lot of the time at such lunches you can actually change their mind set if they are thinking of doing something and they are not too sure. In a much more relaxed environment as opposed to having them at a meeting, if you are in a more relaxed environment, sometimes you can talk them round to doing something that they weren't too sure about, they were nervous about.[9]

Potentially clients with emotional objections (e.g., fear, uncertainty, etc.) can have their concerns allayed by a more relaxing environment.

The amount of time spent at sports events also helps allay concerns and handle objections because potential clients have appropriate time to weigh and consider options, benefits, and concerns. "A day at the races" is literally a *day* at the races. Clearly, that is much different from a phone call or a 15 minute presentation, where a prospect would justifiably feel rushed in making a decision.

"Customer equity" in the form of strong personal relationships which include trust help to facilitate client retention by assisting salespeople in dealing with client problems.

> And it makes life easier, it gets you through difficult situations easier if you have met somebody at a different level or in a non-business sense. It's easier to deal with, certainly it's harder for somebody to be mad at you or to be annoyed with you if you've been out to dinner the night before, or if you were at a show last week or if you played golf.[10]

While there might be tensions between client and salesperson regarding business issues, having a foundation of a strong personal relationship helps to manage the conflict.

Employee relationships

Corporate ticket sales also benefits businesses by helping them to build and maintain strong relationships with employees. Similar to client entertainment, employee relationships can involve both marketing and sales functions. As a brand builder for a company, aligning the company with a sport that most employees happen to like can simply make employees feel good about working there. If there are a lot of NASCAR fans in the company and the company is a NASCAR sponsor, wearing the racing team shirt can be a source of pride and/or enjoyment for an employee. Generally speaking, more satisfied employees are more productive.

Recruiting. Like prospecting in sales, sports events can help companies recruit employees. Sports tickets can be a strong incentive for potential recruits to make contact with a company. Or, the tickets can be part of a larger recruitment strategy. Sports tickets can also assist in retaining employees, both facilitating personal relationships among employees, thereby enhancing morale, and by offering tickets as a performance incentive.

111

Incentives. Sports tickets can be used as an incentive or reward for employees to improve productivity. Sales contests are a common management technique, with sports tickets often proving to be a popular prize. Sports events serve the dual function of rewarding the most productive employees, and facilitating building relationships among top performers.

CLIENT ENTERTAINMENT FEATURES

The most important benefit businesses receive from sports tickets is the opportunity to build and maintain relationships with clients. The features of corporate ticket packages are important to the extent that they facilitate relationships. Common features for ticket packages include:

- **Food.** The quality and quantity of food offerings depend on the nature of the event and the people being entertained. For sports purists, a hot dog and a beer will most often fulfill food desires. For guests seeking more of an "event," where the sports action is secondary, food options and quality can be more important.
- **Branded experiences.** Some corporate ticket packages include branding opportunities, especially luxury suites. By branding spaces hosting guests, businesses can communicate a brand message for the experience. This can include decorating a space in company colors or providing product samples or branded merchandise to guests.
- **Access.** Providing special access to guests is an increasingly common feature of corporate ticket packages, operating under the assumption that relationships will be strengthened if businesses can create unique and meaningful experiences for client guests. The demands for innovation in this area continue to increase as the bar for originality continues to be raised. Some common corporate ticket packages include:
  - Training camp get-aways
  - Fantasy camps
  - Player/coach meet and greet
  - Behind-the-scenes access, such as locker room tours
  - Post-game press conference attendance.
- **Exclusive merchandise.** Businesses can make a long-term impression on guests by creating unique, relevant merchandise.
- **Destination travel.** Creating travel packages which include attendance at big events can provide guests with true once-in-a-lifetime experiences.

CORPORATE TICKET SALES PROCESS

Sports marketers selling tickets to businesses for business reasons need to keep in mind that they are selling business services, not "sports." While sports can be helpful in gaining access to prospects who are themselves fans, the topic can also be seen as frivolous and unrelated to business. Therefore, it is crucial for sports marketers to make a business case for corporate sports tickets.

Specialist, Premium Sales and Service – New York Yankees (Bronx, NY)[11]

Summary

Perform all duties pertaining to the sale and renewal of all Premium inventory (Field Level seats between the bases, Legends, Champions, Delta SKY 360°, Jim Beam, Annual Luxury Suites and Game Day Suites)."

Essential functions

- Identify and sell available Premium inventory
- Generate qualified Premium seating leads via outbound calls, meetings, in-game entertainment and networking
- Assist with the development of Premium Seating sales plans
- Maintain an active role in the renewal process for all Premium inventory
- Develop and maintain concise weekly sales reports for all inventory areas.

In addition to heavy phone work, meetings/conferences and networking events are typical corporate ticket sales prospecting techniques. In-game entertainment is an indication that the Yankees "get high on their own supply" in that they use the techniques they recommend to their clients to build their own business.

Accountability is a key feature in many sales jobs.

Prospecting

The best prospects for corporate ticket sales are companies in industry categories that rely heavily on B2B marketing (see Table 7.1). For this reason, prospects for corporate ticket sales tend to be concentrated in a relatively small number of industry categories. According to a

Table 7.1 Top 10 premium seating industry categories

1. Attorney/legal services
2. Insurance
3. General contractors and home builders
4. Business/management consulting services
5. Doctors' offices
6. Banks
7. Real estate agencies and managers
8. Finance and investments
9. Accounting
10. Business services

Source: Lawrence et al. (2013).[1]

Note
1 Lawrence, H., Contorno, R., and Steffek, B. (2013). Selling premium seating in today's sport marketplace. *Sport Marketing Quarterly*, 22(1): 9–19.

study of 18 North American major league teams across the NFL, NHL, and NBA, nearly half (46 percent) of premium seating clients are represented by only 20 industry categories.[12]

Companies such as Full House, which helped to compile the list in Table 6.1, can be very helpful to corporate ticket salespeople in prospecting more efficiently. However, the full spectrum of industry categories purchasing premium tickets runs into the hundreds. So while contact lists of targeted industry categories is a great starting point, other prospecting techniques are required.

Sports properties have taken a more sophisticated approach to creating sales events which might generate more sales leads. Property-sponsored "industry nights" – in which executives from specific industries such as attorneys or physicians are invited – allow sports properties to deliver a more focused message while also providing a networking opportunity to prospects, thereby providing more value to attending than simply hearing a sales pitch. The NBA's Phoenix Suns reportedly obtained $1.4 million in revenue from a series of five such industry nights.[13] Community-sponsored business functions and networking events, such as those hosted by local Chambers of Commerce, can also be effective prospecting techniques (see Account Executive, Premium Sales – Charlotte Bobcats box on p.116).

Needs analysis

In selling tickets to businesses, sports marketers assume the role of sales consultant. The main selling proposition for corporate ticket sales is that events can help business. The major goals of B2B marketing addressed by corporate tickets are:

1   Obtain new clients
2   Retain existing clients
3   Motivate/reward employees

A rudimentary understanding of prospect needs entails knowing the priorities of the goals. If the company is a local branch of a larger corporation, for example, the prospect might not have responsibility for bringing in new business but have a need for servicing existing clients. In short, *the salesperson must develop an understanding of how the prospect builds and maintains relationships with clients and employees*. That entails learning about business's sales processes. In particular, client entertainment at sports events helps in prospecting and needs analysis, and less so on presentation and closing because of the informal nature of the events.

Prospecting. Sports marketers selling ticket packages face the same challenges for most B2B salespeople: gaining access to the decision maker, getting past gatekeepers, understanding the players are in the decision-making process.

How do you identify prospects and generate leads?
What are your biggest challenges in reaching decision makers?

By identifying business problems, the salesperson can work toward solutions. Having trouble gaining access to prospects? Sports events might help gain an introduction. Do not know who influences the decision maker? An informal conversation during a game might yield some insight.

If sports properties were to take the consultant role more seriously, they could actually provide prospecting services to their sales prospects. Many sports properties are big enough so that they have or have access to huge databases of contacts. Many sports properties also have an inside sales staff available to bang out calls.

> How would you feel about having someone else do all the heavy lifting on prospecting?
>
> How would you feel if we could deliver qualified prospects to you? All you would have to do is show up!

Most premium seating buyers are small companies: 25 percent with fewer than five employees and 75 percent with fewer than one hundred employees.[14] In particular for small, owner-operated professional services, the businesses might not even have a professional sales staff. Plus, imagine the boost in morale to the inside sales staff when they get a product they can sell easily: free tickets to the game!

> Hi, I'm calling from [THE TEAM] and my name is _____. We're reaching out to leaders in the [INDUSTRY] to invite them out to a game. [CLIENT] has sponsored this program so there are no costs to you and no strings attached. Which game would you like to attend?

Ironically, sports properties that rely heavily on client entertainment tend not to practice what they preach, meaning they do not typically employ the practices they recommend for their clients. Instead, most sports properties rely on fan interest in their properties, instead of leveraging interest in other properties, whether sports related or not. Sports properties seeking to expand their businesses to non-fans might consider buying tickets to other events for client entertainment purposes.

At the very least, sports properties should become "thought leaders" in the field of client entertainment and corporate hospitality. "Content marketing" is increasingly used as a lead generation tactic for B2B marketers. As prominent beneficiaries of the practice, sports properties should be at the forefront in promoting the client entertainment value and providing guidance for best practices.

Needs analysis. Identifying business needs can be a big challenge because a certain amount of trust is needed for a prospect to share problems. Goals and priorities can be fairly simple to get at, as most executives are willing to share information along those lines, but problems that need to be solved are more compelling.

> How do you identify customer needs?
>
> How do you learn about the customer's business problems?
>
> What's the best atmosphere for learning about clients' business problems?

One of the goals of needs analysis is also to determine the monetary value of accounts. What is the value of an average account? What is the renewal rate for current accounts? What is the loyalty rate of new accounts? Obtaining answers to these questions can help a salesperson justify investing in tickets to support sales.

Presentation and closing. Strong business and/or personal relationships contribute to more effective presentations and lead to more business.

How do you build strong relationships with your clients?

It is important to understand the prospect's idea of the relationship between business and personal relationships. This is as true for the corporate ticket salesperson as it is for the prospect. Does the prospect wish to build rapport or cut right to the chase with the business proposition? How important are personal relationships in the prospect's industry? Business cultures vary across industries, geographic regions, and between and within different companies. Corporate ticket salespeople must get a feel from prospects about how business is done in their industries.

Presentation

Account Executive, Premium Sales – Charlotte Bobcats (Charlotte, NC)[15]

Essential duties and responsibilities

- *Meet or exceed daily activity expectations of 60 daily activities and 5 appointments weekly.*
- Meet or exceed yearly sales goals as established by manager.
- *Regularly attend networking and chamber events.*
- Create and effectively implement personally developed business plans.
- Prospect and qualify all potential sales opportunities.
- Maintain computerized records of all clients and prospects through CRM system.
- Assist customer service efforts during renewal campaigns.
- Renew and retain luxury accounts as assigned by management.
- *Assist with the planning and execution of all luxury and premium seating special events."* (emphases added)

The quotas here are set for activity (i.e., process goals) as opposed to revenue (i.e., outcome goals), though the account executive will still be accountable for sales goals on an annual basis.

In addition to attending local networking events for prospecting, the account executive is expected to assist with the creation of new sales events. "Influencer parties" in which a current season ticket holder hosts a party at his or her home with the support of team executives and sometimes players and coaches, have become increasingly popular with teams. However, the bar continues to be raised to innovate more creative events.

Tactically, most salespeople use telephone calls in order to set up face-to-face appointments. The NBA's Charlotte Bobcats, for example, set a guideline of 60 "daily activities" per day (probably phone calls or personalized e-mails), leading to five appointments per week. The conversion ratio for activities to appointments is less than 2 percent, which is probably about average. Getting appointments is one of the most important, yet most challenging goals in corporate ticket sales.

The core message of the initial contact is that sports tickets can help business. Typically, the goal of the initial contact is to get an appointment to explain how sports tickets can help business. If successful in getting an appointment, the corporate ticket salesperson must be prepared to effectively argue that sports tickets can help businesses meet their goals. Given the absence of hard data to support the assertion, salespeople can be (1) conceptually rigorous, and (2) provide testimonials.

Being conceptually rigorous means understanding your prospect and thinking through the client entertainment process in a way that links the two together.

> Spending a few hours with a prospect in a fun, relaxed setting would help establish a good relationship, right?
>> It's easier to learn about business problems in an informal setting, isn't it?

Even without rigorous research, it is possible to make a convincing argument by working through the process conceptually and developing logical, well-reasoned conclusions. That sports tend to be well-known to most people makes that job easier as there is already likely to be a fundamental understanding of the product.

Although they are anecdotal, testimonials can provide some much-needed hard data to support the selling proposition of sports tickets and client entertainment. The most effective testimonials are ones that are specific about how the sports property helped achieve business goals. Having "satisfied clients" and "happy customers" is great, but why are they satisfied and happy? Sports properties should take a page from marketing services companies and recruit clients providing testimonials and develop them into full-blown case studies.

Closing and servicing

The key to closing is to convince a prospect that their company's investment in tickets will yield a positive financial return. Here, even basic accounting figures can be helpful and persuasive. Say, for example, an insurance agent has a hundred clients in a $2 million "book" of business. Is it worth $5k–$10k a year to "insure" that business? Or say an average account for an architect is $100,000? Is it worth spending $5000 on season tickets to gain a new client? The architect would only have to get one client every 20 years for the tickets to pay for themselves.

If the presentation of benefits was organized and convincing, then closing should be as simple as restating the benefits. Clearly, an investment of $5000 for a $100,000 return is a good deal. The question is whether the prospect is convinced that the $5000 cost will indeed be an investment that yields $100k.

The initial sale depends on convincing a prospect that tickets are a worthwhile investment. Renewal depends on actually delivering the value. One tactic in doing both is to promise and then deliver on servicing the account. Acting as a personal concierge, for example, in escorting ticket holders and their clients on behind-the-scene tours at the facility is an attractive "value-added" bonus to close a sale, and also a good way to help ticket holders improve relationships with their clients.

MANAGING THE SALES PIPELINE

Sports marketers selling tickets face the same challenge of establishing goals and priorities as sports marketers with other responsibilities. Recording and analyzing sales activity provides sports marketers with some direction in allocating time and effort. As with consumer ticket sales, a customized customer relationship management (CRM) system is a great tool for managing sales efforts for individuals and sales teams.

One sports marketing veteran suggests including the following categories, at minimum, in the sales pipeline:[16]

- *Prospect*. Prospects are all potential customers targeted by the sports property.
- *Likelihood*. Estimates of the likelihood to purchase can be gained from past experience. While the past is not a perfect predictor of the future, analyzing previous results provides a baseline for estimating conversion rates, which can help in allocating time and resources. For example, what percentage of prospects in specific industry categories end up buying? How many sales calls result in appointments? How many appointments end up in sales? How many first-time sales are renewed? Simply making more calls would result in more business if conversion rates held up, but if a salesperson is calling more unqualified prospects and the conversion rate goes down, more calls could be a waste of time and energy.
- *Status*. Status represents a stage in the buying process: prospect, contact, discussions, presentation, proposal, negotiations, sale.
- *Rating*. The rating helps to establish priorities for sales efforts by combining status and likelihood. Highly likely prospects who are far along in the sales process should receive top priority, although it is always important to keep the pipeline full as recommended in the previous chapter.
- *Potential amount*. Salespeople can estimate the potential amount of a deal based on comparative data: what do similarly sized companies in the same industry spend? Baseline data could be combined with other factors: the business owner is a huge fan, the business has ties to the sports property owner, etc.
- *Expected amount*. The expected amount is a simple combination of likelihood times potential amount. If a $100,000 sale is a 50 percent likelihood, then the expected amount is $50,000. Since most sports sales departments establish specific sales goals, this is a helpful tool in determining where an individual salesperson or an entire sales time are in progressing towards their sales goals.

Premium Seating Account Executive – Columbus Blue Jackets (Columbus, OH)[17]

Essential duties and responsibilities

■ Execute effective sales calls and presentations promoting the purchase of the premium seating products in order to meet established sales objectives.

■ *Direct sales of all ticket products to wide range of clientele, including but not limited to corporate executives, business people, hockey fans, and non-hockey fans.*

■ Prospecting calls are required daily for new business generation.

■ Proactively solicit and follow-up on any personal sales leads under the guidelines established by supervisors.

■ *Maintain and be able to produce on a regular basis accurate reports regarding sales, appointments, and account maintenance.*

■ Cooperate in collection and referral of leads for Suite, Loge Boxes, and Terrace Table opportunities. (emphases added)

The percentage of premium seating purchased for business purposes varies by market. For small markets without a big corporate base, such as Columbus, hockey fans can be more important targets for premium seating.

Reports are valuable not only being accountable to your boss, but also for your own organization and planning.

CASE: CALCULATING ROI FOR CORPORATE TICKETS

A common technique for demonstrating a potential return-on-investment (ROI) for corporate tickets is to show how client entertainment at sports events can lead to new business. If the average account size of a company, for example, is $100,000, then surely a $10,000 investment in tickets is worthwhile provided client entertainment can result in at least one sale. Too often, however, the focus is on new prospects and new business only, when client entertainment can be helpful at every stage of the sales pipeline.

While tickets to sports events can be very useful in helping to establish contact with new prospects, they can also be used to increase sales effectiveness at every stage of the sales pipeline. Table 7.2 represents a sample Excel spreadsheet that corporate ticket sales executives can use to demonstrate the potential return within the existing contacts. Conversion rates represent the percentage of accounts in the respective stage of the pipeline that end up in closed business. For example, in Table 7.2, 10 percent of cold prospects end up buying. An ROI worksheet in a spreadsheet is easily amended so that prospects can vary account sizes, number of accounts, and conversion rate.

The augmented conversion rate is the increase a prospect can expect as a result of client entertainment. If the existing conversion rate for cold prospects is 10 percent, it might be reasonable to expect 20 percent for clients who have attended an event with a company

Table 7.2 ROI worksheet for corporate ticket sales

	Average account	Number of accounts	Conversion rate (%)	Expected total	Augmented conversion rate	Augmented total
Repeat business	100,000	10	80	800,000	90%	900,000
Sale complete	100,000	10	100	1,000,000	100%	1,000,000
Contract development	100,000	2	90	180,000	100%	200,000
negotiations under way	100,000	3	80	240,000	90%	270,000
Proposal submitted	100,000	4	70	280,000	80%	320000
Presentation made	100,000	5	60	300,000	70%	350,000
Strong discussions under way	100,000	6	50	300,000	60%	360000
Established contact	100,000	7	40	280,000	50%	350,000
Hot prospect	100,000	8	30	240,000	40%	32,0000
Medium prospect	100,000	9	20	180,000	30%	270,000
Cold prospect	100,000	10	10	100,000	20%	200,000
				3,900,000		4,540,000

salesperson. The added benefit of using this framework is that it can help the corporate ticket sales executive in identifying the needs of the prospect. Where are the weaknesses in the sales pipeline and how can client entertainment help at those stages?

EXERCISE

Conducting a needs analysis

The purpose of this exercise is to conduct a needs analysis with a business executive. As an added benefit, you will learn how to build a professional network when you don't have parents, family, or friends to introduce you into a profession.

Prospect. The first step is to identify a professional working in one of the business categories identified as one of the top buyers of premium seating.[18] A simple way to do this is to run some search terms in Google related to the industry and position titles, which should pull up some LinkedIn accounts for industry professionals. A better way to do it would be to read the trade press in the industry. Local business journals often publish a "book of lists" that includes executives for top businesses across a range of categories, as well as lists of executives who have recently joined new companies or been promoted.

Aim high. You'll be surprised who you can get in touch with. For the purposes of this exercise, you need to choose someone you don't know: no family members, friends of family members, neighbors, etc. This is a cold call.

Research. After identifying a list of individuals, do some research on the industry, the company, and the person. An Internet search is a good place to start – LinkedIn profiles, company websites, etc. – but a library search is even better, especially when searching trade publications. You'll want to prepare some "good"[19] questions in the event you can get someone on the phone. And be prepared. Sometimes prospects will invite you to call them right away. Do your homework. High-level executives are busy and generous in giving you their time. Don't waste it.

Contact. I suggest sending a brief e-mail introducing yourself and asking for 15 minutes of time to learn more about the job and the industry. Tell them why you're contacting them, that you're a student interested in their business, and that you're looking for insight and advice. It's flattering, and most people are really nice, so response rates tend to be high. Then, try to arrange a time to set up a call.

Questions. You're asking for insight and advice, so prepare some genuine questions you have about the industry, the job, and/or the individual's background. Often, opening questions will spur a longer conversation but it's good to have some other questions prepared to keep the conversation flowing. In addition to questions about content, ask for advice: "What advice to you have for someone like me looking to do what you do?" Finally, ask for referrals for other people you should speak with. It's a good habit to get into.

Written summary. Detail your prospecting and pre-approach techniques. How did you choose your prospect? How did you develop questions to ask? You are not selling a product so there is no presentation to the prospect, but write some recommendations about how the company could achieve its business goals through sports tickets. If the company already has sports tickets, evaluate their usage: Do they have the right assets? Are they

121

getting full value from what they're doing? Where can they improve? If the company does not use sports tickets to advance their business, discuss how they might.

THREE MAIN TAKEAWAYS

1 The primary purpose for sports tickets purchased by corporations is to support sales efforts, especially with respect to business-to-business sales.
2 Salespeople use sports events to build strong personal and professional relationships with current and potential clients.
3 Demonstrating the business value of sports events to potential buyers is the key to success for corporate ticket salespeople.

NOTES

1 Murray, B. (2013). SFA chief Regan admits lack of posh seats in Hampden could KO Euro 2020 host bid. www.dailyrecord.co.uk/sport/football/football-news/sfa-chief-regan-admits-lack-2275713, accessed 9/16/2013.
2 Geiger, S. and Turley, D. (2005). Socializing behaviors in business-to-business selling: An exploratory study from the Republic of Ireland. *Industrial Marketing Management*, 34: 263–273.
3 Chantiri, E. (2010). Spend less, network more. *BRW*, Apr 22–28.
4 An analysis of best practices utilized by luxury suite directors. https://alsd.com/content/analysis-best-practices-utilized-luxury-suite-directors, accessed 9/28/2013.
5 Geiger and Turley. Socializing behaviors in business-to-business selling.
6 Ibid.
7 Ibid.
8 Ibid.
9 Ibid.
10 Ibid.
11 http://baseballjobs.teamworkonline.com/teamwork/r.cfm?i=57673, accessed 10/12/2013.
12 Lawrence, H., Contorno, R., and Steffek, B. (2013). Selling premium seating in today's sport marketplace. *Sport Marketing Quarterly*, 22(1): 9–19.
13 Lombard, J. (2010). New tools help NBA build season-ticket sales. www.sportsbusinessdaily.com/Journal/Issues/2010/08/20100823/This-Weeks-News/New-Tools-Help-NBA-Build-Season-Ticket-Sales.aspx?hl=sales%20events&sc=1, accessed 10/12/2013.
14 Lawrence et al. Selling premium seating in today's sport marketplace.
15 http://charlotte.teamworkonline.com/teamwork/r.cfm?i=55868, accessed 10/12/2013.
16 Economou, G. (2009). www.sportsbusinessdaily.com/Journal/Issues/2009/11/20091116/From-The-Field-Of/Pipeline-Helps-Sales-Team-Track-Progress-Identify-Problems.aspx?hl=sales%20pipeline&sc=1, accessed 9/10/2014.
17 http://hockeyjobs.nhl.com/teamwork/jobs/jobs.cfm/Sales-and-Marketing?supcat=219, accessed 10/12/2013.
18 Lawrence et al. Selling premium seating in today's sport marketplace.
19 A "good" question is one in which, after you ask it, the person you are speaking with says, "That's a good question."

Part III
Media

Chapter 8

Sports media

MEDIA GOALS FOR SPORTS PROPERTIES

Media is both an important source of revenue for sports properties and an important vehicle for developing new fans. With advances in digital technologies and increased options for media distribution, sports properties have more control over the distribution of their content. The challenge for sports properties in developing media strategies is to balance monetizing current fans with investing in future fans.

With the increasing number of screens available to sports fans, sports properties have greater choice in selling rights to different media outlets. Given a choice, however, people only pay for sports content if they are already big fans of the property. Media has been a valuable method in developing new fans. If sports content is restricted to current fans, it is more difficult to develop new fans.

There is also an ethical element to the distribution of sports content in media. Even though most professional sports teams are privately owned, many receive some kind of public financial support. In addition to a financial stake in sports, sports fans tend to have a very strong sense of ownership. That is, there is a strong sense among sports fans that team owners have a responsibility to the public, whether or not there has been any financial consideration. In addition to the business considerations about access to sports content, then, there are also ethical considerations. If sports are indeed a public good, then they should be made available to the public.

Of course, the ethical dimension also has business implications. If sports property owners are viewed as greedy and unresponsive to fan needs, then fans might become alienated and disengage. While sports fans tend to be tremendously resilient to poor treatment and have endured poor treatment from sports properties and still remained faithful, there are effects for the brand. Fans might pay the money, but they might also resent it.

Beyond the effects of media strategies on sports property brands, there is also the question of how media relates to other sources of revenue. Sports properties need to understand the influence of media strategies on current revenue in addition to future fan development. In particular, sports marketers need to understand the effects of media strategies on gate and sponsorship revenue. While increased media distribution tends to increase sponsorship value – generally speaking, the higher the number of eyeballs the more value to the sponsorship – there can be the opposite effect on gate revenue.

Technological advances, such as big-screen high-definition televisions, have made home viewing more attractive to sports fans. The effects are significant, to the extent that many sports facilities now include big-screen video screens to replicate the home-viewing experience while at a live event! While early radio and television broadcasts might have been designed to replicate the experience of live attendance for fans who could not attend in person, mediated sports experiences now have come to take on a life of their own.

MEDIA RIGHTS REVENUE

The changing structure of media from a mostly free over-the-air broadcast to pay-TV in the form of cable and satellite introduced more competitors to the market, which in turn led to increased competition for media rights to sports content. While the core of the sports business and the greatest source of revenue remains live events, media rights revenue has become more important to balancing the books for sports properties. Certainly, a big part of the attraction is the huge amounts of money involved.

During the past few decades, media rights fees have continued to increase at exponential rates. As sports media report John Ourand noted,

> [Talk of a sports media bubble] is dead wrong, according to a super majority of my best sources. These executives believe that the sports media industry is no closer to a bursting bubble than it was in 1993, when talk of a sports bubble first emerged.... For as long as I've covered the media business, people have been sounding an alarm about a sports rights bubble. Every five years or so, it gets louder. I don't get the sense that there's any more validity to it today than there was 20 years ago.[1]

In particular, the value of live sports rights continues to grow, representing "the most valuable opportunity in media," according to ESPN's President.[2] Not surprisingly then, TV income for sports properties is huge, especially for US-based sports properties. The US boasts three of the top ten sports properties by media rights revenues, including the world's

Table 8.1 Top 10 sports media rights

Property	Term	Annual rights fee
National Football League	2006–2013	$3.855 billion
Summer Olympics (London)	2012	$2.5 billion
2014 FIFA World Cup	2014	$2.25 billion
English Premier League	2010–2013	$1.85 billion
Italian Serie A	2010–2012	$1.32 billion
UEFA Champions League	2009–2012	$1.195 billion
National Basketball Association	2008–2012	$1.03 billion
French Ligue 1	2008–2012	$955 million
Major League Baseball	2007–2013	$900 million
Spanish La Liga	2009–2012	$840 million

Source: *Sportbusiness in Numbers,* Volume 4 (2010). London: SportBusiness Group.

biggest sports media property, the NFL (see Table 8.1). In addition, the US helps to push media rights revenues for the Summer Olympics past the World Cup despite a smaller global audience.

One of the reasons for US dominance in sports media revenue is the size of the US economy in general. Revenues are higher because there is more money. Unlike European heavily subsidized public television markets outside the US, the US has a very competitive media marketplace. Rights fees escalate because there are a lot of bidders for sports content, especially live sports events. As an ESPN executive said, "Next time we go into a negotiation and there's nobody else bidding, that would be the first time that happens."[3]

Media revenue continues to grow in importance in the financial models of sports properties, especially the bigger ones. Media revenue for the Barclay's Premier League, for example, is responsible for half of all revenue (see Figure 8.1), about double the revenue from matchday and commercial sources, respectively. For the BPL, media rights' dominance in the financial model is a relatively recent occurrence. As recently as the 1999–2000

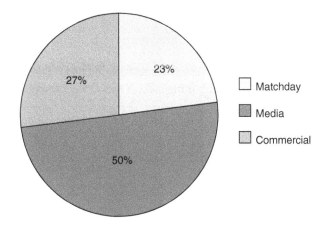

Figure 8.1 Premier League revenue mix (source: Annual Review of Football Finance – Highlights. Deloitte Sports Business Group, June 2013).

season, according to Deloitte, both matchday and commercial revenues exceeded media revenues for the league.[4]

The increased importance of media rights revenues needs to be balanced with overall organization goals for sports properties, such as generating exposure and building the next generation of fans. Therefore, sports media rights strategies have increased in sophistication as revenue has increased in importance.

MEDIA RIGHTS STRATEGIES

Sports properties benefit from increased competition for a limited number of live sports events, especially events which attract big audiences. The International Olympic Committee (IOC) has been historically very dependent on US media rights, which has accounted for more than half of all media revenues for the Olympic governing body. In order to increase competition among broadcasters and increase revenue from non-US sources, the IOC changed its media sales strategy from selling to broadcasting unions that included several countries (e.g., Asia-Pacific, Latin America, etc.) to selling rights on a country-by-country basis. The results were impressive.

For example, Brazilian broadcasters paid an estimated $8–$9 million for Olympic rights as part of a Latin American broadcasting union. For the 2014 and 2016 Olympics, the IOC broke Brazil out of the union and increased revenues to $170 million.[5] The IOC enjoyed similar success in China, increasing revenues from $17.5 million for the Asia-Pacific Broadcasting Union in 2008 to $160 million for CCTV, China's state-owned broadcaster, for the 2014 and 2016 Games.

While the NBC's $2 billion rights deal still makes the Olympics very US focused, the growth potential lies outside the US. According to the IOC's managing director of TV and marketing services, "Other markets are starting to grow. The US can't grow because it contributed for this quad in effect a 50 percent increase [from 2005 to 2008]. Knowing the US is flat, the increase will be contributed by other territories."[6]

Revenue sharing

What industry execs are saying...

"We're a group of 28 fat-cat Republicans who vote socialist on football."[7]

Art Modell, Owner NFL's Cleveland Browns

The NFL negotiates media contracts as a league and distributes the revenue evenly to all teams. The "league-think" policy of thinking about what is best for the league, first formulated by former commissioner Pete Rozelle, has been a big reason for the success of the league.

While overall media rights for sports continues to enjoy healthy growth, the increases are not necessarily shared evenly. The NFL, for example, negotiates television contracts as a league and shares revenue equally with all teams. In contrast, the English Premier League, the league with the next highest media rights revenue, does not share its revenue equally. While all revenue from overseas broadcasters and half domestic revenue is split evenly among the league's 20 members, a quarter of domestic revenue is based on where the team finishes in the league table, and the remaining quarter is distributed based on the number of live broadcasts. For the 2012–2013 Premier League season, league champions Manchester United pulled in $92.7 million in television revenue, compared to the $60.6 million for last place Queens Park Rangers.

While revenue growth from television has been healthy, it is more limited than the possibilities presented by digital technologies that are not limited to networks for distribution. As broadband penetration continues to increase, more sports properties will look toward digital distribution outlets.

Property-owned media

> We started changing our model and started looking at our teams not just as teams on the court, but teams are content. Why are we letting everybody else make money off our content? Why do we need somebody else to distribute our content? Why don't we just distribute our own content?
>
> SVP and CMO, Monumental Sports and Entertainment

Sports properties can generate substantial revenue by selling their media rights to media companies. But as Monumental Sports and Entertainment, the parent company of the NBA's Washington Wizards and NHL's Washington Capitols, asks, why not cut out the middle man? The technical term is "disintermediation," meaning removing distribution channels between producers and consumers.

Since NFL games are national broadcasts, Regional Sports Networks (RSNs) exist primarily to broadcast NBA, NHL, and MLB games to local markets. Games attract the biggest audiences and are therefore the most valuable programs. Following this logic, several teams set out to form their own RSNs. College athletic conferences have picked up on this idea and started their own networks. The Big Ten, for example, successfully launched their own network. The trend has even filtered down to individual college athletic programs with the University of Texas launching the Longhorn Network.

While it is understandable that sports properties seek to maximize revenue from media content, sports property executives must also pay attention to the effects of media distribution on long-term fan development. As the costs of attendance continue to increase and become more elusive to the average fan, connecting to sports through media becomes more important in the fan development process.

While selling media rights to pay television, such as cable and satellite, can increase media revenues to the sports property, those formats reach fewer households than their free-to-air broadcast counterparts. This is especially true for specialized sports networks. The Big Ten Network, for example, is available in 52 million homes, less than half of US television households.

Even when distribution is equal, media partners can provide valuable promotional support. The NBA, for example, airs games on ESPN, which adds NBA coverage on its

129

news and talk shows, creating a comprehensive promotional platform. In contrast, the NHL airs games on NBC, which while it reaches a greater number of households, does not provide promotional support on its other programming. As the SVP and CMO of the NBA's Washington Wizards and the NHL's Washington Capitals put it, "The NBA has an ESPN deal, so they're going to talk up the NBA all the time. On the Wizards side, it's great to have that, but on the Capitals side, you don't." Sports properties must balance revenue generation with fan development considerations in their media rights strategies.

Fan development

Television broadcasts can cannibalize attendance at live events. Why pay to go to the game when you can watch it at home for free? The availability of broadcasts must be balanced with the potentially negative effects of television broadcasts on attendance. While media rights continues to increase in importance to the sports business model, gate revenue remains the primary source of revenue in the industry.

The effects of broadcasting events on television vary but tend to be negative. A study of the effects of satellite television broadcasts of rugby football league games in the UK found a 25.1 percent reduction in attendance for games which aired on television.[8] A study of European soccer attendance found that weekend English Premier League games that were televised on BSkyB's subscription channel had 2.9 percent lower attendance. The same study found a 3.8 percent reduction for weekend games in Spain's La Liga. In both leagues, the negative effects of broadcasting games on attendance was much greater for weekday games.

In addition, for many sports live attendance helps to form long-term relationships with fans. For some sports, such as motorsports, the visceral experience of being at the event cannot be replicated via television. Live sports experiences are strongly related to high levels of fan avidity and long-term loyalty for a sports property.

A notable exception to the primacy of live events might be the NFL, which tends to attempt to replicate the experience of watching the game at home while in the stadium rather than the other way around. Still, the NFL has a controversial "black out" policy that prohibits broadcasting games to local markets if the game is not sold out in an attempt to ensure full stadiums for games.

The choice of media partners for sports properties can have implications for fan development because media itself is increasing in importance as a technique for building fan bases in the face of declining participation. The NHL, for example, chose a media deal with Versus as opposed to ESPN despite Versus being available in millions fewer homes. As a former NHL executive put it, "It gets down to whether 'SportsCenter' and the ESPN marketing machine is more attractive than Versus, where the NHL is the premier property."[9]

THE VALUE OF SPORTS TO MEDIA

Why do media companies pay big bucks for sports rights? Because they're worth it. As the senior executive vice president of 21st Century Fox said, "In the shaky swampy world of television programming, the one solid granite-like area is sports." Live sports events steadfastly remain "must-have" TV, "programming gold" as sports media journalist John Ourand calls it.

Sports media rights have grabbed the attention of investors and can affect the value of media companies. After British Sky Broadcasting PLC (BSkyB) lost UK television rights for UEFA's Champions League to BT PLC – on top of already ceding Barclay's Premier League rights – shares of BSkyB dropped 10 percent in a day. Despite the huge sums of money laid out by BT in rights fees for the Premier League and Champion's League, investors responded favorably, with shares increasing slightly.[10]

BSkyB and BT investors understood that rights fees for high profile sports events can build brands and drive revenues for media companies. Specifically, sports programming can:

- Build network brands and increase viewership to other programs.
- Increase network advertising revenue by:
    - Providing DVR-resistant programming
    - Delivering big audiences with attractive demographics
- Increase network subscription fees.
- Prevent consumers from "cutting the cord" to current pay-TV distributors.

Networks

It is now somewhat common wisdom in the sports industry that sports are vital to the overall success of television networks. That was not always the case. In 1994, Fox outbid CBS for television rights to the NFL, shutting CBS out of NFL broadcasts for four years. While direct revenues from NFL broadcasts did not add up for CBS, the network neglected to consider the ancillary benefits of broadcasting NFL games, such as promoting the network's other shows. CBS ended up losing television audiences and local network affiliate stations to Fox, which was launched into a "big-time" network. As one sports marketing executive put it, "The networks can't afford not to have the NFL on TV."[11]

Building network brands

Television networks that are themselves big brands can seek big name sports properties because, at least in part, it just makes intuitive sense. Sky Deutschland Chief Officer Sports, Advertising Sales and Internet, said, "Without live football coverage, Sky would not be the company it is now." "Sky has its focus set on football, simply because it is the most popular sport in Germany," he added.[12] A big-time network should have big-time events.

For some networks, a long history of an association with a sport can become a big part of the network's brand identity. As Australia's Channel Nine chief executive said, "Cricket is in our DNA and we're very proud of it. A lot of people say we over-invest in it from a broadcasting point of view but it has defined our network ... It is wallpaper."[13]

Promoting other network programming. While there is an emotional element behind a long-term relationship between a sports property and a network, premium sports content is viewed as an important promotional tool for a network's other programming. Cricket Australia's chief executive added:

> Cricket [in Australia], as with premium sport globally, is a great value proposition, bringing viewers to TV networks who then tend to stay on for other offerings from those networks, whether it be evening news and evening programming off the back of a game, or other content the networks promote.[14]

Premium sport is recognized globally as a great value proposition. Television networks heeded the lesson of CBS and the NFL well. CBS, which was outbid by Fox's $1.58 billion offer in 1994, returned to the NFL in 1998 with a $4 billion package. Since then, all of the major television networks in the US have made sure to be involved in the NFL, having heeded the lesson of CBS well.

Driving network revenue

While building brands and promoting other network programming can provide ancillary benefits to media networks, the primary goal of sports programming is to drive revenue through advertising sales and subscription fees.

Ratings. Audiences for prime-time television shows continue to shrink because of increased competition for viewers. More digital capacity means more networks, which leads to more choices for viewers. Premium live sports events are the lone exception to declining ratings. In particular, in the US, NFL television ratings continue to hold steady among the biggest television audiences. The NFL's Sunday Night Football has ranked consistently among the highest rated shows on broadcast television, and Monday Night Football among the highest for cable television.

Ratings for sports programming is not limited to the NFL, however, nor to the US. NASCAR's 36 races per year are down from their highest audiences but still average approximately six million viewers per broadcast. As Fox Sports' co-president said, "Go try and find entertainment programming or other things that do those kinds of numbers on a regular basis. You really have some predictability with sports."[15] Premium sports programming is seen as a reliable and predictable source of big audiences.

As might be expected, soccer in Europe dominates television audiences. The 2012 European Championships, for example, attracted approximately a 50 percent share across Europe, meaning about half of all televisions in use during the games' broadcasts were tuned in.[16] The ratings were even higher in countries with teams advancing in the tournament. Ninety percent of Spanish viewers watched Spain beat Italy in the finals, while the broadcast garnered an 81.7 percent share in Italy. Almost everyone watching television at the time was watching the game. Add the World Cup and Champions League broadcasts to the mix and soccer provides a consistent stream of guaranteed high ratings across the continent.

Attractive demographics. Sports programming not only receives big audiences, it tends to attract demographics that advertisers are most interested in, especially younger adults (18–49) and men. As CBS's Sports Chairman said, "The value of sports content is increasing as it becomes more and more difficult to get people in front of a set – and a specific demographic in front of a set. Sports is still able to attract that demographic."[17]

Advertising effectiveness. In addition to scale (the size of the audiences) and attractive demographics, sports content offers advertisings opportunities to gain increased effectiveness. In particular, sports programming tends to be "DVR-proof" and sports fans are more likely to have positive attitudes about advertising.

Evolving technologies present big challenges for media companies. Digital video recorders (DVRs) further empower consumers to fast forward through commercials. According to a 2006 survey of 133 national advertisers representing $20 billion in advertising spending:[18]

- 78 percent of national advertisers said TV advertising has become less effective.
- 70 percent think DVRs and video-on-demand will reduce the effectiveness of traditional 30-second ads.

While the television advertising is far from dead, and while sports are not a panacea for all of television advertising's woes, live sports events do create value for advertisers.

Live sports events place a premium on watching live, as opposed to recorded shows where it is easier to skip commercials. As Turner Broadcasting System's president of sales, distribution, and sports said, "We know that sports is appointment viewing. We know that five, 10 years from now, this might be the only and final appointment-viewing product in the market, other than news. Nobody's watching the Super Bowl on Monday morning."[19]

News programming is also more likely to be watched live. Nobody is watching the Sunday evening news on Monday morning. Sports networks' combination of live events, sports news, and commentary is therefore liable to attract higher percentages of live viewers. According to ESPN, for example, 96 percent of their programming is watched live, presenting advertisers with a "DVR proof ad environment."[20]

Subscriptions fees. Sports networks recognized the value of their programming and charge television distribution companies accordingly. ESPN, for example, receives $5.40 for every home it is in, nearly five times the amount for the TNT, the next highest at $1.10 per subscriber, according to sports media consultant Neal Pilson.[21] Sports networks are valuable to distributors because, with increased broadband penetration, many television households might "cut the cord" for pay television and get their content through the Internet. A subscription to Netflix, for example, costs roughly one-tenth the average monthly cable bill in the US. As one media analyst commented, "Right now you can basically get anything you want online except HBO, Showtime and sports."[22]

Pay television providers

In the face of younger audiences who are prone to downloading what they want to watch online, pay television providers often look to sports to help secure customers. Why pay for television when you can stream shows online with a broadband connection? Sports.

Satellite television provider DirecTV pays the NFL approximately $1 billion per year for the exclusive rights to broadcast out-of-market games. Fans who live outside the broadcast area of their favorite NFL teams can then watch all of the games at home (Sunday Ticket is also a big attraction for bars and restaurants). An estimated two million of 20 million total DirecTV customers subscribe to the Sunday Ticket. At a list price of approximately $300 for the Sunday Ticket subscription, the fees alone do not make financial sense for DirecTV. Sunday Ticket subscribers, however, must be DirecTV customers so DirecTV successfully

Table 8.2 Out-of-market fans more likely to have satellite television (%)

	In-market	Out-of-market
Cable	65.9*	56.5
Satellite	26.6	33.7*

Source: SRS Baseball Sponsorship Study.

Note
* Z-test for proportions, significant at $p < 0.05$.

leverages the exclusivity of the package to increase the number of subscribers, recouping the rights fees paid by expanding its subscriber base.

Other US sports leagues offer similar out-of-market packages, but they are not exclusive.

- MLB Extra Innings
- NBA League Pass
- NHL Center Ice
- ESPN GamePlan (college football)
- ESPN Full Court (college basketball)
- MLS Direct Kick

According to a national telephone survey of 1000 baseball fans, out-of-market fans were significantly more likely to have satellite and in-market fans, who have easy access to local broadcasts, were more likely to have cable television (see Table 8.2).

While the sports fan demand for programming is great, there are concerns that sports might be pricing themselves out of the market, driving up costs so high that even sports fans will decide to drop their pay television packages. Therefore, cable and satellite television providers must balance demand for programming with overall costs for fans and non-fans. One of the concerns among providers is that, with sports taking up a disproportionate share of costs relative to overall viewership, non-fans might look elsewhere.

Programming strategies, such as those advertised by DISH (see Director, Sports Programming box below) need to develop justification models to demonstrate that sports acquisitions help to grow business. Providers must decide which sports networks to carry and how subscription fees are passed on to customers, either bundled into a package or placed on separate tiers. Providers must also understand the contributions sports networks make in adding to the overall subscription base.

Director, Sports Programming, DISH

Primary responsibilities fall into the following categories:

- Develop and execute acquisition and programming strategy *(including evaluation of its impact on positioning with DISH)*; identify, pursue and source relevant content; provide strategic and analytical guidance on all new content/network opportunities that support internal strategies and customer expectations.

- Evaluate potential channels and develop justification models and strategies.
- *Foster and maintain an in-depth knowledge of the competitive linear, digital and entertainment landscape.*[23] (emphases added)

DISH, a prominent satellite television provider, sought a director of sports programming. Basically, the job entails shopping for sports programs that DISH should carry. The job description recognizes the influence of programming choices on the DISH brand. But there is also an emphasis on "justification models" which would include financial analysis. So, for example, should DISH bid for packages currently held exclusively by competitor DirecTV, such as the NFL's out-of-market "Sunday Ticket" programming?

The job also entails "in-depth knowledge" of the entertainment landscape. Where do you think entertainment is headed?

CASE: BT V. SKY: THE BIG GAME OFF THE FIELD

ESPN as "The Little Channel That Could"?[24] North American observers might be surprised to see ESPN cast as an underdog given its tremendous brand strength in its domestic market. Despite global success in most of the world, ESPN's British venture lasted only four years before the company packed its bags and headed home. Sky, the biggest pay-television operator in the UK, has long been known as "the home of live sport"[25] in the region, having fended off challenges from Setanta and ITV Digital as well as ESPN.

So it was quite a surprise when BT, Britain's leading telecommunications provider, decided to enter the market for live sports and bid for media rights both to the Barclay's Premier League, the top domestic league, and the European Champions League, Europe's premier club competition. As one market analyst described it, "The tastiest battle going on this season is not on the football pitches or even the dugouts, but between BT and Sky as they continue to slug it out over UK's sports fans."[26]

BT's big bet on the Barclay's Premier League rights centered on a strategy to leverage game broadcasts to enlist more subscribers to their broadband service by offering game broadcast free to subscribers. According to BT's chief executive, "Our strategic investments are delivering."[27] Broadband and television customers were up, as were revenue and stock prices. Encouraged by initial success with the Barclay's Premier League, BT decided to double down and bid for the Champions League. Their winning bid surprised many analysts, who thought that BT's strategy was to bid up the price but that Sky would ultimately retain Champions League rights.

While subscriber growth and financial results for BT seem encouraging, and recognizing that the rights fees means windfalls for both the BPL and UEF – there could be long-term implications for the properties. BT sport's Boxing Day (the day after Christmas) game between Manchester City and Liverpool, a game between two top clubs with championship implications on a national holiday, drew 1.5 million viewers.

Leveraging sports content to increase subscriptions is an effective method of monetizing current interest in sports, but ineffective in developing sports interests. In order to watch the game, fans need to be avid enough to pay for the privilege, which leaves out the casual fan and those who might not be able to afford the subscription at that point, which means especially younger fans. The long-term danger for sports properties that pursue this strategy is that casual fans might not temporarily suspend their fan behaviors only to become subscribers when they can afford it. With all of the entertainment and leisure options available, it's easy to find something else to do.

EXERCISE

NFL "blackout" policy. The NFL currently prohibits televised broadcasts of games in local markets if the team does not sell out the stadium, a policy that is very controversial. Many critics make an ethical argument that the public should not be deprived of NFL games because many stadiums are publicly supported and many fans are priced out of attending. From a business perspective, the NFL must balance the need to sell tickets – why brave cold weather and pay high ticket prices when fans can stay home and watch the game on High Definition in comfort – with the need to develop future fans. If home games are not broadcast, how will potential fans get introduced to the sport? How will they be socialized into becoming fans? Should the NFL continue this policy?

THREE MAIN TAKEAWAYS

1   The trend in spiraling sports rights fees looks to continue.
2   Sports properties must balance short-term revenue needs with long-term customer growth.
3   Sports content is a strong factor in shaping the business models of media providers.

RECOMMENDED READING

Comment of sports economists on the FCC's sports blackout rules. http://apps.fcc.gov/ecfs/document/view?id=7021860132, accessed 5/29/2014.
John Ourand's column in the *SportsBusiness Journal*. It's excellent.

NOTES

1 Ourand, J. (2013). Talk of rights bubble bursting is still strong – and still wrong. www.sportsbusinessdaily.com/Journal/Issues/2013/07/22/Media/Sports-Media.aspx, accessed 7/23/2013.
2 Ourand, J. (2013). Three trends worth considering from the upfront season. www.sportsbusinessdaily.com/Journal/Issues/2013/05/20/Media/Sports-Media.aspx, accessed 7/23/2013.

3 Sports: A growing portion of the TV bill, but less than you might think. *Variety*, 321(1): 32.

4 Deloitte, *Annual Review of Football Finance*, 2007.

5 Mickle, T. (2012). Revamped sales strategy helps IOC boost media rights fees. www.sportsbusinessdaily.com/SB-Blogs/Olympics/London-Olympics/2012/08/iocrevenue.aspx, accessed 8/6/2012.

6 Ibid.

7 Mr. Modell's team moved to Baltimore and is now known as the Ravens. John Helyar (1995). Leaguethink links NFL old guarders, *Wall Street Journal*, January 6: B10. As quoted in Mullick, S. (1996). Browns to Baltimore: Franchise free agency and the new economics of the NFL. *Marquette Sports Law Journal*, 7(1): 1–37.

8 Baimbridge, M., Cameron, S., and Dawson, P. (1995). Satellite broadcasting and match attendance: The case of rugby league. *Applied Economics Letters*, 2: 343–346.

9 Mickle, T. and Lefton, T. (2010). Standing at a familiar TV crossroads. www.sportsbusinessdaily.com/Journal/Issues/2010/06/20100614/This-Weeks-News/Standing-At-A-Familiar-TV-Crossroads.aspx, accessed 11/25/2013.

10 Pylas, P. (2013). BSkyB shares battered by soccer rights loss. www.charlotteobserver.com/2013/11/11/v--print/4456776/bskyb, accessed 11/11/2013.

11 Rose, L. (2003). The big picture. http://www.forbes.com/2003/08/28/cz_lr_0828nfltv_print.html, accessed 1/8/2013.

12 Mai, H. J. (2012). Sky Deutschland's Carsten Schmidt talks about the German TV market and digital innovations. www.sportsbusinessdaily.com/Global/Issues/2012/09/14/Media/Sky–Q-and-A.aspx, accessed 1/9/2013.

13 Saltau, C. and Hogan, J. (2013). Windfall TV deal gives cricket new lease of life. www.theage.com/au/action/pringArticle?id=4463921, accessed 6/5/2013.

14 Ibid.

15 Ourand, J. (2011). How high can rights fees go? www.sportsbusinessdaily.com/Journal/Issues/2011/06/06/In-Depth/Rights-Fees.aspx, accessed 11/25/2013.

16 Rolfe, P., Kemp, S., Szalai, G., Lymen, E., and Leffler, R. (2012). About 90 percent of Spanish viewers watched their team's historic 4–0 victory over Italy. www.hollywoodreporter.com/print/344113, accessed 12/10/2013.

17 Ourand. How high can rights fees go?

18 TV advertising is less effective: Survey. http://promomagazine.com/news/tvadvertising_survey_032406/, accessed 3/22/2006.

19 Ourand. How high can rights fees go?

20 www.espncms.com/upfront2013/, accessed 12/10/2013.

21 Cherner, R. (2013). Fox Sports 1 not the usual new kid on ESPN's block. www.usatoday.com/story/sports/mlb/2013/08/11/fox-sports-1-versus-espn/2641247/, accessed 8/12/2013.

22 Futterman, M. (2013). Cable providers revolt over sports costs. http://online.wsj.com/news/articles/SB10001424127887323823004578595571950242766, accessed 7/22/2013.

23 Director, Sports Programming. https://dish-assessment1-dish.icims.com/jobs/22737/director%252c-sports-programming/job?hub=6&mode=job&iis=Internet:+Indeed&iisn=Indeed.com, accessed 11/25/2013.

24 Liew, J. (2013). At the big leaving party, no one spoke to ESPN. www.telegraph.co.uk/sport/football/10067162/At-the-big-leaving-party-no-one-spoke-to-ESPN.html, accessed 5/21/2013.

25 Mance, H. (2013). BT challenges Sky at home and abroad after Champions League deal. www.ft.com/intl/cms/s/0/280c0fc4–4a19–11e3–9a21–00144feabdc0.html#axzz337EkvDJL, accessed 5/29/2014.

26 Pylas, P. BSkyB shares battered by soccer rights loss.

27 Thomas, D. (2014). BT reaps benefits from pay-TV drive. www.ft.com/intl/cms/s/0/047725ba-8a4e-11e3–9c29–00144feab7de.html?siteedition=intl#axzz337EkvDJL, accessed 5/29/2014.

Sports media audiences

MEDIA USAGE AND FAN AVIDITY

There is a strong positive correlation between attending live sports events and following sports in the media. Avid sports fans attend more games; watch more games on television; listen to events and news on the radio; read about sports in print; follow sports in digital formats; and, talk about sports with others. However, there is also a tension between attending live events and watching them on television. As media technology advances and becomes more available, watching sports on television becomes an increasingly attractive alternative to the expense and inconvenience of attending events in person.

The proliferation of high definition (HD) formats, big-screen televisions, and technological advancements in sports broadcasting have combined to make watching sports on television more attractive. According to the ESPN Sports Poll, preferences to attend games in person or watch them on TV have reversed since 1998. In 1998, 57 percent of Americans preferred to attend the game in person and only 37 percent preferred to watch on TV. By 2011, only 35 percent preferred to attend in person and 61 percent preferred to watch on TV (see Table 9.1).

Preferences for attending live events or watching on television vary by sport. The NFL, for example, is a very TV-based sports property. The large fan following combined with the

Table 9.1 Attending in person or watching on TV (%)

	1998	*2011*
Prefer to watch on TV	37	61
Prefer to attend the game in person	57	35

Source: ESPN Sports Poll.[1]

Note
1 Luker, R. (2011). Fans' viewing preferences could have profound effect on strategy. www.sportsbusinessdaily.com/Journal/Issues/2011/09/26/Research-and-Ratings/UpNext.aspx?hl=luker&sc=0, accessed 1/25/2013.

Table 9.2 Live attendance or remote viewing preference (%)

	MLB	*NFL*
Prefer to attend over remote viewing	42	29

Source: ESPN Sports Poll.[1]

Note
1 Luker, R. (2011). Fans' viewing preferences could have profound effect on strategy. www.sportsbusinessdaily.com/Journal/Issues/2011/09/26/Research-and-Ratings/UpNext.aspx?hl=luker&sc=0, accessed 1/25/2013.

comparatively small inventory of games does not leave most fans with much of a choice. MLB, in contrast, has ten times more regular season games to choose from, affording fans greater choices and lower ticket prices. Add weather into the mix – NFL games can be played in blustery conditions – and it is not surprising that 42 percent of MLB fans prefer to attend games in person over remote viewing, compared to only 29 percent of NFL fans (see Table 9.2).

SPORTS MEDIA AS A SOCIAL EXPERIENCE

The tension between media consumption and event attendance applies to the experience of watching sports events remotely, as well as the behavior. It can be argued that early radio and television broadcasts of sports events were designed to allow fans to experience events that were sold out. That is, the broadcasts were meant to provide the experience of attending the event. With advances in technology, however, the tail might be wagging the dog as many sports facilities seem to now try to replicate the experience of watching the game at home.

Even at home, watching sports tends to be a social event. According to the ESPN Sports Poll, 70 percent of sports fans watch games with others. Some fans, however, prefer to watch alone in order to immerse themselves in the sport's action. As one fan put it:

> I don't really mind a group [viewing] situation, but there always seems to be too much talking going on during the game. I prefer being alone or watching a sporting event with you. You usually keep your mouth shut, unless it's Notre Dame football. . . . I prefer to be alone. Therefore, I will not be interrupted by foolish talking.

139

I want my sole attention to be on the game. I want absolutely no distractions. Other sporting events, like the Super Bowl or the NBA Championship games, I like to be in a group. I like to watch these kinds of events in a bar or a place where people can drink, eat, and laugh. I am not as serious, compared to my Michigan and IU viewing games.[1]

For the fan above, interest in being around others for a game decreases as avidity for the sports property increases. While the original intent of sports broadcasts might have been to bring fans who could not attend closer to the action, technological developments in broadcasting have allowed television audiences to gain better viewpoints than fans actually in attendance. As one fan put it in a study published in 1994:

There are just so many damn distractions at the game. I consider myself a sports nut; I like to really get into the game, you know, play calls, statistics on the players and all that stuff. But when you are at the game, you get torn away from the actual game itself and become involved with things like being bugged by the peanut guy or trying to ignore the drunk guy who keeps cussing at the top of his voice.[2]

In recent years, technological advances in sports broadcasting production have increased the appeal for "sports nuts" who really get into the on-field action.

For the majority of sports fans, however, watching sports on television is a social experience that mimics the experience of actually being at the game. Wearing team colors, yelling at the television, cheering the team on, are not typical behaviors for television viewers outside of sports. For many sports television viewers, however, watching at home is the next best thing to being there:

I watched Scott and ten of his friends watch the Bulls versus the Suns basketball game on Saturday.... Since the game took place at the Chicago Stadium, Scott decided to turn his living room into the actual stadium. He turned off all of the lights and gave each of his friends a flashlight. When they announced the starting lineup for the Bulls, everyone turned on their flashlight and waved it around the room as if they were actually in the Stadium. Although some of his friends thought he was a little crazy, this actually made everyone very excited for the game.[3]

The desire to watch at home or outside the home often varies with age. An online survey of 2122 British adults, for example, found that 23 percent of 18–34 Premier League viewers plan to watch games at a pub, and an additional 11 percent plan to watch at a friend's house.[4] While younger viewers are likely to be more social, watching football on television in the US seems to have a broader social appeal. A brand sponsored national survey of US adults found that 78 percent of consumers have hosted a sports television viewing party, with football being the overwhelming sport of choice (74 percent, compared to 8 percent for basketball and 4 percent for baseball).[5]

In poor countries without a lot of televisions in households, fans tend to aggregate in public places in order to see games. Many young soccer fans in Sub-Saharan Africa, for example, look to broadcasts of European teams, often featuring star African players, such as Didier Drogba or Michael Essien. For these fans, soccer bars and soccer video theaters have become de facto stadiums, often providing the only live soccer experiences for these fans.[6] In Africa, soccer is the single most popular sport, far above anything else, and television is the most popular media, far above attending live games.

Sports marketers must be sensitive to the motivations and preferences of sports viewing segments, balancing an intense focus on the action on the field of play with a tone which is suitable for a social occasion.

BUILDING MEDIA AUDIENCES

Media rights fees for sports properties and advertising effectiveness for advertisers depend on a sizable and accessible audience. While the importance of sports programming to other network programming is fairly well documented, the process of building sports media audiences has received comparatively scant attention.

Clearly, there has been a growth in types of sports media. Increased broadband capabilities, social media, smartphones, and other digital technologies provide fans with a huge number of options to connect with sports properties and with other fans. But more media does not necessarily create more media users. While media audiences are in part a consequence of overall fan development efforts, the importance of media rights can lead to conflicts with other fan development goals, especially live attendance.

Sports programming

Sports purists might lament the influence that television has had on altering rules in order to accommodate the demands of advertisers and viewers. "TV timeouts" have been introduced to many sports in order to provide broadcasters with more opportunities for commercial breaks (which is really what they are). The vast NCAA basketball games are not televised but all NCAA competitions must play by the same rules so even games that are not televised take "TV timeouts." In NFL games, timeouts can be called just so broadcasters can catch up on the required number of commercial breaks. As a fan attending a live NFL game, the breaks in the action can be puzzling. Because the timeout was not called by either team for strategic purposes, players tend to just stand on the field and wait for the commercial to be over.

Based on the overwhelming importance of media rights revenue to the NFL and its teams, the priorities regarding the relative importance of live attendees and the television audience is clear. Television is the motor that drives the wheel. For other sports, the financial interests are not as clear cut. In the NHL, gate revenue comprises a greater share of overall revenue than the share of revenue from national broadcasting, so team owners might be less disposed to make concessions for television audiences. There can be a conflict of interests between ticket buyers and television viewers, even if it is something as simple as displacing front row seats in order to accommodate another television camera position.

Scheduling. Scheduling the day and time of games has been an obvious accommodation that sports properties have made for television. The NFL even makes start times for Sunday games flexible in order to ensure a match-up of national interest for NBC's primetime Sunday night broadcasts. Start times for games are complicated further by trying to balance the needs of international audiences. MediaPro, the leading rights holder for Spanish La Liga's TV coverage, sought to have more games moved to mid-afternoon in order to reach Asian viewers more effectively. As MediaPro's president said:

> The Asian market is amongst our most important targets . . . I would really like it if El Clasico between Barcelona and Real Madrid could be played at mid-day. . . . Given the difficulty of making our presence felt in Asia, playing such matches between mid-day and 4 p.m. would be the best time.[7]

Responding to an almost unquenchable thirst for more televised games, the NFL has used its game in London to create a 9:30 a.m. EST time slot for a fourth game window on Sunday. While the 1:30 p.m. local start time might be fan-friendly for attendees, the NFL also said that the start time would "make it easier for a global audience to tune in."[8]

In addition, many sports properties look to occupy a space on the monthly or seasonal calendar. One of the quickest ways to increase the number of viewers for a sports broadcast is to air the broadcast during a time when a lot of people are watching television, especially primetime and holidays. The NFL dominates television viewing during its entire season with an intense buildup from the play-offs to the Super Bowl in late January/early February. Other sports properties carve out time on the sports calendar:

- NASCAR follows up the Super Bowl with the Daytona 500 soon after in mid-to-late February.
- March "Madness" is dominated by the NCAA basketball championships.
- April features MLB's opening day.
- The Olympics and World Cup occupy summer viewing in their respective quadrennials.
- September features the NFL's kickoff weekend.
- MLB seeks to "own" October with the World Series (which ironically now often runs into November).
- Thanksgiving features NFL games.
- Christmas day features an NBA lineup.
- College football used to feature its national championship game on New Year's Day. After moving the game back on the calendar to ensure prime-time viewing not competing with the NFL, the NHL developed the Winter Classic, featuring a series of outdoor games. According to Nielsen, the New Year's Day 2011 broadcast of the winter classic drew 4.525 million viewers for a regular season game, just slightly less than the 4.572 million average viewers for the Stanley Cup Finals.

Production. Increased competition of sports broadcasts has led to increased quality for sports broadcast quality. Sports media consumers have become accustomed to polished presentation so standards are high even to retain viewers, much less grow an audience. Sky came to dominate broadcasting English soccer in no small part because of increased production quality. As a sports media journalist put it, "Viewers have been enticed by the broadcaster's fresh approach to sport, which made even the BBC's coverage look old and dusty. Excellent presenters, 24-hour coverage, super-slo-mo, multi-screen, Fanzone and many other innovations define Sky football."[9]

While broadcasting production has improved steadily, perhaps the biggest contributions to sports production quality were made by one of the sports business's most spectacular failures, the XFL (Xtreme Football League). A joint effort between broadcaster NBC and World Wrestling Entertainment (WWE), the league folded after only one season. After generating a very healthy 9.5 Nielsen rating in its first broadcast, one media researcher remarked, "I can't think of another program that had such rapid ratings deterioration."[10]

The influence of WWE-style promotion, however, sparked experimentation and innovation in broadcasting. While cameras in the cheerleaders' locker room were not widely adopted, many other innovations were. As one former XFL executive said,

> Look at some of the things we pioneered there: the cable cams, miking all the players, sideline interviewers, locker room access, just getting inside the game more than ever – and you realize that now most of that is in practice across sports.[11]

What sports fans are saying...

"Strange as it may seem, I see a huge similarity between sports and soap operas." Many sports television executives would agree. Some sports media properties have actually marketed themselves as "season-long soap operas."

Male sports fan[12]

Storytelling. As a male sports fan said, sports are like soap operas, but it might not seem strange. In fact, I recall TBS one season promoting its baseball broadcasts as a season long "soap opera." Speaking of a recent NBA season, the senior director of programming and acquisitions at ESPN said, "There have been so many plots and subplots that it is great television."[13] One of the recurring themes in the recent NBA has been LeBron James joining an "evil empire" with the Miami Heat. "Great television" requires great characters, heroes, and villains. Beyond the broader drama involving characters, sports broadcasters often develop and communicate a few storylines for viewers to look out for. Here, too, sports broadcasters must balance sensational entertainment, which might appeal to a general audience, with a pure focus on the sport, which might appeal to the broadcast's most avid and loyal fans.

Promotion. The recent decade has seen a great migration of live sports events to cable television in the US, with notable exceptions being the Super Bowl, World Series, and NBA Finals. In addition to being able to pay bigger rights fees because of the money they receive from subscription fees, sports networks on cable television can provide more promotional

Table 9.3 BCS average viewership

Year	Network	Viewers
2011	ESPN	16,729,000
2010	Fox/ABC	19,278,000
2009	Fox/ABC	17,595,000
2008	Fox/ABC	15,554,000
2007	Fox/ABC	18,123,000

support. As one college athletic conference president summed it up, "There's a feeling if cable is the entity that can give the best all-around coverage leading to the game, after the game and the event itself, then it's probably the way to go."[14]

But while cable networks provide more promotional support with publicity generated by ancillary programming, their reach is smaller than that of broadcast networks. In general, it is assumed that cable audiences will be 10 percent smaller than broadcast audiences. In the case of college football's Bowl Championship Series, the move to cable seems to have led to a decrease of about that size (see Table 9.3).

Sports business executives are about evenly split with respect to a sports property accepting a lower rights fee from a broadcast network in order to reach a bigger audience, or accepting a smaller audience on cable but receiving more money for rights. The deciding factor for sports marketers must be to weigh the importance of the organization's goals. Bigger audiences now will likely translate into more long-term growth, but increased rights fees mean short-term revenue. For mature brands with a strong fan development process in place, the short-term revenue might make sense. For less-established brands with more growth potential, the reduced rights fees might be seen as an investment in the future.

MEDIA AUDIENCES

TV is still king

New media technologies attract a lot of buzz, but for most Americans the traditional media of television and radio remain dominant. According to Nielsen, Americans consume nearly 60 hours of media content per week, more than half of that being traditional television (35.1 hours, see Figure 9.1). While Internet usage overall (5.1 hours) and watching videos on the Internet (1.5 hours) and via mobile phones (1.3 hours) is substantial, combined it is still less than the 14 hours Americans spend listening to the radio each week.

For sports, television is even more dominant. While Americans have strong attachments to their computers and mobile phones, especially younger Americans under the age of 25, television is by far the most important device for the enjoyment of sports (see Table 9.4). As veteran sports media executive Neal Pilson commented, even young Americans "apparently are smart enough to realize the emotional wallop of sports on a 50-inch HD TV set is far more rewarding than a two-inch screen on their phone."[15]

Television remains dominant for sports viewing because sports fans plan to watch games live, and with others. Remote viewing away from the television is not much of a factor for

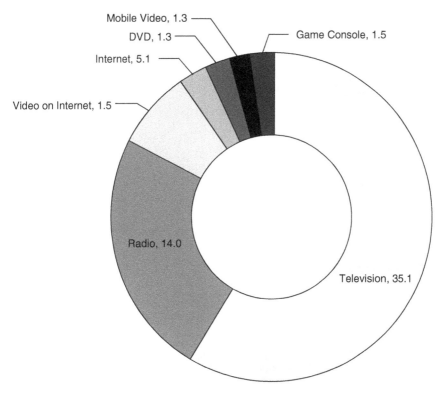

Mobile Video, 1.3
DVD, 1.3
Internet, 5.1
Video on Internet, 1.5
Game Console, 1.5
Radio, 14.0
Television, 35.1

Figure 9.1 Average weekly media consumption (source: Nielsen).

sports because fans plan to be in front of their televisions for the games. Not surprisingly, then, sports programming is the type of programming most likely to be watched live. Only 70 percent of general dramas are watched live or within the same day, as compared to 100 percent of sports commentary and 99 percent of sports events (see Table 9.5). Along with other live events such as awards ceremonies (e.g., the Oscars), sports programming provides advertisers with an audience that is very unlikely to record the program and skip through commercials when playing it back.

Table 9.4 Most important media devices (%)

	"Which of the following devices is most important to you in how you spend your free time?"	"Which of the following devices is most important to your enjoyment of sports?"
Television	46	81
Computer	25	8
Mobile phone	23	5

Source: ESPN Sports Poll.[1]

Note

1 Luker, R. (2013). Even with the newest technology, research shows TV is still king. www.sportsbusiness-daily.com/Journal/Issues/2013/01/21/Research-and-Ratings/UpNext.aspx, accessed 12/16/2013.

Table 9.5 Time shifted television viewing among 18–49-year-old Americans

Type of show	Percent watched live or within the same day of viewing
Sports commentary	100
Sports event	99
News	98
Award ceremonies	96
Reality	85
Evening animation	82
Situation comedy	75
General drama	70

Source: Nielsen.[1]

Note
1 Nielsen. *2012 Year in Sports*.

MEDIA MEASUREMENT

Prior to the development of the Internet and other digital communication, media measurement focused on ratings and shares. For television, that meant ratings and shares as measured by Nielsen:

■ *Rating*: the percentage of total households tuning the program. A "Nielsen rating" provides an indication of total audience size. A rating is the percentage of the total US TV households, 114.2 million as of 2012.[16] Television households fluctuate because (1) a slow economy slows the growth of new households, and (2) some households "cut the cord" for television and watch videos online through companies like Netflix and Hulu.
■ *Share*: the percentage of televisions in use. Program shares are a useful measure because the number of households watching television varies by time and day of the week. A weekend afternoon golf tournament, for example, might put up a modest rating because the weather is nice and people are out, but a respectable share because a high percentage of those watching television are watching the tournament.

With the advent of new media, the question arose about new measures. ESPN executives suggest that there are no new measures; that the main questions for media research remain: How many? How often? How long?[17] "How many?" is reach in television and unique visitors in digital. "How often?" is frequency in TV and visits in digital. "How long?" is the average audience (rating) in TV and total usage in digital. The terms differ but what they measure is the same (see Table 9.6).

Users v. usage. "How many?" and "How long?" are important distinctions. "Who?" must also be added to the list of questions. Sports networks and programs assert to advertisers that sports content is an effective technique to reach young males, who are an attractive but hard-to-reach marketing target. ESPN viewers in total are about equally split between males and females (see Figure 9.2). The reach (i.e., "viewers") of ESPN is 53 percent male and 47 percent female. However, males comprise 75 percent of the total minutes of usage (i.e., "viewing").

Table 9.6 ESPN media measures

	Television	*Digital*
How many?	Reach	Uniques
How often?	Frequency	Visits
How long?	Rating (average audience)	Total usage

Source: ESPN.

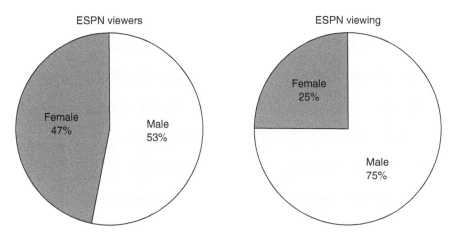

Figure 9.2 Users and usage (source: Nielsen).

TV

In the US, national television audiences are dominated by the NFL. In 2011, top-rated NFL games included more than 27 million viewers for Thursday Night Kickoff, the season opener, to more than 111 million for the Super Bowl (see Table 9.7). The NFL consistently puts up huge numbers of TV viewership, especially for the play-offs and Super Bowl.

In Europe, soccer attracts the top sports audiences. During 2012, the Champion's Leagues, European soccer's club championship, was the most-watched sports event in Spain and Germany, both of whom had clubs in the semi-finals and finals, respectively (see Table 9.8). In Italy, the national club championship final, the Coppa Italia, drew top honors for sports broadcasts, despite the Olympic Summer Games being held in London. Although national audiences in Europe are much smaller than the US because of the

Table 9.7 NFL TV viewership 2011

Thursday Night Kickoff	*Thanksgiving Classic*	*NFC Championship*	*AFC Championship*	*Super Bowl*
27,124,000	30,901,000	51,884,000 (43% share)	54,850,000 (46% share)	111,041,000 (71% share)

Source: Nielsen. *2011 Year in Sports.*

Table 9.8 2012 most-watched sports events

Country	Event	Number of viewers	Share (%)
Germany	Champions League Final	16,786,000	55.0
Italy	Coppa Italia Final	11,587,000	42.4
Spain	Champions League Semi-final	11,271,000	55.8

Source: Eurodata TV.

smaller populations, shares for soccer broadcasts are high, especially for countries playing in the finals of the Euros or World Cup. In the 2010 World Cup, where the Netherlands reached the final, the audience share of the broadcast was an amazing 90.6 percent, meaning 90.6 percent of televisions were tuned into the game, much higher than the 2011 Super Bowl share of 71 percent.

International measurement. Measuring international audiences is difficult because poorer countries are less likely to have rigorous, audited measurements of television audiences. FIFA's estimate of 715.1 million viewers for the 2006 World Cup Final (see Table 9.9), for example, included "guesswork" for most of Africa, used unreliable diary data in big Asian markets, and included repeats, highlights, and delayed showings, plus an additional 100 million plus viewers watching out-of-home. Independent analysts proposed a verified figure of 260 million, and more conservative estimates put the total viewership at about 400 million, though a precise number is elusive.

Consistency. Sports events are also valued as television programming because the audience sizes are consistent. NASCAR, for example, televises 36 Sprint Cup races per year and has drawn consistent audience sizes of 5.8 million (see Table 9.10). Though down from their peaks earlier in the decade, the sizable, numerous, and consistent ratings for NASCAR races make them a very attractive programming option.

Regional. While the big numbers garnered for national audiences attract the most attention, regional audiences can collectively add up to big numbers. MLB's 2011 World Series averaged 16.6 million viewers over seven broadcasts. On Opening Day of that same season, 12.5 million viewers tuned into games across the country featured on both national and regional television. The marquee match-up featuring the big-market Los Angeles Lakers and Chicago Bulls drew 11 million viewers, well below typical NFL numbers. However,

Table 9.9 2006 sports event viewership[1]

Sport	Event	Claimed viewership	Verified viewership
Soccer	World Cup Final	715,100,000	260,000,000
Football	Super Bowl	750,000,000	98,000,000
Olympics	Winter Olympics	2,000,000,000	87,000,000
Soccer	Champions League Final	120,000,000	86,000,000
Auto racing	Formula One Brazilian Grand Prix	354,000,000	83,000,000

Note
1 Why FIFA's claim of one billion viewers was a quarter right. www.independent.co.uk/sport/football/news-and-comment/why-fifas-claim-of-one-billion-tv-viewers-was-a-quarter-right-438302.html, accessed 5/2/2013.

Table 9.10 NASCAR Sprint Cup viewership

Year	Average number of viewers
2013	5,796,000
2012	5,778,000
2011	6,451,000
2010	5,861,000
2009	6,543,000

Source: Nielsen.[1]

Note

1 Mickle, T. and Ourand, J. (2013). NASCAR pleased with viewership consistency. www.sportsbusinessdaily.
com/Journal/Issues/2013/11/25/Media/NASCAR-ratings.aspx?hl=nascar%20pleased%20with%20viewer-
ship &sc=0, accessed 11/25/2013.

Table 9.11 Regional sports ratings

Year	Team	Local market rating
2002	MLB Seattle Mariners	13.2
2012–2013	NHL Pittsburgh Penguins	12.6
2007	MLB Boston Red Sox	12.2
2010–2011	NBA San Antonio Spurs	10.2
1997–1998	NBA Chicago Bulls (Michael Jordan's final season)	8.9

the five NBA games airing on Christmas Day 2011 attracted a total of nearly 35 million viewers, collectively rivaling NFL size audiences.

Local market broadcasts can attract significant audiences in their own right (see Table 9.11). While the overall viewership numbers are low compared to national broadcasts, the local influence of a team can be substantial and of value to networks, advertisers, and sponsors. The NFL attracts sizable national audiences for its primetime games, but even the NFL combines regional broadcasts for its Sunday afternoon games. For MLB, the NBA, and the NHL, fans tend to be more locally concentrated. As evidenced by the $8 billion rights fee secured by MLB's Los Angeles Dodgers for their local market broadcasts, networks have recognized the value of sizable and consistent local audiences.

Radio

Local and unscripted. While portable digital music players such as iPods might have severely affected music radio, sports talk radio remains healthy. According to one industry source, the number of sports talk radio stations has grown 64 percent during the period 2002–2012. Stressing the draw of a focus on local market teams, one executive said:

> Sports talk radio is a local programming platform. While other formats tend to be national and more competitive with satellite radio, it's much more difficult for a sports fan to get a daily fix for their local teams other than in sports talk. Local still matters.

149

In addition to offering a local perspective, a senior vice president of production and business divisions at ESPN suggested that talk radio holds an advantage over television because it is more "authentic" and "unscripted."[19]

Print

Twenty years ago, local newspapers were by far the most used source of sports news. According to the ESPN Sports Poll, nearly two-thirds (65.4 percent) of Americans 12 years of age and older got their sports news from the local newspaper. While the Internet has overtaken newspapers as the most frequently used source of sports news in the last decade, newspapers remain an important source (32.9 percent for Internet and 23.6 percent for newspapers according to the 2009 ESPN Sports Poll).[20]

While the influence of digital formats is certainly substantial, magazine readership overall increased 3 percent to 1.2 billion cumulative readers from Spring 2012 to Spring 2013, according to Gfk MRI's Survey of the American Consumer.[21] Overall magazine readership is still primarily print-based, with digital readership accounting for only 1.4 percent of total readership. Sports-related magazines, likely benefiting from a tech-savvy young male audience, receive among the bigger increases from digital readership: *ESPN the Magazine* got an additional 1.1 million digital readers and *Sports Illustrated* an additional 544,000.

Digital

The Internet has become the favorite method for following sports news. As such, sports-related websites compete to rank highly in comScore's monthly measurement of unique visitors (see Table 9.12). As sports fans have migrated to the Internet for sports news, so too have advertisers seeking to reach those fans. Consequently, media groups such as Yahoo Sports/NBC Sports Network, USA Today Sports Media Group, and Bleacher Report/ Turner Sports Network have aggregated websites to deliver bigger audiences to advertisers. Scale alone, however, tells only a partial story of fan engagement with websites. Time spent on the site and number of page views provide additional insights.

Table 9.12 October 2013 top 10 sports websites

Website	Unique visitors
ESPN	67,721,000
Yahoo Sports/NBC Sports Network	57,409,000
FoxSports.com on MSN	43,071,000
USA Today Sports Media Group	40,576,000
Bleacher Report/Turner Sports Network	36,473,000
NFL Internet Group	34,590,000
CBS Sports	32,139,000
Sporting News Media/Perform Sports	31,409,000
SB Nation	28,559,000
MLB	21,670,000

In particular, video is playing an increasingly important role for sports websites. During October 2011, for example, 35 million fans streamed 463,664,000 videos on sports websites. While social media, especially Facebook, helps to increase video starts, the content of videos is still primarily based on broadcast television, according to one study.[22]

CASE: MEDIA INTEGRATION

One of the concerns about additional media through which fans can enjoy sports was that "traditional" media would get crowded out. In sports media, that does not seem to be the case. To the contrary, as researchers at ESPN found:[23]

- "*A heavy user is a heavy user.*" Fans who watch a lot of sports on television also follow sports a lot on the Internet, radio, and print.
- "*Cross-media usage is not zero-sum.*" Sports fans do not substitute one medium for another – they are more likely to simply add on. While a high percentage of sports fans use different screens simultaneously, they do not do it for long periods of time.

Among ESPN viewers, the more they watch TV, the more they use the Internet (see Figure 9.3). ESPN divided TV viewership into quintiles based on average minutes per day. TV non-viewers spent nine minutes on the Internet, and Internet usage continued to climb as TV viewership increased. The heaviest TV viewers, those who watch nine hours 33 minutes per day, also used the Internet more (35 minutes).

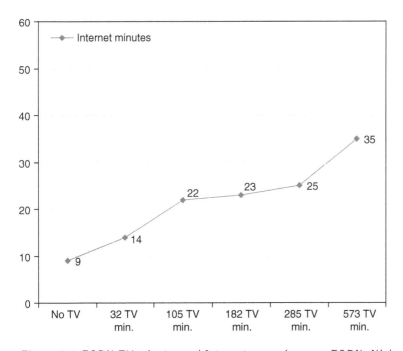

Figure 9.3 ESPN TV minutes and Internet usage (source: ESPN, Nielsen).

Table 9.13 NASCAR media consumption

NASCAR-related media consumption percent: more than once a week by fan avidity

	Percent	Casual	Moderate	Avid	Super
Watch NASCAR on sports news	46.7	8.9	38.3	59.8	87.7
Watch NASCAR races	40.1	16.1	31.6	49.4	68.7
Newspaper	32.8	6.1	24.6	43.2	62.6
Watch NASCAR news shows	26.8	1.6	11.4	33.6	66.9
Internet sports sites	17.6	0.5	4.2	12.7	58.8
NASCAR Internet sites	17.6	1.4	3.8	13.7	57.0
Magazines	6.8	0.4	1.7	4.8	22.8

Source: 2007 Season SRS NASCAR Sponsorship Study.

The pattern of increased media usage across the board holds true for specific sports in addition to sports viewing as a whole. According to a national telephone survey of 1000 NASCAR fans (see Table 9.13), there are consistent strong positive relationships across all types of media for fans following NASCAR. As a measure of fan avidity, media usage is related to other measures of fan avidity that drive revenue for sports properties. Heavy media users also buy more merchandise, attend more events, and are more loyal to sponsors.

EXERCISE

Write a hockey manifesto (or soccer, or women's sports, or German ice hockey – any sport that needs to build a TV audience). For sports properties that rely heavily on gate revenue, future growth depends greatly on developing media audiences, especially television. How can the attendance-driven properties generate media audiences?

THREE MAIN TAKEAWAYS

1 Media isn't social; people are.
2 Sports marketers can build media audiences through scheduling, production, storytelling, and promotion.
3 Despite the rapid growth in digital technologies, television is still king in the sports world; and sport is king in the media world.

RECOMMENDED READING

Mickle, T. (2006). NHL's Shannon takes his broadcast manifesto to the markets. www.sports-businessdaily.com/Journal/Issues/2006/11/20061113/This-Weeks-News/Nhls-Shannon-Takes-His-Broadcast-Manifesto-To-The-Markets.aspx?hl=manifesto&sc=0, accessed 5/29/2014.

NOTES

1 Eastman, S. and Riggs, K. (1994). Televised sports and ritual: Fan experiences. *Sociology of Sport Journal*, 11: 249–274.

2 Ibid.

3 Ibid.

4 YouGov Plc. Premier League out of home viewing attracts key audience. Aug 23, 2010.

5 (2013). Staygating at-home sports viewing parties revealed. www.jsonline.com/sponsoredarticles/food/staygating-athome-sports-viewing-parties-revealed-infographic8083210101–228644311.html, accessed 12/16/2013.

6 Akindes, G. (2011). Football bars: urban sub-Saharan Africa's trans-local "stadiums." *The International Journal of the History of Sport*, 28(5): 2176–2190.

7 (2013). Spanish TV boss wants more matches between 12pm and 4pm. www.insidespanishfootball.com/66826/spanish-tv-boss-wants-more-matches-between-12pm-and-4pm/, accessed 11/9/2013.

8 Associated Press (2013). London NFL game to have earlier start. http://espn.go.com/nfl/story/_/id/10079217/london-nfl-game-start-early-next-season, accessed 12/16/2013.

9 Barrett, S. (2009). When it comes to football, Sky is in a league of its own. http://mediablogged.mediaweek.co.uk/2009/02/11/when-it-comes-to-football-sky-is-in-a-league-of-its-own/, accessed 10/28/2013.

10 Lefton, T. and Ourand, J. (2011). X years after. www.sportsbusinessdaily.com/Journal/Issues/2011/05/16/Leagues-and-Governing-Bodies/XFL-main.aspx?hl=x%20years%20after&sc=1, accessed 12/11/2013.

11 Ibid.

12 Eastman and Riggs. Televised sports and ritual.

13 Lombardo, J. (2011). Drama sells for NBA: League posts gaudy stats as labor issue looms. www.sportsbusinessdaily.com/Journal/Issues/2011/04/18/Leagues-and-Governing-Bodies/NBA-revenue.aspx?hl=drama%20sells%20for%20NBA&sc=0, accessed 12/11/2013.

14 Ourand, J. (2011). The great cable migration: Sports cash in, but pay the price in viewership. www.sportsbusinessdaily.com/Journal/Issues/2011/02/21/In-Depth/Media-story.aspx?hl=great%20cable%20migration&sc=0, accessed 12/11/2013.

15 Luker, R. (2013). Even with the newest technology, research shows TV is still king. www.sportsbusinessdaily.com/Journal/Issues/2013/01/21/Research-and-Ratings/UpNext.aspx, accessed 12/16/2013.

16 Fixmer, A. (2012). Nielsen cuts 500,000 US TV homes on Census, Web viewing. www.bloomberg.com/news/2012-09-25/nielsen-cuts-u-s-tv-homes-by-500-000-on-census-shift-to-web.html, accessed 12/14/2013.

17 Enoch, G. and Johnson, K. (2010). Cracking the cross-media code: How to use single-source measures to examine media cannibalization and convergence. *Journal of Advertising Research*, June: 125–136.

18 (2007). Why FIFA's claim of one billion viewers was a quarter right. www.independent.co.uk/sport/football/news-and-comment/why-fifas-claim-of-one-billion-tv-viewers-was-a-quarter-right-438302.html, accessed 5/2/2013.

19 Ourand, J. (2012). A strong signal. www.sportsbusinessdaily.com/Journal/Issues/2012/02/13/In-depth/Lead.aspx?hl=a%20strong%20signal&sc=1, accessed 10/17/2013.

20 Luker, R. (2010). Use of technology by fans offers industry lots of room to grow. www.sportsbusinessdaily.com/Journal/Issues/2010/03/20100329/Up-Next/Use-Of-Technology-By-Fans-Offers-Industry-Lots-Of-Room-To-Grow.aspx?hl=luker%20newspaper&sc=0, accessed 12/18/2013.

21 Bazilian, E. (2013). Magazine readership growing, survey says. www.adweek.com/news/press/magazine-readership-growing-survey-shows-149863, accessed 12/18/2013.

22 Adobe Systems Inc. *The US Digital Video Benchmark 2012 Review*.

23 Enoch and Johnson. Cracking the cross-media code.

Chapter 10

Sports publicity

Increased media integration by audiences has eroded traditional boundaries between advertising and public relations. Advances in digital technology have allowed brands – both sports properties and sponsors alike – to create more of their own content. Brands can create content that can be used for advertising and also attract outside media attention.

"Paid," "owned," and "earned" media have become popular terms to reflect the way media are structured,[1] reflecting the increased consumer empowered digital environment (see Table 10.1). Traditional television, radio, and print formats now share content on

Table 10.1 Paid, owned, and earned media

	Owned	Paid	Earned
Examples	■ Website ■ Social media	■ Advertising ■ Paid search	■ Media coverage ■ Word-of-mouth ■ Social media mentions and shares
Advantages	■ Control ■ Low cost	■ Can reach mass audiences and drive traffic to other media ■ Control ■ Timely	■ Credible ■ Potentially cost effective
Challenges	■ Requires promotion	■ Lacks credibility ■ Cluttered environment ■ Expensive	■ No control over message, coverage, or timing ■ Difficult to quantify value

Source: comScore.

computers, tablets, and phones, blurring traditional media distinctions. In addition, consumers now play a greater role in creating media and driving traffic through social media.

Branded content, whether it is owned, earned, or paid, ideally converge into a cogent campaign. As the chief executive of MediaLink observed: "Brands as publishers is a big development. They're in the content business. You ask Coca-Cola, they're in the liquid content business. They want to send you content. They don't want to send you commercials."[2] With advances in digital technology, brands are able to communicate with consumers more directly, with less mediation.

Dove Men+Care, for example, has created a series of videos featuring sports personalities, such as NBA star Dwayne Wade, retired tennis great John McEnroe, and sports broadcaster Jay Bilas. The campaign includes 30-second television commercials, which are posted on Dove's branded website: www.dovemencare.com. The videos are shared on social media sites, such as Facebook, Twitter, and YouTube. Dove Men+Care's UK version of the "Scrum Cam," which shows a video of the inside of a rugby scrum, attracted more than 600,000 views on YouTube. The Argentinean version attracted nearly 200,000 views in addition.

Sports properties likewise have the ability to generate their own content. Teams, leagues, and individuals have their own websites, Facebook pages, and Twitter accounts with the ability to produce and distribute their own content directly to fans. As Twitter's head of sports partnerships said of the company's partnership with five MLB teams, "The biggest thing that came out of this is people love media. They want to get closer to the action and they want to get that insider perspective that nobody else has."[3]

MEDIA GOALS

Sports properties and corporations alike are attempting to tap into the potential of new media, but to what ends?

When asked whether Twitter should be used for ticket sales, the company's head of sports partnerships responded, "Twitter's not a commerce platform. Do people want to buy tickets on Twitter? I don't know how much impulse purchase of tickets happen."[4] In contrast, the Local Organizing Committee for the Asian Football Confederations Asian Cup 2015 in Australia sought a Media Manager "to assist in raising awareness of the event throughout Australia." Most media efforts are aimed at increasing awareness and enhancing image.

While "top of the funnel" goals such as awareness and image are the most common goals for media efforts, they can be linked to sales goals. As Twitter's head of sports partnerships explained:

> Surely, if a team has 1,000 tickets left to sell they could potentially send out a tweet at noon and try to drive people to a site. Whether that ever lives on Twitter or not, I don't know. *We're not going to become the commerce platform*, but we may enable other people to do it.[5] (emphasis added)

A senior vice president of university sales and marketing at CBS interactive commented on college athletics website goals, "Some want to use the site more for communicating with the fans and others are more enthusiastic about using it to drive revenue." While all organizations must prioritize tactical goals in order to set budgets, communicating and driving revenue are not mutually exclusive.

The ultimate goal is to converge owned, paid, and earned media into a cogent campaign in order to achieve the larger marketing objectives for the organization. Effective media campaigns build *synergy* among owned, paid, and earned media assets so that the whole is greater than the sum of the parts.

AFC Asian Cup 2015 – Media Manager[6]

Purpose of role:

The [Local Organising Committee (LOC)] is now seeking to appoint a talented and enthusiastic Media Manager to *assist in raising awareness of the event throughout Australia*. The successful candidate will have a passion for the World Game and be from a sporting background. You will also have a proven track record in media, communications or public relations. Reporting to the General Manager Communications, your duties will include:

- Proactively seeking out media opportunities for the LOC.
- Developing creative media strategies to build awareness among football fans and the wider public.
- *Building relationships with key football and general media.*
- *Drafting press releases, magazine articles and general media.*
- *Developing media plans and policies.*
- *Managing media events and press conferences.* (emphases added)

Like advertising, public relations is often used for objectives toward the top of the purchase funnel: awareness and reputation.

Like sales, PR is a relationship-based discipline.

Press releases, media events, and press conferences are standard public relations tactics.

OWNED MEDIA

Disintermediation of traditional media. Ironically perhaps, traditional media is now at risk of becoming disintermediated. As MediaLink's chief asserted, "as brands become publishers, their owned media becomes more important than their paid media."[7]

Brands have a greater ability to reach consumers directly. "Awareness is a big issue, now that there's so much content and so many avenues,"[8] according to the Learfield Sports Chief Content Officer. The challenge for owned media, especially websites, is to create awareness and drive traffic to owned media.

In particular, videos have grown in popularity so that sports properties now hire videographers in addition to writers. The Digital Department at the PGA, for example, sought to hire a video product manager to develop videos that will generate fan interest. For sports properties, generating fan interest not only helps to strengthen relationships with fans, it potentially creates an audience which properties can sell to advertisers.

Video Product Manager – PGA TOUR[9]

Responsibilities:

- Identify and evaluate new and emerging video delivery technologies and develop *innovative digital products* to generate fan interest in the PGA TOUR while also meeting *the goals of larger TOUR initiatives...*
- Manages the day-to-day operational and tactical aspects of video related projects both large and small as they move through the product development life cycle from ideation to launch, and then into regular operations" (emphasis added).

Note the integration of innovations with goals of larger Tour initiatives. Innovative digital technologies can be really cool, which can distract sports marketers from organizational goals. Moreover, digital technologies can generate fan interest without creating a viable business model. Cool for the sake of being cool doesn't necessarily help to attain goals.

To a certain extent, sports properties can enjoy a built-in audience of existing fans, for whom digital assets strengthen an existing relationship. For properties looking to develop content to increase their fan base, the content must be compelling. Major League Soccer, for example, features general news about the sport in addition to news on the league and its teams. The site includes news and commentary about the US national team, American players playing abroad, and big international clubs. Personally, I think it is some of the best coverage around. Other fans seem to agree, as MLSSoccer.com about doubled the average monthly users from 2012 to 2013.

Most owned content does not seek to replace traditional media, but complement it. For corporate brands, that can mean using sports to develop compelling content that will create a buzz. As Anheuser-Busch's vice president of media, sports, and entertainment marketing said, brands are "trying to provide a different type of content that resonates with the consumer and gets them to like us, talk about us, add that social aspect to it."[10]

For properties, the buzz can often move in the other direction, using content to enhance broadcasts and using social media to drive traffic to content. MLS, for example, developed a "second-screen experience" featuring real-time statistics and video highlights that helped to increase traffic 16 percent per game. According to MLS Digital's vice president, the league's 600,000 Facebook likes and 255,000 Twitter followers played a significant role in increasing the number of website visitors.

Corporate brands that engage in business-to-business marketing have developed a wide range of content marketing strategies and tactics. In a survey of more than 4000 B2B marketers, 44 percent have a documented content marketing strategy and 73 percent have someone who oversees content marketing strategy. Commonly used tactics include website articles (81 percent), case studies (73 percent), white papers (64 percent), and research reports (44 percent). Despite the importance of B2B marketing for sports properties in the form of corporate ticket sales, media sales, and sponsorships, there is a notable absence in B2B marketing content available.

PAID MEDIA

Advertising. Advertising is a particularly effective method for generating awareness. Traditional media still draws the biggest numbers. While Internet advertising continues to grow rapidly, the majority of advertising dollars still go to television. For good reason. Television still draws the biggest audiences, especially for sports. GoDaddy.com, for example, has used Super Bowl commercials to drive traffic to its website. According to Akamai, a net usage measurement company, GoDaddy.com experienced a huge surge in traffic during the period the commercial aired on the Super Bowl broadcast.[11] Traffic to online content can be driven by other online techniques. Many websites use search advertising in which websites pay to appear in search engine results, such as Google.

While advertising delivers "scale," or big audiences, the challenge for advertising is a lack of trust. Consumers know that advertisers are trying to "sell" them. As such, consumers tend to be guarded and skeptical. Owned and earned media, in contrast, are more trusted.

According to a global consumer survey conducted by Nielsen among more than 25,000 Internet users worldwide, owned and earned media are much more likely to be trusted than paid media (see Figure 10.1).[12] Earned media was consistently ranked among the most trusted forms of advertising. Word-of-mouth ("recommendations from known people") is the most trusted form of advertising, with 90 percent of participants in the study saying they "somewhat" or "completely" trust recommendations from people they know. Consumer opinions posted online followed with 70 percent, along with owned media in the form of

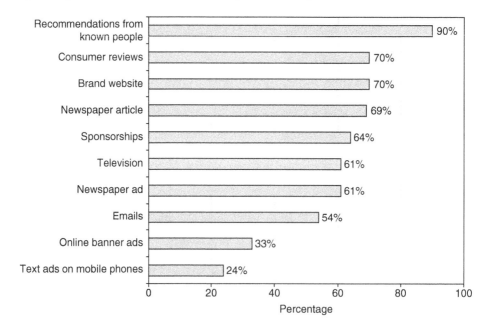

Figure 10.1 Advertising trust (source: Nielsen).

brand websites. Newspaper articles (69 percent) were more trusted than newspaper ads (61 percent).

EARNED MEDIA

Sports properties benefit from fan bases that have a strong demand for media content. Many sports properties have some version of a sports information director, or "SID" as they are called in college athletics. A SID is often responsible for the production and dissemination for the voluminous nature of sports data and stories, including media guides, websites, news releases, and internal records (see Director of Sports Information, University of Pittsburgh at Bradford box below).

Director of Sports Information – University of Pittsburgh at Bradford

Responsibilities include all aspects of sports information for the university's 15 Division III intercollegiate programs, including, but not limited to, writing press releases after the games, working on StatCrew, developing web media guides, writing feature stories for the university's alumni magazine Portraits and other stories as needed, and updating the athletics section of the university's website and social media sites. Additionally, the SID must supervise and train score keepers and statisticians so that duties are performed by AMCC and NCAA rules, assist coaches in gathering current statistical and records files as requested, enter current year statistical data into athletic archives to ensure up-to-date records are maintained at all times, and execute video streaming of home athletic events.[13]

This job ad is for a relatively small (Division III) athletic department. While big name jobs can often add some prestige to a resume, jobs with smaller organizations can provide the opportunity to gain more skills and experience. In larger organizations, entry-level employees might be channeled into specializing early. Smaller organizations lack the staff to specialize. In this ad, for example, note the wide range of duties. This candidate will have an opportunity to get experience in almost all facets of the discipline.

Sports properties with sizable and avid fan bases can keep quite busy simply responding to existing interest. Sports properties looking to gain awareness and almost all corporate brands, however, must actively market and sell their stories. Many sports do not receive regular coverage in national or local news. For soccer teams in the US located in markets with existing "big four" (NFL, NBA, MLB, and NHL), coverage in local news is tough to come by. The New York Red Bulls, for example, play in a market with two NFL, two NBA, two MLB, and three NHL teams. It makes for a crowded sports page and a challenge for other sports properties to gain prominent and consistent coverage. The same is true on a national stage for less prominent (e.g., professional bowling) and controversial (mixed martial arts) properties.

And while sports properties have done a great job getting coverage in the sports pages, they have been noticeably absent from the business press. In addition to not providing much content supporting B2B efforts, sports properties fail to obtain media coverage commensurate with the size of the industry. Entire publications, for example, are dedicated to advertising, which also gets regular coverage in the business sections of mainstream news outlets. While the sports sponsorship industry is much smaller than the advertising industry, it nonetheless represents a multi-billion dollar global enterprise. But you would hardly know that from reading the business pages. Similarly, corporate ticket sales is responsible for billions in global revenue with virtually no media coverage, either owned or earned.

For corporate brands, the challenge to gain media is even greater. While there might be lukewarm interest in professional bowling, there is even less in reading about shampoo. Even when there is consumer interest in a product category, such as home improvement, there is little interest among consumers about specific brands, such as Home Depot. One of the goals for corporate brands in aligning with sports properties is to leverage interest in the sport to gain positive publicity. Sports fans might have little interest in reading about Home Depot per se, but they might have greater interest in reading about what Home Depot is doing with the Olympics.

While sports properties generally do not promote corporate ticket sales or sports sponsorship as overall marketing disciplines, many sports properties recognize the importance of corporate sponsors and "partner" with them to reach their goals. Liverpool FC, for example, recently advertised for a "new" and "exciting" PR opportunity with "the overall objective of raising the profile of the Club's commercial, business and partner marketing activity domestically and in chosen overseas countries" (see Commercial PR Manager, Liverpool FC box below).

Commercial PR Manager, Liverpool FC[14]

Job details

Liverpool FC is seeking a Commercial PR Manager to join their expanding team. This is a new and exciting PR role with the overall objective of raising the profile of the Club's commercial, business and partner marketing activity domestically and in chosen overseas countries. Your focus will be on maximising coverage in domestic and international trade sports, business and brand media. You will also identify suitable profile opportunities with business and sports conventions, trade shows and commercial expos.

Main duties and responsibilities of the role

■   You will develop a multiple bandwidth domestic and international PR/media relations strategy for effectively communicating our commercial and partner marketing activity.

- You will proactively maximize all PR opportunities to capitalise on our retail, hospitality and other business revenue streams (kit launches, hospitality, tourism, catering, etc.).
- You will be expected to work with sponsors and other business Partners to add value and maximise all associated PR opportunities.
- You will act as the initial point of contact for all media enquiries relating to our commercial business activity.

Full disclosure, I'm a fairly avid supporter of the club, but I agree that a commercial PR manager is a new and exciting role not just because it's with Liverpool. The main responsibility for this position is marketing services provided by the club. Like many industries, the sports business can be insular – sports marketers can spend a lot of time talking to each other. Commercial activity for sports properties – advertisers, sponsors, etc. – spans the full range of business categories. Sports sponsorship in particular has not done a very good job of telling its story to the greater business community. Collectively, we should do a better job of it.

Pitching sports media

Whether representing a sports property or corporate brand, any sports marketer seeking to earn media must "pitch" journalists or producers. A PR "pitch" is appropriately named because the process of pitching media follows the same steps as the sales process. Consistent with the premise that the sports industry is a sales-based business, sports publicity is a sales-based discipline.

Objectives. Sports publicity executives must work with clients and/or internal stakeholders to specific objectives of publicity campaigns. What are the program goals and who are the targets? For Home Depot's Olympic sponsorship, for example, agency executives at Manning Selvage & Lee (MS&L) sought to position Home Depot "as the leading supporter of Olympic athletes" to Home Depot customers and potential customers.[15] In addition, secondary objectives included communicating specific messages, such as Home Depot's "You can do it. We can help." tagline, and building awareness of the sponsorship in the run-up to and during the Games.

Prospecting. When seeking to pitch a story to print media, sports publicity veteran Joe Favorito recommends a mix of:

- those who write the news (reporters);
- those who write news and set their own topics (columnists);
- those who ultimately make the decisions on space and story (editors).[16]

For video and audio, Favorito suggests focusing on (1) reporters, (2) producers, and (3) assignment editors. The principles of building and maintaining personal and professional relationships applies to PR pitches as well as sales in general. For example, Favorito recounts a case in which the VP for PR for the Pro Bowlers Tour identified a USA Today writer as an avid bowler and successfully leveraged that interest into national coverage for a sport well past its national heyday in the 1970s. Resources such as Mediabistro.com, Bacon's, and Media Map can help to provide some basic data and interests on editors at major publications.

Sports stories have the potential to reach much broader audiences than those who read the sports pages. As one PR veteran suggested, "Research a wide range of publications that may or may not make sense for a client pitch."[17] A colleague once raised the issue of relevance after learning that I had been mentioned in the *Insurance Journal* for my sports marketing expertise.[18] I explained that many insurance companies are active as sports sponsors so sports marketing is very relevant to their businesses. While sports sponsorship spans a wide range of business disciplines and industry categories, sports properties can also have broader appeal in general lifestyle and special interest publications.

PR practitioners can also respond to journalist requests. In addition to hosting a website that distributes news releases, PRNewsire provides its ProfNet service in which experts can respond to requests from journalists. Expert sources, such as agencies, media managers, and subject matter experts themselves, can register to receive daily queries from journalists on topics of interest.

Needs analysis. Successful PR pitches entail developing an understanding of what journalists are looking for and what their readers are interested in reading, with the latter question being of ultimate importance. The best place to start gaining insights is to read the publications. When MS&L sought to gain publicity for Home Depot's Olympic sponsorship, executives there started with a comprehensive media audit. Home Depot had been involved in the Olympic Job Opportunities Program (OJOP), which gave Olympic athletes jobs and time and resources to train. MS&L executives wanted to understand how and where the program was covered previously. Then, MS&L executives conducted primary research with journalists, gaining feedback from 50 national and local journalists in order to inform a communications strategy.

PR pitchers needs to understand the idea of a good story to journalists and readers. One PR veteran Margo Mateas suggests, "Think like a reporter."[19] Using the many resources available to understand journalists and their readers will help PR practitioners to identify the "hidden story" that reporters and readers will find compelling. In PR practitioner parlance, newsworthy stories need to be "sexy," with a "hook," something that will "make your story jump off the page."[20] Rigorous and diligent analysis helps to inform and fuel strategic thinking, identifying ideas that can be fleshed out and developed.

Presentation. Traditional news releases are still a common PR tactic. Even a casual search for sports-related content on www.PRNewsire.com yields a huge number of releases from a wide variety of sources. News releases are easily lost in the clutter because they are meant for and distributed to general audiences. To increase the odds of getting a story covered, PR practitioners should customize pitches. PR veteran Lorra Brown suggests sending the pitch via e-mail and then following up with one or two phone calls.[21]

Regardless of the format, whether via tradition news release format consisting of a 1–2 page summary or a brief e-mail, the pitch needs a clear and succinct headline. In a news release, the headline must contain the idea behind the story and offer enough of a hook to entice the reader to continue reading the entire release and perhaps cover it. In e-mails, the subject line must convince the reader to open the e-mail.

For example, I responded to a ProfNet Query for a story about renting versus buying a house. *U.S. News & World Report* has a national circulation so I was interested in the exposure even though it is not sports marketing related. Thinking that there would be a lot of responses providing statistics and research, I decided to go with an anecdote about "Lou," the maintenance guy at my old apartment building. The quote ended up being used as the lead for the story.[22]

ProfNet query

I'm writing an article for *U.S. News & World Report* about renting versus buying. When is it better to buy and when is it smarter to continue renting? I'm looking for insight, advice, anecdotes, statistics, research – whatever anyone has that can help answer that age-old question: Is it smarter to buy a house or rent one? I'm a freelancer.

Response to ProfNet query

Subject: Long-time renter recently bought a house

And I miss renting. The best thing in my old place was "Lou." Faucet leaking? Call Lou. Air conditioning not working? Call Lou. Now that I'm a homeowner, I got no "Lou." You know anyone who does gutters in Indianapolis?

For most approaches, PR pitches need support to be credible. Personally, I like the dot-dot-dot approach. In either an e-mail or news release format, the story needs to be boiled down to a single thesis statement. Then, offer three supporting points, preferably research-based. For example, in response to a ProfNet query about US sports leagues playing games overseas, I proposed that leagues look overseas because of limited growth opportunities domestically, then supported it with more detailed arguments in two additional paragraphs. The main point of my response was succinct and compelling enough to be used in the story's lead.[23]

ProfNet query

MLB, NFL, NBA, and NHL seem determined to play more of their games overseas. Why are they doing this (money? branding?) and are they losing US fans in the process as well as putting extra burdens on the players who have to travel internationally? Are players subject to tax laws from other countries? This story is for the CNBC.com website. All interviews by phone or e-mail. Not all source submissions will get replies. Not all interviews may make final story edit.

ProfNet response

Subject: Sports leagues fan development overseas

Hi Mark,

The main reason many sports leagues are staging events overseas is because the US sports market is very mature and cluttered, so the growth opportunities lie outside the US.

The recent trend in events is an outgrowth of a long-term media strategy. The NFL, MLB, NBA, and NHL have all had international offices for quite a long time, which have been successful in gaining carriage on media outside the US. Since it's an already existing product and there are minimal additional costs, it's been a profitable venture.

In order to develop individuals into fans, however, live events are the next step. The keys to becoming a long time, avid fan of a sport are (1) play it, (2) attend an event, and (3) consume the media in all of its forms. Basketball enjoys fairly widespread international participation, as does baseball to a lesser extent and in fewer markets. For the NFL, increasing participation would be prohibitively expensive. While exhibition games can be successful in generating some interest, they are not a substitute for regular season games. Compared to the expense of NFL Europe and a full league, occasional regular season games are a cost-effective fan development strategy, which can still generate a lot of fan excitement. And it works for the NFL because the league can schedule games adjacent to by-weeks for teams to compensate for travel.

The travel schedules for sports with more games in the regular season are a significant barrier for NBA and MLB regular season games overseas, which have tended to stick to tours and exhibitions. Of course, MLB also launched the World Baseball Classic, largely as an effort to develop fans in other markets.

Good luck with the story and feel free to call my cell if you'd like to discuss further.

Best, Larry

Closing. Like salespeople, many PR practitioners fail to ask for the business. With PR, that means asking for the story. As one PR veteran stated:

> Your pitch needs to have a close. Give reporters several dates and times to talk with you, then you can call to follow up and see which one works for them. Don't be wishy-washy and leave it up to chance.[24]

It helps to be specific in what you are asking for. If the pitch was based on sound strategy informed by a rigorous and thorough needs analysis, then closing should be a matter of simply restating the benefits to the journalist's audience members.

Measurement. One of the bigger challenges for PR, like the marketing discipline overall, is accountability. Many PR practitioners will supply clients with voluminous clip books of media mentions and impressions, both of which can tally huge numbers for a big campaign. MS&L's campaign for Home Depot, for example, yielded 580 total media placements, totaling 650 million impressions. More importantly, however, MS&L also developed a positioning evaluation tool to determine if media placements communicated the campaign's key messages. While MS&L found 86 percent of all media coverage communicated the key messages, there is still a measurement gap between message communication and financial results.

Attempts have been made to quantify PR efforts through providing advertising equivalencies. Suppose a client is covered in a newspaper article. The way an ad equivalency works is the article's space is measured and then compared to how much it would cost to buy advertising in the newspaper for the equivalent space. For television coverage, the time of the story is equated to what it would cost to buy a commercial during the broadcast. Of course, as we have seen, a story is not the same as an ad. Sometimes it is better because it is more credible. Other times it is worse because the story might not contain key messages. However, while ad equivalencies are not valid measures of the financial value of PR efforts, communicating key messages to a target audience is measurable and can be linked to sales and profits.

CRISIS MANAGEMENT

> Get it right; get it fast; get it out; and get it over.
>
> Warren Buffet on crisis management[25]

Sports marketers can control athlete behavior neither on nor off the field of play, though they must contend with both. Often, it is behavior off the field of play that is most challenging to deal with. For sports PR agencies and player representatives, crisis management is a primary and recurring responsibility, especially in the age of social media and ubiquitous cameras and videos through mobile phones.

Steroids, fights, trouble with the law, on-the-field, off-the-field. The timing and nature of crises are not predictable, but that they will happen is. Therefore, it is important for sports organizations (and sponsors) to plan accordingly. Warren Buffet's advice about crisis management is simple but sound. Crises are dealt with best when they are dealt with quickly. Pete Rose regrets not admitting to betting on baseball earlier. If he had, he very well might have saved his baseball career. Among Lance Armstrong's biggest transgressions was the repeated lying over years and years.

Some general principles for crisis management:

1 *Take control quickly*. As Warren Buffet says, "get it fast." The longer you wait, the greater the chance the crisis will dictate the story, not you.
2 *Tell the truth*. "Get it right." Don't say you took performance enhancing drugs to recover from an injury if you did it to enhance performance.
3 *Tell your story*. "Get it out." Explain the facts surrounding the story. Was your client in the middle of a brawl attempting to break up a fight?
4 *Make it right and/or accept the consequences*. Fans love a good redemption story. Athletes and sports personalities who admit to their failings and atone for their transgressions can sometimes end up becoming even more endeared to fans.

165

CASE – WHAT YOU CAN EXPECT IN YOUR FIRST SPORTS PR JOB

Lorra Brown, a former senior vice president at Ogilvy Public Relations Worldwide, provided the following summary of an entry-level practitioner in entertainment, most of which can be applied to a sports setting:

"An entry-level entertainment PR practitioner can expect to spend time performing the following tasks:

1 Staring at a computer screen monitoring news stories about his or her clients or cutting, pasting, and photocopying clips;
2 Making hundreds of follow-up calls to event invitees or journalists;
3 Tracking down obscure vendors to fulfill seemingly impossible requests;
4 Booking and confirming car service and hotel reservations;
5 Conducting dozens of site inspections of venues to meet detailed event specifications;
6 Taking red-eye flights and heading directly to the office for work;
7 Standing in the rain, snow, and cold to check in guests;
8 Stuffing hundreds (even thousands) of gift bags in a windowless closet;
9 Deflecting nasty come-ons from smarmy clients – politely;
10 Earning a barely livable salary and being expected to work crazy hours, including weekends."[26]

- Entry-level PR jobs involve a lot of desk research.
- Like sales, PR requires great phone skills. In many respects, PR is more about talking than writing.
- In general, you can see that these jobs require a lot of "organizational skills" – there are a lot of details to be attended to, and senior level executives LOVE entry-level employees who can take care of the details to free them up for strategic thinking and client management.
- In sports, remember that you work during hours most people are off.
- The sports business is male-dominated, especially at the senior levels. Locker room culture often gets extended to sports board rooms, so there's no shortage of smarmy clients or nasty come-ons, especially in disciplines in which there are a lot of women, such as PR.
- Long hours, short pay. I call that the "sports tax." The benefit is that you get to sell a product you believe in, but you really need to decide for yourself if it's worth it.

EXERCISE

WHEN LANCE ARMSTRONG AND OTHER CYCLISTS WERE BUSTED FOR **DOPING**, THEY LOST THEIR **TITLES**.

WE'RE HERE TO REPOSSESS YOUR YELLOW JERSEYS, **DRUGFIEND**!

ACCORDING TO THE EXPERTS, DOPING WAS/IS PERVASIVE IN PRO CYCLING.

THEY **ALL** DID IT.

COULDN'T WIN WITHOUT DOPING.

THAT WAS THE SYSTEM.

STILL, THERE MUST HAVE BEEN **ONE** CLEAN CYCLIST. ONE. IN, FOR EXAMPLE, FRANCE. AFTER STRIPPING PLACE FINISHERS WHO **CHEATED**...

Tour de France
1. OXYGENATED BLOOD
2. STEROIDS
3. EPO
4. TESTOSTERONE
5. HUMAN GROWTH HORMONE
6. BOVINE GROWTH HORMONE

...SHOULDN'T THAT ONE, NAÏVE, HONEST CYCLIST GET THEIR **RIGHTFUL AWARD NOW?**

Jacques Renard
3rd grade
Placed #5182

Figure 10.2 Who really won the Tour de France?

Most people are familiar with Lance Armstrong's story and fall from grace (see Figure 10.2). Suppose you've been hired to repair his public image. Brainstorm some ideas for Lance Armstrong's redemption.

THREE MAIN TAKEAWAYS

1   With advances in digital technology, brands can create their own content.
2   Earned media helps to add value to both the paid and owned media.
3   Earning media involves sales elements, such as prospecting, needs analysis, presenting, and closing.

NOTES

1   Corcoran, S. (2009). Defining earned, owned and paid media. http://blogs.forrester.com/interactive_marketing/2009/12/defining-earned-owned-and-paid-media.html, accessed 12/17/2013.
2   Fisher, E. (2013). MediaLink's Kassan talks technology, content. www.sportsbusinessdaily.com/Journal/Issues/2013/10/14/Opinion/From-the-Executive-Editor.aspx?hl=medialink&sc=0, accessed 12/17/2013.
3   Madkour, A. (2013). Overheard at the Sports Marketing Symposium. www.sportsbusinessdaily.com/Journal/Issues/2013/10/14/Opinion/From-the-Executive-Editor.aspx?hl=overheard&sc=0, accessed 12/17/2013.
4   Ibid.
5   Ibid.
6   AFC Asian Cup 2014 Media Manager. www.isportconnect.com/index.php?option=com_content&view=article&id=19779:afc-asian-cup-2015-media-manager&catid=81:job&Itemid=230, accessed 6/10/2013.
7   Fisher. MediaLink's Kassan talks technology, content.
8   (2012). IMG Intercollegiate Athletics Forum: Realm of intellectual properties expanding in sports. www.sportsbusinessdaily.com/Daily/Issues/2012/12/06/Colleges/IMG-Forum-Intellectual.aspx?hl=college%20athletics%20content%20video&sc=0, accessed 12/19/2013.
9   http://pgatour.teamworkonline.com/teamwork/r.cfm?i=60509, accessed 12/19/2013.
10 Madkour. Overheard at the Sports Marketing Symposium.
11 Miller, R. (2010). Go Daddy ad drives huge traffic spike. www.datacenterknowledge.com/archives/2010/02/08/go-daddy-ad-drives-huge-traffic-spike/, accessed 12/19/2013.
12 The Nielsen Company (2009). *Nielsen Global Online Consumer Survey*.
13 http://ncaamarket.ncaa.org/jobs/5850851/director-of-sports-information, accessed 12/20/13.
14 Commercial PR Manager. http://sportsrecruitment.com/jos/details/310/commercial-pr-manager, accessed 11/17/2011. I know this violates lesson number two in *Scarface* ("don't get high on your own supply") as I am a fairly avid Liverpool fan, but this job ad is the first and only one I have seen for a sports property targeting the business press.
15 The Home Depot empowers Olympic and Paralympic athletes to do-it-themselves. http://prfirms.org/resources/the-home-depot-empowers-olympic-and-paralympic-athletes-to-do-it-themselves, accessed 5/29/2013.
16 Favorito, J. (2013). *Sports Publicity: A Practical Approach*. London and New York: Routledge. Check out his blog: http://joefavorito.com/.
17 Brown, L. (2009). Pitch perfect: How to succeed when client or media marching orders don't make sense. *PR Tactics*, March: 16.
18 St. Onge, K. (2008). Insurers keen on NCAA's basket-full of opportunities. www.insurancejournal.com/news/national/2008/04/08/88958.htm, accessed 12/20/2013.
19 Mateas, M. (2003). Advice on pitching and working with the media. *PR Tactics*, January: 21.
20 Cannon, J. (2006). The 60 second pitch. *Public Relations Quarterly*. Winter: 28–30.
21 Brown, L. (2007). Faulty pitches: How to avoid sending irrelevant, infuriating material to editors. *PR Tactics*, December: 17.

22 Williams, G. (2013). Renting or buying a home: Which is smarter? http://money.usnews.com/money/personal-finance/articles/2013/12/13/renting-vs-buying-a-home-which-is-smarter?page=2, accessed 12/20/2013.

23 Koba, M. (2013). US pro teams give "away game" a whole new meaning, www.cnbc.com/id/101095638, accessed 12/20/2013.

24 Mateas. Advice on pitching and working with the media.

25 www.prdaily.com/Main/Articles/Get_it_right_get_it_fast_Warren_Buffett_on_crisis_4522.aspx, accessed 1/9/2014.

26 Brown, L. (2012). Glamour? Ha! The realities of entertainment and fashion PR. www.prdaily.com/Main/Articles/Glamour_Ha_The_realities_of_entertainment_and_fash_10701.aspx, accessed 5/28/2013.

Chapter 11

Sports advertising sales

CHAPTER OUTLINE

1 Ad markets

2 Digital advertising

3 Why sports advertising?
   a Demographics
   b Cross-media synergy
   c Engagement

4 Identifying prospects
   a Agencies
   b Direct selling to brands
   c Sports sponsors

5 Developing valid business reasons for sports advertising

Sports properties do not have a challenge in creating media. Clearly, there is strong demand for television, radio, print, and digital sports content. With a cluttered sports media marketplace, the challenge is to "monetize" the content. Whether a sports property creates and owns its content or sells the rights to a media company, having an audience does not mean much without revenue. Media rights fees that exceed revenue generated is not a sustainable business model; and neither is a sports property's production costs exceeding revenue. That means selling advertising.

Advertising sales for sports media spans two industries: sports and media. The relationship can be complicated when sports media is included on networks with other programs, such as broadcast networks. Still, buying advertising on sports media is very much a "sports" buy. Advertisers must ask themselves, "How does my product play in the world of sports?" Sports advertising sales executives must help to answer that question.

AD MARKETS

Like media usage, advertising spending is dominated by television. According to Nielsen, nearly two-thirds (62.8 percent) of global advertising spending was spent on television in 2011 (see Figure 11.1).[1] Traditional media, such as print (newspaper and magazine) and

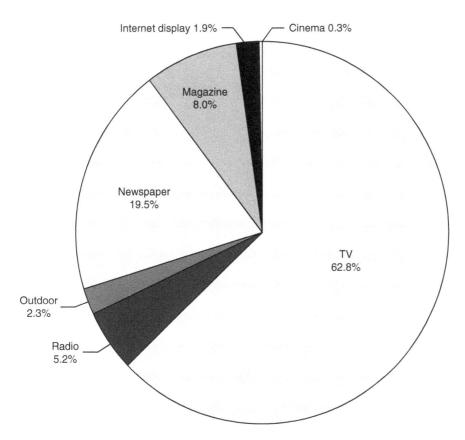

Figure 11.1 2011 global ad spending by media type (source: Nielsen).

radio, still generate substantial revenue as compared to Internet display advertising, though it must be recognized that display advertising accounts for only about 20 percent of total Internet advertising.

Many of the biggest advertisers on televised sports programs are also the biggest advertisers in general. According to Nielsen, sports event programming accounted for 23 percent of the total US television advertising spend for 2012, which is roughly equivalent to percentage of total viewing. Automotive and telecommunications companies spend the most on television advertising so it makes sense that they also spend the most on sports advertising.

Keeping in mind the question, "How does your product play in the world of sports?" it is not surprising that beer companies spend a much higher percentage of their total ad spending on sports. In 2011, Anheuser-Busch spent nearly two-thirds (65.7 percent) of its total television advertising spend on sports (see Table 11.1). An airline, however, is a less intuitive company for a sports advertiser. However, Southwest Airlines heavily leveraged its relationship with the NFL, spending the highest percentage of its television ad spend on sports (68.7 percent) among sports' biggest 50 advertisers. Among automotive companies, luxury brands Lexus and Mercedes determined that their products play well in the world of sports, both spending more than a third of their total TV ad budgets on sports.

171

Table 11.1 2011 TV advertising spending on sports

Company	Total sports TV ad spending (in millions)	Percentage of company spend
Southwest Airlines	$165.5	68.7
Anheuser-Busch	$299.7	65.7
MillerCoors	$203.0	56.3
DirecTV	$138.0	38.7
Lexus	$120.6	37.3
Coca-Cola	$86.6	36.2
Mercedes-Benz	$101.4	35.2
Sprint	$171.1	30.6
Apple	$95.1	28.1
Nissan	$153.2	26.5

Source: Nielsen.[1]

Note

1 Broughton, D. (2012). Verizon tops among ad spenders. www.sportsbusinessdaily.com/Journal/Issues/2012/06/04/Research-and-Ratings/Ad-spending.aspx, accessed 8/19/2012.

DIGITAL ADVERTISING

While traditional media continue to garner the majority of advertising revenues relative to Internet display advertising, Internet advertising revenues are growing most rapidly and becoming more important to sports properties and media companies. For NBC, for example, digital revenues doubled as a percentage of ad revenue between the Olympic Summer Games in Beijing in 2008 and the 2012 Games in London.

Digital advertising continues to evolve in format as well as grow in revenue. Digital video commercials, sponsorships, and rich media now account for almost half of all display-related Internet advertising revenues (see Table 11.2). As ESPN's executive vice president of digital and print media said, "We set ad innovation as one of our priorities for 2013."[2] As part of ESPN's effort to identify new forms of digital advertising, company executives hosted a "hackathon" to spur innovation. Fifteen teams spent 24 hours developing a pitch for ESPN sales executives. The winning team came up with an idea for video advertising built around highlight footage for ESPN's Gamecast service, which provide real-time reports for events not available on television.[3]

"Native advertising" is a recent innovation in digital content. The concept is based on "advertorials" in print publications, but the digital format makes the sponsored status less noticeable. In native advertising, paid content appears alongside unpaid content. For advertisers, the benefit is that they conceivably receive the trust levels of unpaid content but the control of paid content. The challenge, then, is to develop paid content that would be equally appealing to website visitors as unpaid content. Mainstream news publications such as *Forbes* and the *New York Times* have adopted the practice.

Native advertising is not without controversy, especially for news organizations in which there has been a firm line between journalism and advertising. Critics are concerned about compromising journalistic integrity. Still, native advertising has shown early signs of success in both increasing advertising revenues and attracting visitors. According to the Forbes Media group

Table 11.2 2012 Internet advertising revenues

	2012	
	Percent of total spend	*Total spend (in millions)*
Search	46.3	$16,916
Classifieds and directories	6.6	$2430
Lead generation	4.6	$1689
Email	0.4	$156
Mobile	9.2	$3370
Display-related		
■ Digital video commercials	6.4	$2330
■ Ad banners/display ads	21.1	$7721
■ Sponsorships	2.3	$845
■ Rich media	3.0	$1113
Total display-related	**32.8**	**$12,009**

Source: IAB.

publisher and chief revenue officer, "If it's great, it gets a lot of page views."[4] The challenge for sports-related digital content providers, then, is to create native advertising content that is "great." Sports-related seems particularly well-positioned to take advantage of native advertising because brand-sponsored video content is more successful in going viral than print content.

WHY SPORTS ADVERTISING?

With the numerous options available to advertisers, why choose sports? Sports advertising sales are successful to the extent that sports media can deliver value to advertisers. Sports media's unique selling proposition (USP) typically entails:

1   Attractive and unique audience demographics;
2   Cross-media advertising synergy; and
3   Positive attitudes toward advertising.

Demographics

Sports properties typically promote the attractiveness of their audiences. Young, male, and affluent are elusive audiences for advertisers because they are difficult to reach efficiently. The CEO of apparel company William Rast (founded by Justin Timberlake) led a group that invested in the Global RallyCross motorsports circuit. He said of the investment, "When I saw this business, I said, 'Wow, this is such an incredible model because of the demographic.' Every retailer is trying to get the 18–35-year-old and no one has it."[5]

ESPN, for example, promotes its audience to advertisers as a "premium audience." As promoted on ESPN's customer marketing and sales website, through the ESPN.com website, advertisers can:

173

Connect with young, upscale, educated and highly engaged sports fans on the #1 sports website for men.

Median Age: 33
Men: 81%
Men 18–34: 45%
Median Income: $62,545
HHI $100K+: 26.6%

GfK MRI, Spring 2012[6]

Young, upscale, and educated is highly suggestive of certain consumer behaviors but not very precise. Advertisers today seek data about purchase consideration in addition to brand recall measures, and product usage and brand preference in addition to demographics. As ESPN's director of advertising analytics said, "It used to be about high ratings and reach, and that was enough. Now, there's a lot more accountability, so we have gotten much more granular."[7]

Demographics alone do not ensure efficiency or effectiveness for advertisers, who are primarily interested in current and potential customers in their product category and of their brands in particular. Men's grooming products, for example, have moved into sports media to promote their products and brands. Procter & Gamble leveraged sports in ad campaigns for its Head & Shoulders shampoo. Unilever has used sports for both its Dove Men+Care and Axe brands. As ESPN's president of customer marketing and sales said, "We were able to show that the kind of men ESPN attracts are high-margin customers that any brand wants. These are high-margin consumers that shop quickly, are more brand loyal, and tended to not shop for price."[8]

Cross-media synergy

Sports are not the only place where consumers with demographics that appeal to advertisers can be found. Advertisers seeking young men can also find them at *Maxim*, for example. What makes sports different from *Maxim*? As ESPN's vice president of integrated media research said:

> Sports fans are the biggest consumers of media via cross-platform devices, because of this urgent need to stay connected to sports all day. Whether it's game-casting or managing fantasy leagues, or just keeping up with headlines, that's what makes sports fans different.[9]

So, sports fans can be reached via different platforms and spend a lot of time with a lot of different media platforms. Based on its cross-platform research on the 2010 World Cup – which included measures across television, radio, Internet, mobile, and print – ESPN asserts that, "There is a positive correlation between multimedia and advertising effectiveness."[10] Based on the findings of its ESPN XP research, ESPN argues that "advertisers must have presence across all platforms to ensure not only exposure but also authenticity of sponsorship. In fact, advertisers who put together the most cohesive story saw the greatest impact."[11]

Table 11.3 Strengths and weaknesses of advertising media

	Television	Digital	Radio	Magazine	Newspaper
Strengths	■ Reach ■ Easy to buy	■ Can link to purchase ■ Cost-effective	■ Frequency	■ Lifestyle targeting ■ Production	■ Older, affluent audience ■ Geographic targeting
Weaknesses	■ Cost	■ Clutter ■ Lack of engagement	■ Small audiences ■ Sound only	■ Small audiences	■ Older, declining audience ■ Poor production

Recognizing the value of cross-media synergy, advertisers seek to buy television and digital together. According to sports media expert John Ourand, advertisers "believe that taking advertising position on second screens will complement what's being done on television."[12] Consequently, sports media organizations tend to sell across platforms. NBC, for example, packages digital ads with television sales for its Olympics ad sales. That means that sports media sellers seek sports advertising executives who can work with different media platforms. For example, a sports talk radio station in Ohio sought a "Radio Sales Account Executive" who could also sell digital and on-site opportunities: "This position is perfect for the salesperson who knows how to integrate radio, digital, and on-site opportunities into a results driven marketing program for their clients."[13] Similarly, ESPN seeks advertising sales executives with cross-platform expertise. In a job ad for "Account Executive Television Sales," ESPN sought a candidate who: "participates in the development of multimedia marketing opportunities to grow new or current revenue."[14] Likewise, ESPN sought a "Director Audience Sales" with digital expertise who can also: "contribute to and become fluent in the ESPN conversations/presentations that are expected to be delivered in the marketplace with multi-media sales teams."[15] The main point here is that advertisers are seeking integrated media programs that will help them attain their business goals, not just an audience.

Different media vehicles can create synergy because each medium brings something different to the table (see Table 11.3). Television advertising can reach mass audiences effectively. Television advertising is also easy to buy because it has been around for so long, but can be very expensive. Digital advertising continues to grow rapidly because it is cost-effective in reaching consumers and can reach consumers when they are ready to buy, although there are still concerns about low click-through rates for banner advertising and a lack of engagement. Consumers regard some digital advertising as overly intrusive and/or easy to ignore. Radio advertising allows advertisers to place frequent ads for consumers, but reaches small audiences with sound only. Magazine advertising allows advertisers to reach market segments who share a lifestyle with good production values, but readership for even the biggest sports magazines is comparatively low. Newspaper advertising reaches an older, affluent demographic in a well-defined geographic region, but production quality is poor and readership continues to decline.

Engagement

While it might be intuitive that increased exposure across platforms can increase brand recall for advertisers, as ESPN pointed out, advertisers that put together a cohesive story are the most effective. Telling a cohesive story means that the advertisements across media platforms are connected to each other and also to the programming. Relevance for advertising works outside of sports as well. A study of magazine advertising found that "endemic ads," in which advertising messages are related to article content, are the most effective in driving traffic to advertiser websites.[16]

Perhaps because many sports advertising messages are created to be endemic to sports, sports fans have more positive views toward advertising in general. In a national online study of US adults, avid sports fans, the top quartile of sports media users, are almost four times as likely to "like" advertising than non-fans (see Figure 11.2). Positive attitudes toward advertising in general tend to be related to positive attitudes toward specific advertisements.

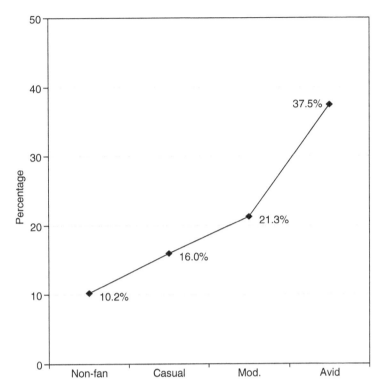

Figure 11.2 Sports fans' attitudes toward advertising: percent "like" advertising (source: UIndy Sports Report).

ESPN created a fictitious candy bar to test advertising effectiveness on its NFL programming. Based on the results of its research, ESPN found that the NFL gave the brand a "lift" to the fictitious brand. Dubbed the "High 5" bar, ESPN commissioned an advertising agency to create a commercial which it could compare to three ads for real candy bars. Results of the research indicated that favorable ratings increased 40 percent for "High 5" when shown in ESPN's NFL coverage compared to non-NFL programming. In addition, NFL fans said they would pay 10 percent more after viewing the commercial.[17]

Endemic sports advertising works for real brands, too. According to Nielsen, the best-liked television commercial during NASCAR's 2011 Sprint Cup season belonged to M&M's. The ad consisted of M&M red and yellow candies kidnapping NASCAR driver Kyle Busch and driving the car in his place. The ad's 40 percent likeability score as measured by Nielsen was double the 20 percent average for other ads in the series.

IDENTIFYING PROSPECTS

Selling advertising often involves working with some combination of brand and agencies. Most big advertisers have ad agencies that they work with and many engage a separate media buying agency as well. Even when advertising is sold directly to brand executives, agencies are likely to become involved at some point.

177

Agencies

The main benefit of working with media buying agencies is that they have already received a financial commitment to buy from their clients. Sports media sales executives do not need to sell agencies on the idea of doing advertising, just that the brand should buy time on their property. With a commitment to spend already in place, media sales executives are left to negotiate price and volume with media buying executives.

One media sales executive recounts a negotiation early in his career in which a media buyer asked for a 50 percent discount from the previous year. Although new to the job, the sales executive realized he was being tested and replied that, although he could not meet that price, he hoped they could find common ground. Eventually, the media buyer ended up with a higher total dollar amount than the previous year at a discounted rate that was agreeable to both parties. The media sales executive summed up the experience as follows:

> What I learned in dealing with agency buyers is that selling is a two-way street. It is a process by which a person helps others get what they want and in return both sides receive a fair and equitable deal. Selling is not a manipulative exercise in which salespeople get others to do something that is not in their best interest. This experience with Western International also taught me the most important lesson in negotiating with seasoned agency negotiators: "Always say 'no' to an initial offer, but always say it nicely and come back with a reasonable alternative."[18]

The key to the successful negotiation here was that both sides had a degree of empathy for the other's position. The media buying executive has a responsibility to get the lowest prices and the best deals for the agency's clients. Understanding that position allows a salesperson to negotiate a deal that works for both sides.

Direct selling to brands

In selling to media buying agencies, media sellers can enter into a race-to-the-bottom price war. If price is the distinguishing feature for buying advertising time, then competition can get fierce to offer the lowest prices and thereby reduce revenues. The most effective technique for marketers to justify higher prices is to deliver more value. Sports media sales executives can create more value for advertisers by creating customized, comprehensive marketing solutions.

As RadiOhio put it, they seek "Relationship driven marketers not 'list' babysitters or 'numbers' sellers – this is about selling solutions not ratings."

Here, sports media sales executives should consider "getting high on their own supply." One of the main features of selling sports is that many prospective advertisers are themselves sports fans. One sports media sales executive ended up making contact with the owner of a chain of muffler repair shops by using basketball tickets.

> Bob, I'm the new kid on the block at KOVR-13. I'm looking forward to meeting you in the near future to see if there's any way I can be of service to you and your

business. No strings attached. I hope you and your son enjoy the pair of front-row seats I've enclosed for next Tuesday's Sacramento Kinds vs. Los Angeles. Enjoy, Mark Chassman, KOVR-13.[19]

The muffler shop ended up buying an advertising package for the NFL's Monday Night Football broadcasts in an effort to reach young males.

Sports sponsors

It is important to keep in mind that sports media advertising packages are "sports buys." Many sports leagues require their sponsors to commit a specific dollar amount in related advertising. One of the ways sports media properties can acquire guaranteed commitments in advertising from sponsors is to become a preferred media supplier for a respective league. By forging partnerships with sports leagues, sports media properties can get placed on a short list to receive required media spending by sponsors. Even without required media spending, sports sponsors are qualified prospects for sports advertising as a way for the brands to leverage their sponsorships.

DEVELOPING VALID BUSINESS REASONS FOR SPORTS ADVERTISING

While sports advertising is very much a "sports buy," it must also make business sense for the overall marketing goals. In developing a pitch for a prospective advertiser, sports advertising sales executives must identify a valid business reason (VBR) for contact. A typical e-mail to a contact might look something like this:

Subject: Kick [YOUR COMPETITOR] where it hurts . . .
Dear [PROSPECT],
I hope this finds you well.
I have an idea where you can use my [MEDIA PROPERTIES] and that cool ad from a few years ago to kick [YOUR COMPETITOR] where it hurts.
I have all kinds of research that shows how we perform against [YOUR PRODUCT].
Would you want to talk?[20]

But then if there is interest on the part of the potential advertiser, there must really be an idea and research to back it up.

Syndicated research studies, such as Simmons, Scarborough, or Gfk/MRI are common tools for sports media sales executives to identify VBRs for potential advertisers. Syndicated research studies measure consumer product usage, media behaviors, attitudes, interests, and opinions. By comparing brand users with the average American, these studies point out areas in which advertisers can be more efficient in the media spending and effective in their advertising creative. By combining items in which a consumer segment indexes highly to the general population, these studies can provide marketers with profiles of consumer segments.

Table 11.4 Hispanic Red Bull drinkers

	Percent more likely to...
Listen to Hispanic radio	629
Go dancing/partIcipate in dance	171
Claim to be "fashionable on a budget"	142
Watch boxing on TV	124
Read sports magazines	74

Source: Gfk/MRI.[1]

Note

1 www.gfkmri.com/ConsumerInsights/InsideBrands.aspx, accessed 9/12/2014

For example, Table 11.4 draws on data from Gfk/MRI's *Survey of the American Consumer* to create a profile of Hispanics who drink Red Bull. With respect to media behaviors, Hispanic Red Bull drinkers are 124 percent more likely to watch boxing on television and 74 percent more likely to read sports magazines. A media property that could combine televised boxing with sports magazines would have a good reason to contact Red Bull about reaching its Hispanic customers. The data might also be used to develop some "spec spots," or sample advertising creative. "Spec spots" are particularly popular in radio formats because production costs are low. Based on Gfk/MRI's results, Hispanic Red Bull drinkers are 171 percent more likely to go dancing than the average American, and 142 percent more likely to claim to be "fashionable on a budget," so dressing up to go out dancing might make sense to include in advertising creative somehow.

CASE: DEVELOPING A VBR FOR FIDELITY INVESTMENTS

In Table 11.5, Gfk/MRI creates a profile of users of Fidelity Investments. Fidelity users are 50 percent more likely to listen to a sports event on the radio. They are also interested in travel, as they are 127 percent more likely to read airline magazines and 100 percent more likely to make travel plans on the Internet. Fidelity used "Turn here" as a marketing slogan, which presents an advertising sales executive with an opportunity to leverage sports media behaviors and interest in travel.

Table 11.5 Fidelity investments consumer profile

	Percent more likely to...
Read airline magazines	127
Attend classical music/opera performances	109
Make travel plans on the Internet	100
Participate in casino gambling	60
Listen to a sports event on the radio	50
Be willing to pay more for high-quality items	30

Source: Gfk/MRI.[1]

Note
1 www.gfkmri.com/ConsumerInsights/InsideBrands.aspx, accessed 9/12/2014.

Suppose you are selling radio time for NASCAR broadcasts. Fidelity's "Turn here" campaign seems like a good fit for a sport based on left turns. In addition, racing fans travel 250 miles or so on average to attend a NASCAR race, so a promotion that involves trips to a race or races and includes "high-quality items" as prizes could be featured in the ads. The radio ads could be bundled with a digital ad buy, especially one that's heavy on travel-related sites based on the consumer profile. Maybe the radio ad could feature classical/opera performances.

Lastly, let's think about the high index for casino gambling. There's a NASCAR race in Las Vegas, which presents an added opportunity. But lots of other racetracks have casinos in relatively close proximity. How could casinos be integrated into the program? How could this work for other sports content?

EXERCISE

Needs analysis. Repeat the exercise from Chapter 7, but this time focus on the list of sports advertisers, either national or local.

THREE MAIN TAKEAWAYS

1   Sports offers advertisers attractive demographics, cross-media synergy, and unparalleled consumer engagement.
2   Sports advertising salespeople must develop and document valid business reasons for contacting potential advertisers.
3   Sports ad sales is most effective when advertising is included in customized, integrated marketing proposals made directly to advertisers.

RECOMMENDED READING

Warner, C. and Buchanan, J. (2004). *Media Selling: Broadcast, Cable, Print, and Interactive,* 3rd edition. Ames: Iowa State Press.

NOTES

1   The Nielsen Company (2012). *Global AdView Pulse Lite.*
2   Spangler, T. (2013). ESPN goes for the extra point with hackathons. http://variety.com/interstitial/?ref=h ttp%3A%2F%2Fvariety.com%2F2013%2Ftv%2Fnews%2Fespn-goes-for-the-extra-point-with-hackathons-1200482075%2F, accessed 5/18/2013.
3   http://frontrow.espn.go.com/2013/05/more-than-120-new-ideas-hatched-for-first-espn-ad-innovation-hackathon/, accessed 12/22/2013.
4   Mandese, J. (2012). The natives are restless: New publishers move line distinguishing edit, ad content. www.mediapost.com/publications/article/184085/the-natives-are-restless-news-publishers-move-lin.html, accessed 9/20/2013.
5   Mickle, T. (2012). Youth appeal draws investment to RallyCross. www.sportsbusinessdaily.com/Journal/

Issues/2012/11/12/Leagues-and-Governing-Bodies/Global-RallyCross.aspx?hl=youth%20appeal%20draws%20investment%20to%20Rallycross&sc=0, accessed 5/2/2013.

6 www.espncms.com/Advertise-on-ESPN.aspx, accessed 2/4/2013.

7 Lefton, T. (2012). ESPN's well-researched sales pitch. www.sportsbusinessdaily.com/Journal/Issues/2012/01/02/In-Depth/ESPN.aspx?hl=espn%27s%20well-researched%20sales&sc=0, accessed 2/4/2013.

8 Ibid.

9 Ibid.

10 ESPN. A surround strategy for cross platform research. http://som.yale.edu/sites/default/files/files/ESPN%20XP%20Yale%20pres%20051013.pdf, accessed 12/23/2013.

11 (2010). ESPN presents results of World Cup cross-platform research project – ESPN XP. http://espnmediazone.com/us/press-releases/2010/09/espn-xp-results/, accessed 5/3/2013.

12 Ourand, J. (2013). Three trends worth considering from the upfront season. www.sportsbusinessdaily.com/Journal/Issues/2013/05/20/Media/Sports-Media.aspx, accessed 5/20/2013.

13 www.971thefan.com/content/topic/services/employment.html, accessed 12/23/2013.

14 http://jobs.espncareers.com, accessed 10/15/2013.

15 Ibid.

16 *Advertising Age.* From print to Web: The magazine ads that best drove readers to websites. Wide ranges of products succeed in moving consumers from one medium to another. http://adage.com/print/245330, accessed 11/25/2013.

17 Crupi, A. (2011). High 5: ESPN, NFL prove their mettle with mystery candy bar. www.adweek.com/news/television/high-5-espn-nfl-prove-their-mettle-mystery-candy-bar-133360, accessed 12/23/2013.

18 Chassman, M. (2004). Broadcast television. In Warner, C. and Buchanan, J. (Eds.), *Media Selling: Broadcast, Cable, Print, and Interactive*, 3rd edition. Ames: Iowa State Press, pp. 351–369.

19 Ibid.

20 Thanks to John Kesler at Emmis Communications for providing the example.

Part IV
Sponsorship

Sponsorship

What it is and how it works

Like many men my age, I played Little League baseball when I was a kid. And like many leagues, our teams were named after local businesses. I played for Dianem Trucking Co. After years of dominance by Vito Stamato & Co. (a garbage hauling company) and despite surprisingly strong play from Tom's Florist, we battled it out with Kitchen Masters for the division title during my final season and ended with a respectable though disappointing second place finish.

Even as kids, we understood why our teams were not named after our favorite major league teams, like the Mets or Yankees. These local companies donated money to buy equipment and uniforms. Players did not have to pay high user fees in order to participate – most costs were covered by sponsors. In turn, the players wore the company names across our chests and sponsors were featured on signs on the outfield fence.

Why is it that after 30 years after I played Little League baseball, I still remember Dianem Trucking Co. with fondness? The answer lies at the heart of sports sponsorship's rapid growth as a marketing discipline during the past few decades. I loved playing Little League baseball. I understood the contribution that sponsors made to allow me to participate in what was the National Pastime. I appreciated the contribution the sponsors made to my team and the organization as a whole. Even now, if I needed flowers in my old neighborhood, the first number I'd call would be Tom's Florist.

Sponsors have used the underlying principles of sponsoring a Little League team – tapping into fan passion to achieve marketing goals – to develop a sophisticated marketing discipline. The growth of sports sponsorship has been impressive over recent decades and is largely responsible for the rapid growth of the sports industry as a whole.

WHAT IS SPONSORSHIP?

Sponsorship is often referred to as a marketing communication option similar to tools in the traditional marketing communications mix: advertising, public relations (PR), direct marketing, sales promotions, and/or personal selling. Alternatively, sponsorship has been defined not as a communication option but as an "investment, in cash or kind, in an activity, in return for access to the exploitable commercial potential associated with that event".[1] Similarly, Cornwell, Weeks, and Roy distinguish sponsorship from advertising in that "sponsorship involves a fee paid in advance for future potential communication values."[2] According to these definitions, sponsorship relationships represent *potential* marketing communications, not existing ones. Strictly speaking, a sponsorship is a contract between a sponsor and a property, not a marketing program. In order to become an active marketing program, sponsors must implement one or (typically) more communications options.

Cornwell[3] coined the term "sponsorship-linked marketing" to reflect the required coordination among sponsorship's communications options, such as advertising and sales promotions, among others, and sponsorship's key constituents, such as employees and audiences. Tripodi[4] recommends that sponsors use all marketing promotions tools – advertising, sales promotions, public relations, and personal selling – in order to maximize sponsorship effectiveness. Sponsors are increasingly employing a combination of sponsorship-linked marketing communications such as advertising, public relations, and sales promotions to achieve their marketing goals.[5] Signage at events is visible during news coverage, combining advertising and public relations. Advertising is used to generate awareness for the sponsorship as well as other sponsorship-linked marketing communications, such as sales promotions. Sales promotions are tied to sponsorships by offering exclusive prizes for contests or sweepstakes or premium items licensed by the sponsored property. As Cliffe and Motion observe,[6] firms use sponsorship as a platform upon which marketing communications can be integrated. By integrating marketing communications around a sponsored property – NASCAR, an art museum, or a charity – "the design and execution of any communication option reflects the nature and content of other communication options that also makes up the communication program."[7] As such, sponsorships can be considered IMC programs.

Sponsorship-linked marketing, however, does more than coordinate the nature and content of communication options. Rappaport's engagement model of advertising[8] might apply to sponsorship programs in that sponsorship increases relevance and deepens the emotional connection to brands. Where sponsorship distinguishes itself from an advertising engagement model, however, is in its ability to access well-defined target markets; its potential to tap into consumers' emotional connections with sports, arts, and charitable organizations; and its capacity to integrate more than one communication option.

WHY SPONSORSHIP?

Sports sponsorship is big business. Sponsorship rights fees were estimated at $51.1 billion globally in 2012, 69 percent of which was spent on sports.[9] And that figure is just rights fees. It is safe to assume that sponsors spend approximately an equal amount on other marketing activities leveraging their sponsorships. According to industry estimates, the growth in sponsorship spending has consistently outpaced other marketing promotions, such as advertising and sales promotions. Sponsorship's growth has been fueled by changes in the marketing communications landscape (e.g., media fragmentation, ad avoidance, skepticism of advertising), and an increasingly sophisticated, creative, and rigorous approach to sports sponsorship practice.

Cross-media integration. Before the Internet and the proliferation of television channels, marketing communication was a fairly straightforward proposition. With three television networks dominating the airwaves in the US, advertisers could reach broad audiences with great efficiency. Fundamental changes in the media landscape coincided with the rapid growth of sponsorship, especially relative to advertising. Technological advancements such as cable TV, VCRs, the Internet, and digital video recorders have fragmented the media audience into hundreds of pieces. From the three national networks, most TV viewers now have 50, 100, or even 500 choices. Consequently, while people are watching more television overall, audiences for individual networks and programs continue to get smaller.

In addition to the increased number of TV channels, consumers also have almost limitless options via the Internet and their cell phones. Taking into account media multi-tasking, consumers spend much of the day connected to media, but the increasing number of choices challenges marketers to reach audiences consistently enough to make a lasting impression.

Targeting. Since advertisers purchase media time based primarily on the size demographic characteristics of audiences, it's difficult to gain efficiency in reaching a targeted audience. With increasing media fragmentation, almost all audiences are targeted niches – even the most popular prime time network programming lacks a majority of TV viewership. For example, approximately one-third of US adults describe themselves as fans of the NFL, the most popular sport in the country. Younger males are more likely to be interested in the NFL, but even with tightly defined demographic categories, sports-themed marketing targets only half the audience at best.

In contrast, by definition 100 percent of NFL fans like the NFL. It's tautological, but an important benefit of sports sponsorship. The Super Bowl, for example, reaches a national audience, perhaps the only regular television programming to deliver one. Commercials that air during the Super Bowl broadcast rarely have a tie to the NFL. Budweiser dominates Super Bowl Sunday advertising but Coors is the official beer sponsor of the league. Because the Super Bowl enjoys a national audience, many are not fans of the NFL and most are not fans of the team playing. Consequently, advertisers create commercials designed to appeal to the general audience, rather than the segment of avid NFL fans watching the game. But what the Super Bowl gains in reach, it loses in effectiveness. Super Bowl commercials are funny and entertaining, but not tied to the sport in a way that's meaningful to fans.

Conversely, the Daytona 500 is NASCAR's biggest race of the season and draws very strong television ratings, but most viewers are NASCAR fans. Most advertisers are also connected to NASCAR and/or its teams with substantial sponsorship agreements, and most commercials feature the sport and/or its drivers. Using a NASCAR platform, advertisers reach their target more efficiently (almost 100 percent), and more effectively because fans of the sport like commercials more when they are tied to NASCAR and/or its drivers. So even though the Super Bowl might attract three or four times the number of viewers than the Daytona 500, the net effectiveness of television ads might even out because of the value

Table 12.1 Traditional advertising v. sponsorship

Traditional advertising	Sponsorship
Media fragmentation	Vertical integration
Targeting by demographics is inefficient and ineffective	Target by interest is 100% efficient and more effective
Ad avoidance	Communications embedded in programming
Lack of credibility for advertising	Link to credible organizations
Single, one-way marketing promotion	Integrated marketing communications with potential for interactivity

of sponsorship ties in reaching a targeted audience. Sports sponsorship taps into the passion fans have for their sports.

Ad avoidance. Technological advancements such as the remote control and digital video recorders make it easier for television viewers to skip commercials. Sports sponsorship allows brands to embed the message into the programming so that viewers can't "zap" it. In addition, sports are more resistant to video recording than other programming because fans want to watch the live action as it unfolds.

Credibility. Advertising lacks credibility. More than two-thirds (68.6 percent) of US adults said they have felt misled by advertising.[10] On the other hand, consumers are more likely to regard sponsorship as a credible marketing effort because of the tie to a credible, respected, and/or well-liked property.

Cross-tool integration. Because of advertising's limitations and environmental changes such as increased media fragmentation and technological developments, marketers have been expanding their promotional mix beyond traditional advertising to include a larger variety of communication channels. Since promotional elements are often handled by different sections of a company, marketers are challenged to integrate their marketing communications into a clear and consistent message. Sports sponsorship presents a simple solution: integrate a communications program around a sport. Of course, the implementation of sponsorship-linked marketing communications is much more complex, but the trend toward targeted, integrated marketing communications has helped fuel the growth of sports sponsorship, particularly compared to traditional advertising (see Table 12.1).

HOW SPONSORSHIP WORKS

Descriptions of how sponsorship works tend to be heavily laden with ambitious but vague claims. Sponsorship is said to "touch the soul," and "pull at the heartstrings." Sponsorship is "active," while advertising is "passive." While the jargon leans toward the hyperbolic, there is an element of truth here. When sports sponsorship works, it effectively taps into fans' passion for the sports they love.

How sponsorship taps into fan passion is unique among the many tools available to marketers in a way that transcends typical relationships between company and customer. The broad objective of sports sponsorship is to build and maintain relationships, particularly between company and customer (but also including the sports property).

Let's think about relationships in general. Suppose you're introduced to someone at a bar through a common friend. What's a typical reaction? "Let me buy you a drink." Now suppose, your new friend beat you to it and bought the first round. What's the typical reaction? "I'll get the next round." Why? There's no financial obligation. I wouldn't even argue that there's a moral imperative. The social contract of reciprocity, rather than a business contract, dictates the exchange. The drink, despite a comparatively small financial value, can have a very high sentimental value.

Anthropologist Marcel Mauss observed similarities in gift giving and receiving in cultures across the world. He argued that the gifts are voluntary in theory, but in reality they are reciprocated obligatorily. That is, in theory your new friend buys you a drink out of the goodness of his or her heart, but in reality there's an obligation to reciprocate. As a fundamental element of human society, gift-giving is complicated in industrialized commercial societies. As Mauss says, "the round of drinks is ever dearer and larger in size."[11]

When executed well, sports sponsorship is a gift from sponsor to fan. At the deepest level, the gift is the very sport itself. As Ray Bednar says, sponsorship "communicates that the brand likes its consumers enough to sponsor things that they care about."[12] In theory, the sponsor's gift is voluntary. There's no legal obligation to return the favor. Unlike patronage rewards such as frequent flyer miles, you don't have to buy the product before you receive the free flight. Unlike promotional premiums, you don't have to send in proofs of purchase before you get the prize. In theory, sports sponsors voluntarily provide financial support to sports properties.

In reality, sports sponsors expect a return. Of course, sports sponsorship is not a pure gift economy like the potlatch ceremonies in the American Northwest, in which villages would exchange almost all of their possessions. Sports sponsorship is a marketing promotion, a fact of which sports fans are acutely aware. However, "gift marketing" can be subject to the same principles of reciprocity in general. Sociologist Alvin Gouldner,[13] in his famous work about the norm of reciprocity, argued that obligations of repayment are contingent upon the following:

- The perceived value of the benefit – the debt is in proportion to the perceived value of the benefit.
- The motives imputed to the donor – "without thought of gain."
- The resources of the donor – "he gave although he could ill afford it."

Following Gouldner's framework, the gift of sports sponsorship works when (1) fans place a high value on the sponsors' contribution; (2) fans recognize the sponsor's contribution as substantial in relation to the sponsor's resources; and (3) fans perceive sponsors' involvement is commensurate with its resources.

Since the sports products provided by sponsors tend to be experiences rather than tangible goods, perceived value varies – though not randomly. Here, fan passion increases perceived value. Simply put, the more passionate the fan, the more valuable the experience and, consequently, the more valuable the sponsor's contribution. MasterCard's "priceless" advertising campaign highlights the intense emotions fans have for sports, suggesting that the sports experiences are of infinite value to sports fans. The idea is that you can't put a price tag on these intensely personal experiences. However, sponsors can bring them to you.

189

So, when a sponsor makes it possible for a fan's favorite NASCAR driver to pass a rival on the final lap of the Daytona 500, that sponsor just gave that fan a gift of tremendous value. According to the rules of reciprocity, a fan receiving the gift entails an obligation to return, which in the case of sports sponsorship means loyalty to the sponsor's brand and products. Loyalty has both behavioral and psychological components. Behavioral loyalty basically means repeated purchases and a higher share of the customer (i.e., the customer buys the sponsor's brand more frequently relative to other brands). Emotional loyalty is a feeling of allegiance to the brand or company because of the sponsor's gift. Emotional loyalty drives brand equity and behavioral loyalty drives sales. Sports sponsorship creates both emotional and behavioral loyalty.

The act of purchasing a sponsor's product completes the gift exchange between sponsor and fan. The sponsor "gifts" the sports experience and, in return, the fan becomes a loyal customer. In this sense, sports sponsorship is an "active" marketing promotion rather than a "passive" effort, such as advertising. Sponsor-loyal fans feel like they are contributing to the sport when they buy a sponsor's product. In this sense, consumers are empowered by the sponsorship relationship. It's a way for a fan to be "part of the team." However, when sponsorship works, it's more than a business transaction or a rational decision that purchasing a product supports the financial health of the sports property.

Fans understand that companies sponsor sports in order to market their products. But sports sponsorship can "pull at the heartstrings" and "touch the soul" when fans believe that there are more motives in addition to selling products. It could be that the sponsor likes its customers enough to sponsor things they care about, as Ray Bednar says. Or, it could be that the sponsor shares similar interests with customers; or, that sponsors think the sport is cool, too; or, the sponsor thinks it's a worthwhile cause. The "warm and fuzzy" feeling that fans have for sponsors is a consequence of the imputed sincerity of the sponsor's motives.

So far, we've discussed how sponsorship works, but it doesn't always work. But the principles of norms of reciprocity are still at play. Often – and it varies greatly by sport – sports fans see only a cost of sponsorship, not a benefit. So, there's no "gift." Some consumers believe that the sponsorship costs get passed on to consumers in the form of higher prices. Many sports fans feel that sponsors are an intrusion – sullying an otherwise pristine environment; they see sponsors as an uninvited guest, crashing an otherwise fun party. Skeptical fans regard sponsors' motives as disingenuous – money-grubbing, greedy corporations muscling their way into a sport. Many sports fans feel that sponsors have an obligation to support their teams and leagues because of the vast corporate financial resources, a capitalist *noblesse oblige*. There's no obligation for fans to be loyal to sponsors if the view is that corporations already owe a debt to society.

Sports sponsorship doesn't work in a vacuum – so the results are not predetermined according to some black box formula. Whether sponsorship works or not has more to do with how it's done than on inherent characteristics or immutable psychological processes. Fortunately, there's a lot that both sponsors and sports properties can do to make sponsorship work.

The sponsorship funnel

Sponsorship is often referred to as "multi-faceted" or "multi-pronged" without specifically mentioning what the "facets" or "prongs" are. Like marketing programs in general, sponsorship managers identify sponsorship goals based on an analysis of the situation, then develop sponsorship strategies and implement sponsorship tactics to achieve the desired sponsorship outcomes. And like marketing programs in general, a funnel is a helpful conceptual tool for making sense out of sponsorship components.

Like the marketing funnel, the sponsorship funnel is not meant to present a "unified theory" of sponsorship. Recognizing that sponsorship is in fact "multi-faceted" – composed of varied media and communication tools – the funnel provides a systematic approach to planning, implementing, and evaluation sponsorship programs. And, like the marketing funnel, the sponsorship funnel can be helpful in identifying sponsorship goals.

Strategies

Audience characteristics. Sponsorship properties deliver value to sponsors by providing access to their audiences. In sports settings, that means providing sponsors access to fans. The logical follow-up, then, is that sponsorship properties are more valuable if they can provide more and better access to bigger and better fan audiences. But what makes an audience bigger and better? And how can audiences be "delivered" to sponsors to achieve sponsorship and broader marketing goals?

- **Size.** The size of a sponsorship audience determines the overall potential of the sponsorship. But because a sponsorship can reach audiences beyond just fans who watch broadcasts or attend events – when a property's logo is included on packaging, for example – the audience could include all people who have a favorable attitude toward a sport. The growth of sponsorship is in large part a recognition of the pervasive presence of sports across the world.
- **Demographics.** The efficiency of a sponsorship will depend on how well the sports property's audience matches up to the brand's target. In general, sports audiences tend to be more male than female, so brands that target men tend to sponsor sports.
- **Purchase behaviors.** Demographics can be good predictors of desired behaviors but ultimately brands are interested in customers. Young men who do not drink beer, for example, are not targets for beer companies even though they are men. In general,

Table 12.2 The sponsorship funnel

Audience Fan Passion Message	Strategy
Activation	Tactics
Brand image Sales	Outcomes/Goals

audiences with greater purchasing in a category are more attractive to sponsors because they represent greater sales potential.

- **Brand preferences.** A fan base that has high overall purchases in a brand category might be attractive as a sponsorship property, but the market share among those fans for a particular brand might be low. Brands have to balance the overall demand among a fan base with current brand preferences in order to set realistic goals and identify opportunities.
- **Attitudes.** Some groups of people are more receptive to marketing efforts than others. Even if sports audiences represent sizable demand in a product category, fans must still somehow be delivered to the sponsor. In traditional marketing terms, we might say that the segment must be actionable. More favorable attitudes toward advertising, greater awareness of sponsors, or an increased inclination to participate in promotional games, contests, and sweepstakes, for example, contribute to the overall attractiveness of a market segment.

Fan passion. Fan passion is at the core of effective sponsorships and a distinguishing characteristic of sports. It is fan passion that sponsors hope to somehow leverage into desired sponsorship outcomes. The President and CEO of Octagon Worldwide, responding to a bleak outlook following the financial crisis said, "Fan passion will carry the day."[14] He was right. In general, the more passionate the fan, the more effective the sponsorship, but sponsors need to understand what is driving the passion in order to develop programs to leverage it.

- **Points of attachment.** Fans love theirs sports. But what do they love? Sports brands can be comprised of leagues, teams, owners, coaches, players, and the fans themselves.
- **Intensity.** Who has the "best" fans? A small but passionate fan base can reach market segments more efficiently. Brands want to focus on people with whom their efforts will get the best results. But a larger fan base yields better total results because it is bigger.
- **Sources of pleasure.** Brands can leverage fan passion more effectively if they can understand what triggers that passion. Brands must identify the emotional underpinnings of fan experiences in order to leverage fan passion into marketing results.
- **Fan culture.** For most fans, sports are not experienced individually, but as part of a larger community. Fan groups share common histories, languages, and experiences. In order to be recognized as a part of the team and receive the attendant membership benefits, sponsors must be sensitive to the fans' cultural norms and beliefs.
- **Brand image.** Sports brands differ by levels of prestige and attributes. Sponsor brands do not necessarily have to be inherently similar to sports property brands because sponsorship programs can communicate the meaning of the sponsorship, but the respective images must be taken into account in order to develop effective programs.
- **Fan behaviors.** Sponsors need to understand how and where fans interact with sports. Media usage, including frequency, media, and level of engagement are all crucial to understand in developing sponsorship programs.

Messaging. Sponsors both explicitly and tacitly "say something" through and about their sponsorships.

■ **Communicating a message through sponsorship.** Most commonly, sponsors use a sponsorship to help communicate their overall brand message. For example, Allstate uses college football sponsorships to support its "you're in good hands with Allstate" message by placing its "good hands" logo on nets behind the goal posts and by using goalkeepers in themed advertising airing during game broadcasts. The imagery is consistent and supports the explicit "good hands" message.

■ **The medium is the message.** Sponsorships also tacitly "say something" about the brand, or more specifically about the relationship between the brand and the sponsorship property. As long-time sponsorship executive Ray Bednar says, sponsorship "communicates that the brand likes its consumers enough to sponsor things that they care about."[15] Sponsorships can communicate other messages to consumers tacitly – that is, sponsorships can "say something" without the sponsor saying something – but too often sponsors and properties allow consumers to infer these meanings on their own, despite the general lack of public knowledge about the nature of sponsorship and role sponsors play in sports. Unlike advertising, sponsorship lacks a ready frame of reference for sports fans. Even sponsorship industry professionals can have difficulty clearly explaining sponsors' role in sports!

Tactics

Activation and leveraging

"Activation" and "leveraging" are terms often used interchangeably to describe sponsorship-linked marketing efforts, especially marketing promotions (advertising, sales promotions, direct marketing, personal selling, and public relations). Strictly speaking, however, activation and leveraging do not mean the same thing.

In mechanical terms, a lever allows a person to lift several times his or her body weight. In finance, leverage is a small investment used to gain a much larger return. If we envision a sponsorship as a mechanical lever, then "leveraging" a sponsorship means using the sponsorship to get marketing results. In financial terms, sponsorship is the investment that is used to gain a higher return in the form of better marketing outcomes. To "activate" means to set in motion, which focuses on sponsorship effectiveness as the goal. Among practitioners, the distinction is rarely made between activating and leveraging but the underlying concept is important. Sponsors need to both build some equity in a sponsorship – goodwill, favorable attitudes, sponsorship awareness – in order to leverage the sponsorship into the desired marketing outcomes related to brand image and sales.

There has to be something to leverage, but the process of leveraging also helps to activate the sponsorship. So, it is not just a case in which sponsors activate, then leverage. Rather, sponsorship-linked marketing communications both activate and leverage sponsorships in an upward spiral in which the sponsorship and its linked marketing communications support each other. Specific communication tools include:

■ *Advertising*. Sponsorships can be activated by advertising in which the meaning of the sponsorship is articulated to fans. Sponsorship can be leveraged in themed advertising that features content from a sports property, which can make the advertising more likeable and memorable.

- *Sales promotions.* Sponsorship can be activated by sales promotions in which the association between sponsor and property is made clear. Sponsorship can be leveraged by sales promotions linked to a sports property, which can increase participation and make the promotion more likeable.
- *Public relations.* Sponsorship can be activated by public relations when media coverage of the sponsorship increases awareness and/or favorability. Sponsorship can be leveraged by PR when the sports provides a media-worthy setting for a brand to gain publicity it would not otherwise.
- *Direct marketing.* Sponsorships can be activated by direct marketing when a sponsor uses a database of fans to communicate the sponsorship's benefits to fans. Sponsorship can be leveraged by direct marketing when the brand uses a sports property to acquire a customer database and/or increase response rates to communications.
- *Personal selling.* Personal selling in sponsorship is typically leveraged in a business-to-business setting in which salespeople use a sports appeal to develop and maintain relationships with clients.

Sponsorship outcomes

Awareness. Sponsorship awareness has often been looked to as a proxy for sponsorship effectiveness, probably because it is easy to measure. While some sponsors might seek to increase brand awareness as a primary goal, sponsorship awareness is a means to an end, not an end in itself. Sponsorship awareness can indicate how well a sponsorship is working to a certain extent, but is a weak indication of how well the sponsorship is being leveraged into more important marketing outcomes, such as enhancing brand image and sales.

Knowledge. Awareness of a brand name will not yield other more important marketing outcomes on its own. Consumers need to know what the brand stands for, what the company does, and why it's important to consumers.

Liking. Fans might love their sport and know who sponsors are but not really care. Therefore, sponsors need to focus on how to develop favorable attitudes toward the sponsorship and ultimately towards their brands. Fan passion needs to somehow be converted into passion for the sponsor's brand.

Sales. Ultimately, sports sponsors are most concerned with acquiring new customers and retaining and increasing sales among existing customers.

CASE: WHEN SPONSORSHIP GOES BAD

Corporate sponsorship has grown rapidly as a marketing discipline in recent decades, but it is not without controversy. While attitudes toward corporate sponsorship tend to be favorable in general, the process can also elicit strong negative feelings among sports fans who feel like sponsors are taking something away from their sports, not contributing to them.

Attitudes toward corporate sponsorship tend to become more negative as sports fans get older. For younger fans, most sports properties have always had corporate sponsorships:

naming rights for facilities, college football bowl games. Older fans, however, saw corporate names added to and sometimes replacing existing names. Older sports fans have a psychological reference point in which sports spaces are not pristine, but have much less corporate presence. As a focus group participant in an industry study said:

> I think like anything else it's just a matter of being overdone. It's getting to the point to where everything's being sponsored now. Now if a few things were just corporate, it wouldn't be so bad, but now you hear everything, the "Blank" Marathon, the "Blank" this. Even PBS, which used to say they never accepted advertising . . . now you see it all the time on there.[16]

While naming rights for sports facilities is commonplace, there are some stadiums that will never be renamed because of the backlash it would incur from fans. It would be difficult to envision Old Trafford and Lambeau Field getting corporate names, for example. Even when a new stadium is being built, such as the new Yankee Stadium, iconic names cannot be replaced. When Denver's Mile High Stadium was replaced with a new stadium and a new name (Invesco Field), there was a very vocal minority of Denver residents who were strongly opposed to the corporate name.

Even though it is an irrational belief, most sports fans feel a sense of ownership in the sports properties they love. "Our" club, "our" team. In reality, with rare exceptions, sports are not owned by the fans, but by wealthy businessmen. Yet, if sports sponsorships are to be effective, they must anticipate and deal with negative attitudes. And attitudes toward corporate sponsors can be intensely negative.

A participant in focus groups about corporate sponsorship talked about the *danger* of sponsors taking too much control over sports events:

> . . . there was a major sporting event that was sponsored by Pepsi and a Coca-Cola logo was not allowed within so many miles of any of the sports arena or any of the sports events that were going on at that time. . . . That's kind of dangerous.[17]

Another participant suggested that it is the intent of corporate sponsors to take over:

> [Corporations] want to go all the way, they want everything.

Another participant compared corporations to inhuman monsters:

> An individual is like a person, and actual person that you can see. A corporation is like a big monster.

In a gift economy, there are negative consequences to an unwanted gift. In the case of corporate sponsorship, many consumers have a negative reaction to the corporate efforts, questioning the motives of the sponsor. Corporate sponsors must be cognizant of the potential backlash from consumers, especially with respect to overly aggressive programs.

EXERCISE

Wrigley Field in Chicago is a historic, landmark baseball stadium that is scheduled to undergo major renovations. Renovations to existing facilities are expensive, often more expensive than just building a new stadium. Revenue from corporate naming rights for Wrigley Field would be substantial if it could be done without a severe fan and resident backlash. Would it be possible to create a communications plan that could persuade fans to accept and maybe even welcome a corporate name?

THREE MAIN TAKEAWAYS

1   Sponsorship is a platform upon which integrated marketing communications can be integrated across both tools and media.
2   Sponsorship provides brands with efficient targeting, embedded exposure, and greater credibility than advertising.
3   Sponsorship functions as a gift economy; sometimes the gifts are welcome, other times they are resented.

RECOMMENDED READING

Mauss, M. (2000). *The Gift: The Form and Reason for Exchange in Archaic Societies*. New York: W.W. Norton. This book does not relate directly to sponsorship but provides insights into the foundations of gift economies.

Bednar, R. (2005). *Sponsorship's Holy Grail: Six Sigma Forges the Link Between Sponsorship and Business Goals*. Lincoln, NE: iUniverse. A practice-oriented book written by one of sponsorship's top practitioners.

NOTES

1   Meenaghan, T. (1991). The role of sponsorship in the marketing communications mix. *International Journal of Advertising*, 17(1): 36.
2   Cornwell, T.B., Weeks, C.S., and Roy, D.P. (2005). Sponsorship-linked marketing: Opening the black box. *Journal of Advertising*, 34(2): 21–42.
3   Cornwell, B (1995). Sponsorship-linked marketing development. *Sport Marketing Quarterly*, 4(4): 13–24.
4   Tripodi, J. (2001). Sponsorship – a confirmed weapon in the promotional armoury. *International Journal of Sports Marketing & Sponsorship*, March/April: 1–20.
5   Weeks, C.S., Cornwell, T.B., and Drennan, J.C. (2008). Leveraging sponsorships on the Internet: Activation, congruence, and articulation. *Psychology & Marketing*, 25(7): 637–645.
6   Cliffe, S.J. and Motion, J. (2005). Building contemporary brands: A sponsorship-based strategy. *Journal of Business Research*, 58: 1068–1077.
7   Keller, K.L. (2001). Mastering the marketing communications mix: Micro and macro perspectives on integrated marketing communications programs. *Journal of Marketing Management*, 17: 825.
8   Rappaport, S. (2007). Lessons from online practice: New advertising models. *Journal of Advertising Research*, June: 135–141.
9   IEG Sponsorship Briefing. www.sponsorship.com/IEG/files/6b/6bca0a93–47cc-4eb8-b514-c4cc3debc7d4.pdf, accessed 2/10/2013.

10 Shavitt, S., Lowrey, P., and Haefner, J. (1998). Public attitudes toward advertising: More favorable than you might think. *Journal of Advertising Research*, 38(4): 7–22.

11 Mauss, M. (2000). *The Gift: The Form and Reason for Exchange in Archaic Societies*. New York: W.W. Norton.

12 Bednar, R. (2005). *Sponsorship's Holy Grail: Six Sigma Forges the Link Between Sponsorship and Business Goals*. Lincoln, NE: iUniverse.

13 Gouldner, A. (1960). The norm of reciprocity: A preliminary statement. *American Sociological Review*, 25(2): 161–178.

14 Dudley, R. (2010). Faith in passion, live sports, measurement fuels optimism. www.sportsbusinessdaily. com/Journal/Issues/2010/04/20100412/Opinion/Faith-In-Passion-Live-Sports-Measurement-Fuels-Optimism.aspx, accessed 2/10/2013.

15 Bednar. *Sponsorship's Holy Grail*.

16 TBG Feasibility Study (July, 2002). Prepared by The Bonham Group for the City of Houston.

17 Ibid.

Chapter 13

Sponsorship goals and strategies

Job Description: Corporate Account Manager, Fremantle Dockers (Australian Football League)

"A rare opportunity has arisen for a hardworking and dynamic sales professional to join our Commercial Partners team as one of our Corporate Account Managers. Many job descriptions for sponsorship executives stress the importance of strategy and accountability. This one is no exception. The Fremantle Dockers sought a candidate who would take a strategic approach and use research to identify new revenue streams.

This role will take a *strategic* approach to maximizing corporate revenue streams within the Commercial Partners department by working closely with the Business Development Manager and the other Account Managers.

In addition to managing the relationship with existing clients this role will be responsible for generating new leads using outbound telemarketing/cold calling and *using research and trend analysis to identify potential areas to drive revenue.*"[1] (emphases added)

SPONSORSHIP OBJECTIVES

What industry execs are saying...

"For us, more than ever, it's specifically about how can we sell more beer."[2]
Anheuser-Busch VP Media, Sponsorship & Activation

The ability to link sponsorship to sales is becoming increasingly important to sponsors, especially for fast-moving consumer goods.

Sponsorship is best when you use it to drive passion and commitment to your brand.[3]
Former MillerCoors Sr. Director, Sports and Entertainment Marketing

As is the case with marketing in general, sponsorship executives are increasingly accountable for demonstrating financial returns for their marketing investments. As sponsorship rights fees continue to escalate, the pressure continues to mount to demonstrate a positive ROI. Consequently, many sponsors, especially in fast-moving consumer goods industries, have developed a laser-like focus on sales.

Sales and financial returns, however, are outcome goals and do not address the process of how a company gets there. There is a very strong relationship between brand image and sales, but brand and sales objectives can often be in conflict within sponsors' companies when it comes to establishing priorities. Some executives have noticed a pendulum swing away from brand building and toward sales. As the former Sr. Dir. of Sports and Ent. Marketing at MillerCoors put it, "Certainly retail push is important, but so is consumer pull. You can't depend on an 8.5-by-11-inch case card to do that."[4]

Companies with mature, strong brands, such as Budweiser, might be focused on "selling beer" rather than building the Budweiser brand, but it is specifically *how* they can sell more beer. And, more specifically, it is about *how* they can sell more beer through sports sponsorships. That is, it is necessary to develop specific *sponsorship goals* that are designed to achieve overall marketing goals.

As with any other marketing activity, sponsorship programs need to contribute to overall marketing objectives, such as building brands and increasing sales. Sponsorship goals must be developed with strategies and tactics that will lead to the desired outcomes. And, as with any effective goal-setting techniques, sponsorship goals are most effective when they are measurable and specific, which can present a challenge.

As a comprehensive, integrated marketing program, sponsorship can address numerous different goals. A review of sponsorship objectives found a total of 61 specific, distinct sponsorship goals.[5] Establishing clear priorities can be a big challenge given the large number of choices and strategic directions, yet clearly defined sponsorship goals are essential to successful sponsorship programs. At some point, sponsorship managers need to develop focus and priorities to allocate funding. Too many goals means stretched budgets and weakened success.

There are no set limits for the number of sponsorship goals are optimal. Collett and Fenton recommend two to three goals for optimal performance with an absolute limit of five goals.[6] Skildum-Reid, on the other hand, notes that sponsors usually compile a list of 8–12 goals based on her experience.[7] The large number of potential sponsorship goals increases the importance of establishing priorities and focus. And goals should be not only specific, but measurable. IEG recommends that sponsors establish numerical weights for each sponsorship goal based on priorities developed by management, and then align goals with sponsorship strategies and tactics.[8] The problem there, as Skildum-Reid points out, is that the relationship between goals and strategies can be somewhat untidy: "Sometimes, one strategy will address three different objectives. Other times, it will take three strategies to achieve one objective."[9]

Assigning quantitative weights to subjectively determined sponsorship goals lends an air of legitimacy to professional judgments but does not yield valid measurements of sponsorship performance. A more valid approach would be to weight objectives based on measures of how different elements of sponsorship programs contribute to overall marketing objectives, especially sales. That is, let customers tell you how important specific sponsorship objectives are with respect to achieving broader marketing goals.

The overall number of goals depends on establishing a clear path to the desired outcomes. In goal-setting terms, sponsors need to identify goal-achievement strategies and focus on process goals. Therefore, it is necessary to link outcome goals, such as sales and brand equity, with process goals, such as sponsorship strategies and tactics. The "sponsorship funnel" again is a useful conceptual tool for establishing goals. In order to achieve outcome goals, sponsors should set strategic and tactical goals specifically related to their sponsorship programs.

Sponsorship sales goals

While it is important to understand the relationship between process goals and outcome goals, it is also important to break down outcome goals into specific, measurable goals. "Increase sales," for example, is broad and ambiguous and can be broken down into more specific components:

- **Consideration.** As there can be many external factors that affect sales figures (e.g., economic, political, etc.), increasing purchase *intent* can be a more valid measurement of marketing effectiveness and, hence, an effective sponsorship goal. Attention should still be paid to conversion rates between purchase intent and actual purchases.
- **Trial.** Product sampling at live events is a common component of sponsorship programs, especially for consumer products in which touch, smell, or taste are prominent features. If Coca-Cola is looking to introduce a new flavor, consumers might want to taste the product before purchasing it. Car buyers would need to test drive a car before buying it. As product modifications can be difficult by the time they are brought to market, product trial can be a priority among marketing goals.
- **Purchase.** Sales increases are typically the end goal for sponsors, but could be broken down further into acquiring new customers or increasing sales amounts from existing customers.
- **Brand loyalty.** According to a survey of 105 sponsorship managers conducted by IEG and Performance Research,[10] the most important objective when evaluating potential

properties is to "increase brand loyalty." Almost three-quarters (72 percent) of respondents ranked the factor a 9 or 10 on a 10-point scale where 10 is "extremely valuable." The sample size of the study is somewhat small and not weighted to reflect the sponsors' size, but brand loyalty consistently ranks high in importance in sponsor surveys from previous years. Brand loyalty can be a particularly effective way to increase profits because loyal customers buy a product more often and require less marketing investments or price inducements to buy in addition to buying more of the product. Moreover, sponsorship is well-positioned among marketing tools to facilitate loyalty when programs can tap into the passion audiences hold toward sponsorship properties.

Strategic sponsorship goals

Like any type of marketing program, sponsorship strategies consist mainly of identifying desired targets and developing messaging. Sponsorships are no different. Figure 13.1 illustrates how a traditional marketing funnel can be adapted to sponsorship. Sponsors need to identify the audiences they want to reach via sponsorship and decide what they want to say about their brands to members of those audiences.

Reach an audience. Sponsors often look to sponsorship in order to reach desired market segments more efficiently and effectively. Heineken, for example, identified young adult Hispanic males as a desirable demographic because it is a fast-growing population in the US. Drawing on Hispanic males' interest in soccer, Heineken developed a social media

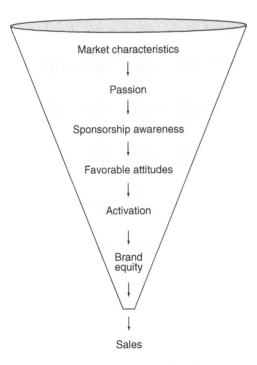

Figure 13.1 The sponsorship funnel.

201

Strategic Sponsorship Goal: Reaching an Audience

"We have a focus on Hispanic males age 21–34 because it's the fastest-growing demographic in the US."

VP of Marketing, Heineken.[11]

One of sponsorship's main advantages is its ability to reach targeted audiences efficiently.

---

initiative during the UEFA Champions League, airing television spots and digital advertising on outlets such as Fox Deportes, ESPN Deportes, and Goal.com.[12]

While sponsorship is often used to reach tightly defined audiences, such as Heineken's focus on 21–34-year-old Hispanic males with an interest in soccer, many sponsors look to sponsorship in order to reach mass audiences as well. Sponsorship can provide exposure very cost-effectively when sponsor logos are embedded in the properties themselves. The sponsorship industry has been criticized for placing too much emphasis on media exposure and sponsorship awareness, and for good reason. Media exposure and sponsorship awareness are relatively easy to measure, so both sponsors and sponsorship properties could fall back on these measures as indications of sponsorship effectiveness. Mere exposure, however, is rarely, or rather should be rarely, a primary goal in sponsorship.[13]

But we should not throw out the baby with the bath water. Sponsorship awareness and exposure can contribute to building strong brands. While exposure should not be a primary goal for sponsors, it is still an important goal: 70 percent of sponsors in the IEG/Performance Research survey rated "Create Awareness/Visibility" as a 9 or 10 on a 10-pt. scale, marginally below increasing brand loyalty (72 percent).

Strategic Sponsorship Goal: Reaching an Audience

"We're in the partnership business and out of the sponsorship business. I'm not looking for someone who says, 'Your logo can be in these 17 places and you'll have access to tickets.' We're looking for engagement and access."[14]
Executive Director of Media, Engagements and Integration, Verizon Wireless

Exposure alone is rarely sufficient for sponsors by itself. However, sponsors should be cognizant of the way in which awareness can contribute to other elements in the sponsorship funnel, especially activation.

Link to fan passion. As a marketing tool, sponsorship distinguishes itself in its ability to tap into fan passions. "Effective marketing is no longer tied to eyeballs but rather heartstrings," according to IEG. ". . . companies are creating loyalty by tethering their products and services to the issues, events and organizations their customers care about."[15] Sponsors understand the passion sports fans hold for the sports they love, and seek to associate their brands with fans' strong emotions.

The primary goal for sponsorships by Verizon Wireless was described as "engagement" and "access." Rather than simply gain rights to marks, hospitality, and signage, Verizon Wireless developed a focus on acquiring content it could own exclusively, providing a direct conduit between fan passion and the brand. For example, Verizon's deal with the NFL included exclusive access to the NFL RedZone Channel for Verizon subscribers.[16]

Strategic sponsorship goal: Communicate a message

Following a successful partnership with the USOC in 2012, we wanted to evolve it to include areas of our business, such as personal investing and wealth management, that are growing in importance for Americans. Our theme, "It's amazing how far you can go with a little help along the way," is a powerful message that speaks to all of us, whether you are an athlete going for the gold or an individual investor planning your financial future. We look forward to sharing those inspirational stories to our clients, associates and fans across the country over the next three years.[17]

President and CEO, TD Ameritrade

This is a good example of linking a brand message to sports. Sports fans will be more receptive to receiving the message if it's placed in a sports context rather than simply a straightforward brand message.

Communicate message. As noted in the preceding chapter, sponsors often use sponsorship to communicate a brand message and to say something about the sponsorship itself. For sponsors whose products are endemic to sports, the link can be natural and self-evident. Athletic equipment brands, for example, are easy to link to sports properties when the equipment is used to play the sport (e.g., Nike and basketball). Sponsors in non-endemic links to sports need to establish a reason for their involvement.

Sponsors without a built-in link to a sports property need to find a way to establish a link between their brands and a sports property. Jon Kander suggests that sponsors find a way to link their brand message with some attribute of the sponsorship property that connects with fans in a meaningful way.[18] TD Ameritrade looked to the United States Olympic Committee to help communicate its brand message: "It's amazing how far you can go with a little help along the way." TD Ameritrade executives link competitive athletes making plans to win Olympic gold with individuals planning their financial futures.

While sponsors often use sponsorships to communicate their brand messages, much less attention is paid to the tacit messages communicated by the sponsorship itself. Just being an Olympic sponsor says something about the sponsoring brand. In fact, an Olympic sponsorship *could* say a lot of things: that the brand is a big company; that the executives at the company are patriotic; that people who work at the company care about the same things their customers care about.

Tactical sponsorship goals

Activation. In an environment of rising marketing costs, many marketers are concerned increasingly with getting the most value for their marketing dollars. "Integration" ranks among marketers' top challenges year after year, according to surveys of high-level corporate marketers.[19] Sponsorship can address issues both of value and integration. Therefore, a common sponsorship objective is to "create a focal point" for other marketing promotions (advertising, sales promotions, etc.).[20] That is, sponsorship can provide a platform upon which to integrate various marketing promotions.

Strategic sponsorship goals: Activation

"It's not 'How can the most people see my sign? It's 'How can I get our new razor in front of them?' Being in Fenway Park or Yankee Stadium is nice, but I have to be in CVS and Wal-Mart, or wherever consumers are making purchase decisions. We've got to drive retail...

We index fairly high among any teen-adult consumer group and our market share is substantial, so it's not like we have this desperate need for more name recognition or brand exposure. We have to be able to make those rights come alive at retail. It's activation, activation, activation; leverage, leverage, leverage; that is what makes our brand come to life."[21]

Global Director of Sports Marketing, Gillette

Of course, Gillette indexes fairly high among consumer groups because it has historically spent a lot of money on media. While it's true that retail presence is the ultimate goal, it's important to identify strategies for success in getting there, which might include brand exposure and sponsorship awareness.

Many brands also use sponsorship programs as a "catalyst"[22] in order to improve promotional effectiveness. Brands can use sponsorship to increase effectiveness across the entire spectrum of marketing promotion tools: advertising, sales promotions, direct marketing, etc. to:

- *Increase advertising engagement.* Sports fans like advertising more than non-fans, so there is a built-in fertile marketing environment for brands to use advertising connected to sponsorship. Further, advertising which is themed around a sports property and targeted to an audience of fans is more likely to be watched, remembered, and liked.
- *Increase effectiveness of sales promotions.* Brands can use links to a sports property to increase participation in promotions and, more importantly, make them more enjoyable. As the global director of sports marketing at Gillette said, activation efforts need to "come alive at retail."
- *Build/access database of prospects.* Brands can use sports properties to build a database of prospective customers, especially when combined with a sports-linked sales promotion, or brands can use the sponsorship to access to an existing database of sports fans provided by the property.
- *Earn and create more media.* Brands can leverage sports properties' newsworthiness and fan interest to earn coverage across media (print, TV, digital). Brands can also use

sports properties to create their own branded content, leveraging fan interest and the efficiency of digital platforms and social media to distribute.

- *Establish business relationships*. Corporate hospitality is a common feature in many sponsorship programs, most often used for client entertainment with the goal of establishing and maintaining business relationships. Sports properties can also serve as platforms for businesses to connect. UPS, for example, uses its NCAA sponsorship to "open the door" for discussions with other NCAA corporate partners. "Over the past few years, the college platform has really blossomed for us," said the company's director of sponsorships and events.[23]

Sponsorship brand goals

Vodafone increases awareness through F1

We've achieved very high levels of recognition and awareness for the Vodafone brand, supported by our investments in sponsorship. We now want to focus on our own marketing engagement platform to showcase the key attributes of our brand directly to our customers, using digital interactions and live events in ways that are both locally relevant and globally consistent.[24]

Chief Commercial Officer, Vodafone

It's always important to think about "what's next" in terms of marketing goals. This is a good example of a brand achieving goals and then setting new ones based on past successes.

Awareness. Sponsorship's ability to generate mass exposure for brands has been a double-edged sword. On the one hand, brands that seek to increase recognition and awareness can turn to sports properties with broad international reach, such as F1, the World Cup, and/or Olympics. Vodafone, for example, reported "ubiquitous" levels of awareness in excess of 90 percent in all markets where the company operates, which company executives attributed to the results of its global sponsorship strategy. On the other hand, if sponsorship is viewed merely as a vehicle to gain exposure, then sponsorship relationships end after awareness has been achieved. Vodafone ended its F1 McLaren sponsorship after finding that its goals for recognition and awareness had been achieved.[25] Established, mature brands tend to look beyond mere exposure.

Brand perceptions

"If you go to a person and say, 'If you were going to buy insurance, what name comes to mind?' We want to be top of mind there."[26]

President of Market Management, Farmers Insurance

Top-of-mind awareness is a good indicator of overall brand strength.

Brand image. Most brands look beyond using sponsorship for mere exposure and seek to attain brand-related goals related to consumers' image, including perceptions and experiences. Perceptions could include overall salience, as Farmers Insurance seeks in its sponsorships as measured by top-of-mind awareness. Brands can use sponsorship to develop overall goodwill to the brand. Farmers Insurance, for example, seeks sponsorships that provide a platform to promote its community programs, such as programs feeding school children or helping bring businesses and jobs to local areas.[27] Or, brand image can seek to support more specific brand attributes, such as brand "personality" of knowledge.

Scotts uses sponsorship to "educate" and "connect." So, Scotts attempts to increase brand knowledge but also to influence brand "experiences." Scotts complements its national MLB sponsorship with several team deals, leveraging the picturesque fields of MLB ballparks to connect with fans in an effort to "simplify" lawn care.[28] It is an effort to forge what many marketers refer to as "brand experiences," linking perceptions and image with lived experiences. The immediate goal of "brand experiences" is to shape perceptions of the brand and the related experiences. The ultimate goal is to shape behaviors, especially sales.

Sponsorship goal: Knowledge and experience

"We have almost universal brand recognition, so increased awareness is almost a moot point...

Lawn care is a category that's confusing to most consumers, so our strategy is to connect, educate and demystify. We want to be the brand that connects homeowners with nature. If we can amplify that experience in an endemic way, then we're doing the right thing – and that should increase sales."

Sr. Brand Mgr of Sports Marketing and Sponsorship, Scotts Miracle-Gro Co.[29]

Many industry categories can be confusing, unpleasant, or just plain boring. Who wants to talk about 'supplemental insurance'? Sports-related platforms can make consumers more open to learning about a product or service.

SPONSORSHIP SELECTION

Potential sponsors now face a dizzying array of sponsorship opportunities, especially for companies that operate internationally. In addition to choosing which sport/s to become involved with, sponsors must choose from different levels. "Olympic" sponsors, for example, can be part of the exclusive TOP program which provides global rights; but sponsors can also become involved with National Organizing Committees, like the USOC; organizing committees for specific Games; National Governing Bodies, like USA Swimming or USA Track and Field; or individual Olympic athletes. Adding advertisers during event broadcasts to the equation increases the clutter.

Sports properties' need to increase revenue has led to sponsor clutter, which continues to be a big concern for sponsors. Most sponsors have given up on "owning" a sport through category exclusivity a long time ago. In a survey of 54 sponsor and advertiser executives, clutter (28 percent) was considered one of the greatest threats to sponsorships, while exclusivity

(4 percent) was barely mentioned (see Table 13.1). Though the sample size of the survey is small, the indications are fairly strong that exclusivity is barely considered a threat. Competitors can always find a way into the sport or event, whether through a sponsorship level with the property itself, or a sponsorship through some affiliated property. As the sr. director of alliance marketing for McDonald's said, "I gave up on exclusivity [in 2002]."[30]

While ambush marketing continues to be a topic of interest in academic circles, sponsorship executives tend to focus on creating effective programs rather than protecting their "rights" in a sponsorship property. Sometimes, efforts to protect sponsors from competitor involvement in a sports property can backfire, as Visa found when controversy stirred around its decision to be the exclusive card provider to the London Olympic Games.[31]

What sponsors want properties to know

Sports price themselves out of the market – the cost per customer is too much.

As rights fees rise, there are not as many dollars for activation, and under-activating a property is the death of it. When properties are doing partnerships, they should have as much in the purchasing as in the activation.

Properties and rights holders need to understand that they need to help their partners sell more products instead of just focusing on their own business objectives or reaching their sponsorship revenue goals.

You have to look at properties that continue to carve up their categories. It used to be the 'official car' or whatever. But now it's the 'official foreign car,' the 'official domestic car' ... the 'official truck.' Sponsors will end up saying, "Enough."

Participants, NSF Corporate & Industry Survey[32]

As the sponsorship executives quoted above argue, sports properties are under pressure to generate incremental revenue, which results in rapidly increasing fees and more clutter. In this case, the best defense is a good offense. One of the principals at Team Epic, a

Table 13.1 The greatest threat to sponsorships (%)

Lack of measurement	31
Clutter	28
Cost	15
Activation	11
ROI	11
Category exclusivity	4

Source: GMR Marketing, NSF Corporate & Industry Survey.[1]

Note
1 Spanberg, E. (2012). The challenge: Stand out amid the clutter. www.sportsbusinessdaily.com/Journal/Issues/2012/03/26/In-Depth/Clutter.aspx, accessed 4/30/2013.

sponsorship agency, advises clients to forget about "ambushing" concerns and concentrate on putting together an effective program.[33]

In the face of spiraling rights fees, sponsors need to select sports properties judiciously in order to get value, and they can afford to. Sponsorship is a buyer's market. There are more properties than sponsors, and there is greater property need than sponsorship dollars. The two major decisions sponsors face in selecting sponsorship properties and/or creating a sponsorship portfolio are (1) choosing the sport, and (2) choosing the sponsorship level.

By sport

Puffs tissue and US skating's "kiss and cry" zone

"We realize that's an emotional place for the skaters, and Puffs is all about helping people put their best face forward, so we realized it was a natural fit."[34]

Puffs Communications Manager

The "kiss and cry" zone at figure skating competitions refers to the area where skaters await judges' scores. It tends to be a highly emotionally charged area as skaters who just finished their programs find out if they should "kiss" or "cry." During televised broadcasts of skating competitions, the area can receive as much as 10 minutes in air time as competitors anxiously await their scores. Executives at US Figure Skating, according to one report, regarded this asset to be one of its most valuable marketing prizes.[35] But valuable to whom?

Brands seek sports properties that will somehow "fit" their company, product, brand, and/or marketing goals. In some cases, sports properties can be "made to fit" through communications programs, but an existing fit gives potential sponsors an edge. If you were an executive at US Figure Skating, what kind of companies would you target?

US Figure Skating executives met with beauty companies, makeup brands, hair care products, and bottled water brands before landing Puffs as a partner. Why target those brands? What makes Puffs a "natural fit"? Broadly speaking, sponsors seek a fit with the audience and the sports property's brand. In this case, Puffs gains access to a sizable audience reachable through media; demographically, the female-skewing figure skating audience is a match for Puffs customers; and, brand-wise, Puffs can tap into fan passion for a sport characterized by style and putting one's "best face forward."

Selecting sports audiences

Reach. The greatest driver of value for sponsorship properties is their reach, that is the size and location of the audience. Exposure alone is not a guarantee of sponsorship success but the size and scope of the audience provides a foundation for value. Therefore, sports properties with the most reach – the biggest audiences and the broadest footprint – tend to be the most valuable.

Reach, according to a *Financial Times* report, is the key to Formula 1's commercial success, estimating the audience at 45 million viewers per race. "Global reach," according to

---

BlackBerry sponsors F1 to reach "emerging markets" such as India and Brazil

"That was the first consideration. We are a completely global brand."[36]

Chief Marketing Officer, BlackBerry

Rolex's chief executive, was the key to remaining in F1. Adding a race in the US strengthened the global appeal: "Now, it is an ideal global platform. For the audience we want to touch, [F1] is a unique platform in the world of sports," said BlackBerry's CMO.[37] Of course, not every brand seeks a global reach, so sponsors must seek out sports properties that match their marketing targets and identifying sports properties' audience size and scope is a logical first step.

Demographics. While demographics alone are not completely effective in identifying marketing targets, they can be useful tools in gaining efficiency. Financial services companies, for example, often set their sights on the "mass affluent," or upper middle class.[38] Soft-drink companies might be interested in targeting younger consumers. Noting population growth trends, young Hispanic males might capture the attention of beer companies.

In choosing sports properties, sponsors consider the balance between efficiency and overall reach. Stanley tools identified a primary objective of increasing brand awareness among its 18–35-year-old target demographic.[39] In order to gain efficiency, Stanley should look for sports with the highest percentage of young fans. According to Scarborough Sports Marketing, the major pro sports league with the highest percentage of 18–34 fans is MLS; the lowest, MLB (see Table 13.2). Stanley sponsoring MLS would make a lot of sense based on efficiency.

Perhaps counter-intuitively, Stanley forged sponsorships in MLB, the least efficient of major league sports in reaching young fans according to Scarborough. The percentage of young fans in a sport, however, does not speak to the overall number of young fans. MLS might deliver young fans more efficiently but it will deliver fewer young fans overall because there are fewer fans of the sport. Attendance in MLB, for example, is approximately 10 times attendance in MLS (see Table 13.3). Even when controlling for differences in the

Table 13.2 Interest levels in US pro sports leagues by age (%)

Age	MLB	MLS	NASCAR	NBA	NFL	NHL
18–34	28.0	37.8	29.4	31.9	29.6	33.4
35–49	28.8	31.8	30.0	28.9	29.1	32.1
50 plus	43.1	30.4	40.6	39.2	41.3	34.4

Source: Scarborough Sports Marketing.[1]

Note

1 Fan demographics among major North American sports leagues. www.sportsbusinessdaily.com/Daily/Issues/2010/06/Issue-185/The-Back-Of-The-Book/Fan-Demographics-Among-Major-North-American-Sports-Leagues.aspx?hl=fan%20demographics%20among%20major&sc=0, accessed 5/2/2013.

Table 13.3 Estimated 18–34-year-old attendees

	2011 regular season attendance	*Percent 18–34*	*Total*
MLS[1]	5,468,849	37.8	2,067,225
MLB[2]	73,425,568	28.0	20,559,159

Notes
1 www.sportsbusinessdaily.com/Journal/Issues/2011/11/07/Research-and-Ratings/MLS-Turnstile-Tracker.
  aspx?hl=mls%20turnstile%20tracker&sc=0, accessed 9/12/2014.
2 www.sportsbusinessdaily.com/Journal/Issues/2011/10/03/Research-and-Ratings/Turnstile-Tracker.
  aspx?hl=mlb%20turnstile%20tracker&sc=0, accessed 9/12/2014.

percentage of younger fans, MLB still delivers far more members of the target demo to Stanley. Moreover, as Stanley sees to build awareness, the signage available in MLB ballparks combined with media coverage and broadcasts make MLB a suitable vehicle to the extent that, according to Stanley, the brand increased awareness by 12 percent in a year, though the increase could not be attributed solely to the MLB sponsorships.[40]

Purchase behaviors. Demographics can be a crude marketing tool, serving as a proxy for the more precise market segments based on purchase behaviors. Why does Stanley target 18–35-year-old males? Probably because they are likely to buy a lot of tools. Ever wonder why there are so many beer companies that sponsor sports? Sports fans drink beer. A lot of it. According to a national survey of US adults, avid sports fans are more likely to drink, more likely to drink beer, and drink more beer per week (see Table 13.4). The more people like sports, the more they drink.

While there is a positive relationship between sports interest and beer consumptions, fans of some sports drink more beer than others. NASCAR fans, it should come as no surprise, are likely to drink beer and a lot of it: 5.0 12-ounce services per week, much higher than the 3.8 servings for figure skating fans, and higher than the 4.6 for NFL fans (not shown). But while the 3.8 beers per week among figure skating fans is lower than the national average of US adults (4.1), it should be kept in mind that about 75 percent of figure skating fans are women and that they are more likely to drink beer than average. So, more likely to drink but drink less. Keeping in mind that if 80 percent of beer volume is consumed by men, then 20 percent is consumed by women, which could represent a sizable opportunity depending on a brand's goals.

Brand preferences. Brand preferences are of strong interest to sponsors because even if an audience reports high usage levels in the product category, they might purchase

Table 13.4 Beer consumption and sports

	Drink alcohol (%)	*Drink beer (%)*	*Beers per week*
US adult 21 plus	68.1	45.0	4.1
Avid sports fan	74.2	63.8	4.7
NASCAR fan	69.2	53.6	5.0
Figure skating fan	65.7	54.3	3.8

Source: The UIndy Sports Report.

someone else's brand. For sponsors, looking at brand preferences for audiences identifies the kinds of opportunities a sports property might present. If fans of a sport report a preference for a sponsor's brand, it is an indication of good "fit" and an opportunity to perhaps increase the "share of customer," i.e., to sell more to existing customers. If the preference is low, it is an opportunity to gain market share relative to competitors.

According to Scarborough Sports Marketing, fans of the NHL's Phoenix Coyotes are much more likely to visit quick service restaurants than residents of the Phoenix Designated Marketing Area (DMA) in general. Some brands, however, are more strongly preferred than others. As shown in Table 13.5, Subway enjoys a very strong preference among Coyotes fans as compared to Phoenix residents in general (16 percentage points), while Wendy's 4-percentage point difference is much more modest in comparison. While a relationship between any QSR and the Coyotes makes some sense because of the increased usage, there are very different opportunities presented to Subway and Wendy's. Subway might use a Coyotes sponsorship to maintain its preference among fans and increase sales among an already brand loyal segment. Wendy's, on the other hand, might use a sponsorship with the goal of increasing market share relative to QSR competitors.

Attitudes. One of the basic characteristics of successful market segmentation is that segments must be actionable. Having a large fan base with appealing demographics is not helpful if fans are not affected by marketing efforts, and sports fans differ greatly with respect to sponsor loyalty. A high percentage of a brand's marketing targets in a larger audience is an indication of *efficiency*. The ability to influence sports fans' perceptions and behaviors is an indication of *effectiveness*.

By most measures, the NFL has roughly double the number of fans as NASCAR. So do NFL sponsors get double the value of NASCAR sponsors? They would if fans were equally influenced by the respective sponsors, but they are not. While a great deal of effectiveness depends on what sponsors do with their sponsorship rights – that is, how they activate their sponsorships – fan attitudes toward sponsors provides a foundation for effectiveness. Low levels of sponsor loyalty among fans of a particular sport would require greater activation efforts to influence attitudes and behaviors. High levels of sponsor loyalty allow a sponsor to leverage positive attitudes into desired results for the brand.

Table 13.5 Quick service restaurants visited in the last 30 days (%)

	Coyotes fan	Phoenix DMA
McDonald's	47	40
Subway	45	29
Taco Bell	41	30
Burger King	36	29
Wendy's	26	22

Source: Scarborough Sports Marketing.[1]

Note
1 Tackle the new business challenge. www.scarboroughsportsmarketing.com/dia_tackle_the_new.php, accessed 5/2/2013.

So, while the NFL enjoys about double the number of fans, according to a series of studies conducted by Turnkey Sports and Entertainment, NASCAR (70 percent) enjoys about double the percentage of NFL fans (40 percent) who are more likely to consider trying a product or service because a brand is a sponsor of the sport (see Table 13.6). While attitudes toward sponsors are not automatically converted into tangible results, there is a definite indication of value to NASCAR sponsors relative to other sports, according to these studies. Consequently, existing attitudes toward sponsors should be a consideration in choosing which sports to sponsor.

Fan passion. Fans love their sports. By definition, that is what makes them fans. Emotional intensity and behavioral loyalty tend to be highly correlated for sports fans. The more fans love the sports, the more likely they are to follow in the media, attend in person, and purchase merchandise. While fan bases for different sports can differ along the lines of emotional intensity and behaviors, they are still fans.

Non-fans of sports, however, demonstrate vastly different attitudes toward sports properties. Depending on how sponsors activate around their sponsorships, non-fan attitudes have the potential to profoundly affect a sponsorship program. Sponsors who activate at retail, for example, cannot target their efforts specifically to fans, unlike sponsors who activate through targeted media.

While only 5 percent of Americans say that they "hate" sports in general (using that specific word: "hate"), significantly more "hate" individual sports. Professional wrestling's WWE, for example, enjoys solid attendance at live events, excellent television ratings, and is among the leaders in ppv buys. Yet, sponsorship revenues lag despite the large audience. While WWE fans demonstrate loyalty that translates into significant revenue, non-fans have equally strong feelings in the opposite direction. According to the UIndy Sports Report, 45 percent of US adults "hate" professional wrestling (see Figure 13.2), so sponsors who promote a relationship with WWE outside the "WWE Universe" run the risk of alienating a sizable segment of consumers.

Antipathy toward sports extends beyond controversial properties such as professional wrestling and mixed martial arts. While the "bubba" image of NASCAR seems to alienate a lot of Americans, so too do the more "refined" sports of golf and tennis. Women's sports, too, seem to generate a backlash, all factors sponsors should consider in choosing sports properties and developing sponsorship programs.

Table 13.6 Percent more likely to consider trying a product or service because it is a sponsor

NASCAR	70
PGA Tour	67
NHL	63
NBA	53
MLB	49
NFL	40

Source: Turnkey Sports and Entertainment.[1]

Note

1 Broughton, D. (2012). NHL sponsor loyalty numbers move to top tier. www.sportsbusinessdaily.com/Journal/Issues/2012/06/18/Research-and-Ratings/NHL-Sponsor-Loyalty.aspx?hl=sponsor%20loyalty&sc=1, accessed 5/3/2013.

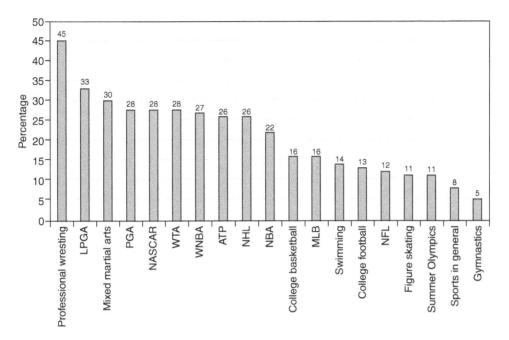

Figure 13.2 Sports Americans "hate" (source: UIndy Sports Report).

Brand image. Brand image "fit," or congruence, between sponsor and property can be a consideration. Some sports properties seem to have a natural "fit" between sponsors and the sports in property selection. Think "NASCAR sponsor" and images of alcohol, tobacco, and motor oil might come to mind. While there are some characteristics endemic to sports – race cars use motor oil – much of what has come to be understood as "fit" is based on historical context. For a long time, NASCAR did not have any auto insurance companies as sponsors. The common wisdom was that it would not be a good "fit" because of the wrecks in NASCAR. Now, auto insurance brands are peppered throughout the sport, almost to the point where it now seems "natural."

Sponsors do not need to avoid sports properties that on initial examination do not seem to fit. Properties can be made to fit with a substantive, consistent presence in the sport combined with a communications program that provides a reason for being there.

Creating a sponsorship portfolio. Sports fans are often described as fans of individual sports: "football fan," "basketball fan," "baseball fan." Most sports fans, however, are fans of several sports. Fans might have a favorite sport or team but most fans follow more than one sport and more than one team. In fact, according to Rich Luker, founder of the ESPN Sports Poll, Americans are fans of nine sports on average.[41] Sponsors that engage in more than one sport need to keep the relationships between and among sports in order to understand if they are reinforcing efforts among the same people or reaching new market segments.

For example, which is better for an NBA sponsor seeking to expand its portfolio: an NFL sponsorship or an NCAA basketball sponsorship? On its face, it might seem that NCAA basketball is a better "fit": they are both "basketball." In planning an activation program, that might be true. A sponsor could integrate the NBA and NCAA basketball sponsorships into a basketball-themed program. However, a much higher percentage of avid NBA fans are also avid fans of the NFL (70.8 percent) than of NCAA basketball (58.0 percent), according to Luker on Trends.[42]

In terms of brand image, NCAA basketball might be a better fit. Given the separation of fan bases between the NBA and NCAA basketball, however, there might be a challenge to integrating along a common theme. In terms of reaching your existing audience, the NFL is a better fit. In terms of reaching a new audience, NCAA basketball is a better fit. Ultimately, the decision rests on aligning the sponsor's goals with the opportunities to put together an integrated program.

What industry execs are saying...

"Right from the start you have to look at your portfolio of partnerships and determine, ultimately, are you well-positioned to sell more beer. That's our number one goal."[43]

Director of Sports and Entertainment Marketing, MillerCoors

Sponsorship strategy is goal-driven. If a sponsor's primary goal is to sell more beer, then it should select the properties best-suited to achieve that objective.

By sponsorship type and levels

Even after sponsors choose an appropriate sport, they have many options within those sports based on the type of sponsorship: league, team, facility, event, athlete. In addition to different sponsorship types, many sports properties create tiers of sponsorships that include varying levels of benefits. It is necessary to choose a specific property within a sport because it is impossible to sponsor the sport itself. Partnerships must be forged with specific organizations, which then may offer different levels of sponsorship packages. As sports properties continue to be pressured to increase revenue, sponsors face an ever increasing array of choices.

Sports fans do not typically distinguish between sponsorship types and levels. In fact, sports fans often have difficulty distinguishing between sponsors and advertisers, as a sponsorship research executive observed in the course of watching numerous focus groups with fans.[44] While there is no single path to become a sponsor of a sport in general, the major organizations within sports consist of:

- *League.* Sponsors may partner with sports at the league level. Opportunities range from title or presenting sponsorships of the league itself at the top level to smaller relationships with fewer benefits. The Australian Football League (AFL), for example, is sponsored by Toyota at the "Premier Partner" level with Toyota's name and logo appearing on the league badge itself. The AFL also has three "Major Partners" – Coca-Cola, nab, and Carlton Draught – in addition to more than 20 "Official Partners."
- *Team.* In rare cases, category exclusivity for a league-level sponsorship extends to teams in a league as well. Mostly, however, team-level sponsorships are independent of the

league and another avenue for sponsors to gain access to a fan base. Holden, an Australian subsidiary of General Motors, sponsors the Collingwood Football Club, an AFL team, despite the fact that Toyota is the Premier Partner of the league.

- *Facility*. Naming rights sponsors for sports facilities have become so commonplace during recent decades that it is easier to name facilities that do not have corporate names than the ones that do, with facilities without corporate names being iconic, like Fenway Park or Old Trafford, or just not sellable. Fans typically associate the naming rights sponsor with the tenant/s of the facility, though technically the sponsorship is with the facility, not the team. Of course, most naming rights sponsors also have additional sponsorships with the tenant team but that usually requires two separate deals.
- *Event*. In individual sports, such as golf and tennis, events are independently owned and thus another potential entry into a sport. Even in team sports with leagues, separate events or tournaments are available for sponsorship, such as all-state games and championships.
- *Individual*. Lastly, sponsors have the option of bypassing teams, leagues, and events and partnering directly with players, coaches, retired players, or media personalities. Developing a partnership with an "athlete endorser" allows brands to gain access to sports fans without formal relationships with teams, leagues, or governing bodies. Nike, for example, has made great use of developing relationships with individuals in sports rather than leagues or teams.

League or team?

The question comes up ... how impactful is having the NFL shield versus the ability to do specific promotions with particular teams. People are Green Bay fans and Dallas fans, not NFL shield fans.[45]

Director of Sports and Event Marketing, MillerCoors

Points of attachment. The relative value of different types of sports properties depends on the emotional attachment fans have within the sport. Take the example of college football. A fan could be attached to the sport of football itself, college football in general, the conference the school plays in, the school's football team, the school itself, the state the school is in, the city where the school is located, the coach, or a player or players or former player/s. A fan might have been attached to college football at one or all of these points to varying levels. So which offers the most value to sponsors?

As one sports marketing executive noted, NFL fans tend to be fans of their favorite teams, like the Green Bay Packers or Dallas Cowboys, not the NFL "shield." But many fans can be, and in fact are, fans of the "NFL," meaning they watch games even when their favorite team is not playing. Further, while many people are "Green Bay fans," many people are not. In fact, many people hate the Green Bay Packers, such as Chicago Bears fans. Well, that might not be a big deal in Green Bay, Wisconsin. You are not likely to find many Bears fans there, but fans of sports teams tend to be geographically dispersed, especially among popular teams that can have national followings.

SPONSORSHIP MESSAGES

What industry execs are saying...

"Whether it was complaints over burgers in the shape of Olympic rings or any other problem, it came down to blaming sponsors. We as an industry are doing a bad job and sponsors are failing to show their worth to consumers."

Former Director, Olympic Marketing, Lloyds Banking Group[46]

Unlike advertising and public relations, the sponsorship industry lacks a professional organization to communicate its message.

Sports fans know that brands sponsor sports in order to market their products or services. If marketing your product is the *only* reason for being involved in a sport, however, the brand will likely experience a consumer backlash as being selfish, intrusive, and, in extreme cases, evil. Sponsors need a reason for being involved other than selling a product.

Most sponsors have existing brand messages that they would like to communicate through a sponsorship. Unlike other marketing tools, sponsorships must also pay attention to what the medium itself says to consumers. BMO Harris Bank sponsors the NHL's Chicago Blackhawks. While many sponsors call themselves "proud sponsors" of a sport, BMO Harris says they are "Proud Sponsors and Loyal Fans" of the Blackhawks, sending a "we're just like you" message to Blackhawks fans. The messaging is supported by activating the sponsorship in a TV commercial in which an actor playing a bank executive skates through the bank office with an ice floor to pick up a printed application for a customer and ends by telling the customer, "We're big fans of the Chicago Blackhawks."[47]

Creating sponsorship messages

Anybody can align a property with an audience. That's not the difficult part. Having that reason for being is what makes all the rest pay off.[48]

SVP, Consulting, Velocity Sports and Entertainment (now Team Epic)

By identifying a "reason for being" for a sponsorship, sponsors can establish a logical, meaningful link for fans. But in order to develop a meaningful link, sponsors must understand the fans they seek to influence.

■ **Sources of pleasure.** Not all fans enjoy sports the same way or for the same reasons. Different sports attract different kinds of fans and even within sports, there are segments of fans based on the "benefits" they get from being a fan. Baseball fans, for example, are more likely to be driven by memories and nostalgia when compared to the more team-devoted NFL fans; and can be divided into three different segments, according to Octagon's Passion Drivers research:[49]

■ "*Field of Dreamers*," according to an analysis of the study, couple nostalgia for their love of the team, and are typically older and more affluent.

■ "*Team Obsessors*" connect avidly with a team and like to connect with other fans, still affluent but younger than Field of Dreamers.

■ "*Family Connectors*" like baseball because of the opportunities it provides to spend time together as a family, although they also love their teams and appreciate baseball history. These fans are more likely to be female, married with children, and be middle income.

Developing a meaningful "reason for being" for a baseball sponsorship entails an understanding both of baseball fans in general and of specific fan segments.

■ **Fan culture.** Fans of sports, teams, and leagues share a common history, language, and culture, which sponsors need to understand in order to craft a meaningful sponsorship message. Think about the relationship between soccer clubs and fans singing songs that are historically associated with the club or new songs invented for specific players. Nike drew upon Liverpool fans' "Liverpool number 9" song in tribute to Fernando Torres, creating a commercial in 2008 that translated the English version into Spanish, a nod to Torres' home country.[50] Countering Adidas' team sponsorship of Liverpool, Nike drew upon Torres' star power with the club at the time and leveraged the Liverpool fans' song to create a fun advertisement.

Align brand and sponsorship messages. Lastly, brands must keep in mind that the sponsorship message must be consistent with the brand message. A fun, irreverent tone might work for a sponsorship but not for the brand, or vice versa. Charmin toilet paper signed a deal with Charlotte Motor Speedway for two NASCAR races, which the brand activates with banners featuring tire skid marks on the back of men's briefs. Irreverent? Definitely. Fun? Maybe, depending on one's taste, but I doubt you would ever see an activation like this at Wimbledon.

CASE: LOCAL BRANDS, NATIONAL AUDIENCES IN MLB

According to the SRS Baseball Sponsorship Study, a national telephone survey of 1000 baseball fans, nearly two-thirds (64.1%) of baseball fans are bigger fans of their favorite team than the sport of baseball in general (30.4%) or their favorite player (5.5%) (see Figure 13.3). Following this, it would make sense that the biggest value for sponsors is with team sponsorships. The problem is that many more fans of a team live outside the local area (65.0%) the team plays in, according to the same study (see Figure 13.4). The New York Yankees, Boston Red Sox, and Atlanta Braves all have significantly more fans outside their local area than in. People might be Yankees fans and not "MLB" fans, but trying to put together a promotion with a team that has a geographically dispersed fan base can be a challenge unless it were limited to a digital platform.

Where fans are located has implications for sponsors' portfolio selection. For example, a sponsor of the New York Yankees might be attracted to the team's status as most popular team (see Table 13.7) with the most popular point of attachment (see Figure 13.3). But

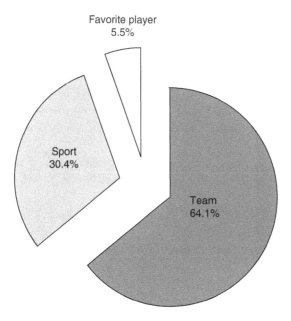

Figure 13.3 MLB points of attachment (source: 2007 SRS Baseball Sponsorship Study).

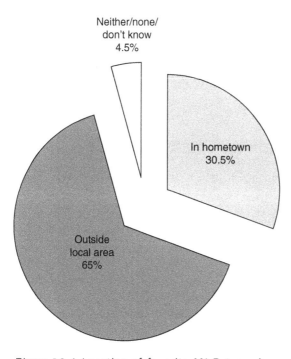

Figure 13.4 Location of favorite MLB team (source: 2007 SRS Baseball Sponsorship Study).

Table 13.7 LB team popularity

MLB team popularity

Team	% like	% don't like
New York Yankees	13.0	30.4
Boston Red Sox	11.6	8.0
Atlanta Braves	8.4	3.4
Chicago Cubs	7.5	2.8
St. Louis Cardinals	6.8	1.1
Cleveland Indians	5.7	0.3
Detroit Tigers	4.4	0.6
New York Mets	3.4	3.4
Minnesota Twins	3.0	0.4
Los Angeles Dodgers	2.9	2.3
Philadelphia Phillies	2.7	1.0
Seattle Mariners	2.7	0.3
San Francisco Giants	2.6	2.0
Cincinnati Reds	2.4	0.1
Houston Astros	2.4	0.1
Chicago White Sox	2.3	2.4
Milwaukee Brewers	2.2	0.3
Baltimore Orioles	1.9	0.4
Texas Rangers	1.9	0.3
Los Angeles Angels of Anaheim	1.8	0.6
Kansas City Royals	1.4	0.0
Arizona Diamondbacks	1.3	0.4
Oakland Athletics	1.3	0.6
Pittsburgh Pirates	1.3	0.5
Colorado Rockies	1.1	0.4
Florida Marlins	0.5	0.5
San Diego Padres	0.5	0.4
Tampa Bay Devil Rays	0.3	0.2
Washington Nationals	0.2	0.1
Toronto Blue Jays	0.0	0.2
None	1.3	45.9

Source: *SRS Baseball Sponsorship Study* (2009). Colorado Springs: Sponsorship Research & Strategy.

more fans don't like the Yankees than do; and, the top three teams in MLB by popularity all have more fans outside the area than in (see Table 13.8).

Activation efforts can present a huge challenge geographically. If a brand sponsors the Yankees, where do you activate? The New York market seems like a safe bet but then the

Table 13.8 MLB team popularity in and out of local market area (%)

MLB team popularity in and out of local market area

Team	Total	Local	Outside
New York Yankees	13.0	9.5	14.3
Boston Red Sox	11.6	7.9	13.8
Atlanta Braves	8.4	5.2	10.0

Source: *SRS Baseball Sponsorship Study* (2009). Colorado Springs: Sponsorship Research & Strategy.

brand fails to reach the majority of Yankees fans. Digital media can reach fans directly but then it is difficult to obtain a substantial reach. A league sponsorship with MLB mitigates the negative effects of team associations but then fails to provide the emotional attachment that teams do.

EXERCISE

Create a sponsorship portfolio for a sponsor. Based on the data presented in the case study, recommend sponsorship assets for a prospective MLB sponsor. Make sure you consider sponsor goals and potential activation efforts in your choices.

THREE MAIN TAKEAWAYS

1   Sponsors seek to build brand and drive sales through sponsorship programs.
2   Lack of measurement is one of the greatest impediments to sponsorship growth.
3   Sponsorship assets should be chosen based on their demonstrable ability to achieve sponsorship goals.

NOTES

1   Corporate Account Manager: Fremantle Dockers. www.afl.com.au/news/2013–04–26/corporate-account-manager-fremantle-dockers, accessed 5/9/13.
2   (2009). SBJ/SBD Relay Worldwide Sports Sponsorship Symposium kicks off. www.sportsbusinessdaily.com/Daily/Issues/2009/09/Issue-13/Events-Attractions/SBJSBD-Relay-Worldwide-Sports-Sponsorship-Symposium-Kicks-Off.aspx?hl=Dan%20McHugh&sc=1, accessed 3/7/2013.
3   Clark, D. (2009). Sponsors should return to brand building. *IEG Sponsorship Report*, 28(19).
4   Ibid.
5   O'Reilly, N. and Madill, J. (2012). The development of a process for evaluating marketing sponsorships. *Canadian Journal of Administrative Sciences*, 29: 50–66.
6   Collett, P. and Fenton, W. (2011). *The Sponsorship Handbook*. San Francisco: Jossey-Bass, p. 16.
7   Skildum-Reid, K. (2012). *The Corporate Sponsorship Toolkit: Using Sponsorship to Help People Fall in Love With Your Brand*. Australia: Freya Press.
8   Measuring High Performance Sponsorship Programs. www.marketingpower.com/ResourceLibrary/Documents/Content%20Partner%20Documents/IEG/2009/IEG_Measurement.pdf, accessed 3/21/2013.
9   Skildum-Reid. *The Corporate Sponsorship Toolkit*, p. 51.
10 Sponsors rely less on ads, signage: Findings released from 2012 Sponsorship Decision-Makers Survey. www.sponsorship.com/Resources/IEG-Performance-Research-Study-Highlights-What-Spo.aspx, accessed 4/9/2013.
11 Botta, C. (2013). Heineken targets US fans of UEFA Champions League with new social media contest. www.sportsbusinessdaily.com/Journal/Issues/2013/03/25/Marketing-and-Sponsorship/Heineken.aspx?hl=heineken%20targets&sc=0.
12 Ibid.
13 Skildum-Reid. *The Corporate Sponsorship Toolkit*.
14 Lefton, T. (2011). The Gatekeepers: Suzy Deering. www.sportsbusinessdaily.com/Journal/Issues/2011/05/30/In-Depth/Suzy-Deering.aspx, accessed 9/12/2014.
15 IEG's Guide to Why Companies Sponsor (2008). www.sponsorship.com/Resources/What-Companies-Sponsors.aspx?print=printfriendly, accessed 6/16/2008.
16 Lefton. The Gatekeepers: Suzy Deering.
17 Cutler, M. (2013). TD Ameritrade expands USOC sponsorship. www.sportbusiness.com/news/188392/td-ameritrade-expands-usoc-sponsorship, accessed 4/11/2013.
18 Kander, J. (2010). Sponsorship messaging: Creating a link between sponsor and property. www.sponsorship.com/About-IEG/Sponsorship-Blogs/Jon-Kander/October-2010/Sponsorship-Messaging—Creating-a-Link-between-Spo.aspx, accessed 4/1/2013.

19 Lukovitz, K. (2011). ANA: Accountability heads list of top issues. *Marketing Daily*. www.mediapost.com/publications/article/142755/#axzz2Fc9fVBcT, accessed 12/20/2014.

20 Skildum-Reid. *The Corporate Sponsorship Toolkit*.

21 Lefton, T. (2011). The Gatekeepers: Greg Via. www.sportsbusinessdaily.com/Journal/Issues/2011/05/30/In-Depth/Greg-Via.aspx, accessed 9/12/2014.

22 Skildum-Reid. *The Corporate Sponsorship Toolkit*.

23 Smith, M. (2013). NCAA sponsorship delivers business customers for UPS. www.sportsbusinessdaily.com/Journal/Issues/2013/04/01/Marketing-and-Sponsorship/UPS.aspx, accessed 4/9/2013.

24 Vodafone concludes global sponsorship review. www.vodafone.com/content/index/media/group_press_releases/2013/sponsorship_review.html, accessed April 29, 2013.

25 Ibid.

26 Mickle, T. (2011). The Gatekeepers: Paul Patsis. www.sportsbusinessdaily.com/Journal/Issues/2011/05/30/In-Depth/Paul-Patsis.aspx?hl=the%20gatekeepers%20paul%20patsis&sc=0, accessed 9/12/2014.

27 Ibid.

28 Lefton, T. (2011). The Gatekeepers: John Price. www.sportsbusinessdaily.com/Journal/Issues/2011/05/30/In-Depth/John-Price.aspx?hl=the%20gatekeepers%20john%20price&sc=0, accessed 9/12/2014.

29 Ibid.

30 Relay Sports Symposium. www.sportsbusinessdaily.com/Journal/Issues/2007/10/20071001/This-Weeks-News/Relay-Sports-Sponsorship-Symposium.aspx?hl=lewicki%20exclusivity&sc=0, accessed 4/30/2013.

31 Kemp, N. (2013). Lloyds Olympic marketer warns sponsors are seen as a "necessary evil." www.marketing-magazine.co.uk/article/1180100/Lloyds-Olympic-marketer-warns-sponsors-seen-necessary-evil, accessed 4/29/2013.

32 Spanberg, E. (2012). The challenge: Stand out amid the clutter. www.sportsbusinessdaily.com/Journal/Issues/2012/03/26/In-Depth/Clutter.aspx, accessed 4/30/2013.

33 Ibid.

34 Mickle, T. (2013). US Figure Skating finds "kiss and cry" partner. www.sportsbusinessdaily.com/Journal/Issues/2013/01/21/Marketing-and-Sponsorship/Figure-skating.aspx, accessed 5/1/2013.

35 Ibid.

36 Allen, J. (2013). Sponsorship: Brands beat a path to F1's door despite drop in TV viewers. www.ft.com/intl/cms/s/0/17fccc94–85bc-11e2-bed4–00144feabdc0.html#axzz2S4yCOMd9, accessed 5/1/2013.

37 Ibid.

38 O'Daniel, A., and Spanberg, E. (2012). Bank of America's cuts make turn to NASCAR. www.bizjournal.com/charlotte/print-edition/2012/03/16/bofa-cuts-make-turn-to-nascar.html?page=all, accessed 5.2.2013.

39 Lefton, T. (2010). SportsNet sees ad sales uptick; Stanley tools around in sports. www.sportsbusinessdaily.com/Journal/Issues/2010/04/20100412/Marketingsponsorship/Sportsnet-Sees-Ad-Sales-Uptick-Stanley-Tools-Around-In-Sports.aspx?hl=primary%20objective&sc=1, accessed 5/2/2013.

40 Ibid.

41 Luker, R. (2011). Fan base complexity sets up intense competition for attention. www.sportsbusinessdaily.com/Journal/Issues/2011/06/27/Research-and-Ratings/Up-Next.aspx, accessed 5/8/2013.

42 Ibid.

43 Carpenter, J. (2013). Minding my business with MillerCoors sports & entertainment marketing dir. Adam Dettman. www.sportsbusinessdaily.com/Daily/Issues/2013/04/10/People-and-Pop-Culture/Minding-My-Business.aspx?hl=minding%20my%20business&sc=1, accessed 5/16/13.

44 Spanberg. The challenge.

45 Kaplan, D. (2003). Beermakers take different tacks to reach fans. www.sportsbusinessdaily.com/Journal/Issues/2003/03/20030324/Special-Report/Beermakers-Take-Different-Tacks-To-Reach-Fans.aspx?hl=beermakers%20take%20different&sc=0, accessed 5/9/13.

46 Kemp. Lloyds Olympic marketer warns sponsors are seen as a "necessary evil."

47 Chicago Blackhawks "Ice Bank" Commercial | BMO Harris Bank. www.youtube.com/watch?v=ao9QddhiDHc, accessed 5/13/13.

48 King, B. (2009). Sweet spots. www.sportsbusinessdaily.com/Journal/Issues/2009/06/20090622/SBJ-In-Depth/Sweet-Spots.aspx?hl=sweet%20spots&sc=1, accessed 5/13/13.

49 King, B. (2010). What makes fans crazy about sports? www.sportsbusinessdaily.com/Journal/Issues/2010/04/20100419/SBJ-In-Depth/What-Makes-Fans-Crazy-About-Sports.aspx?hl=what%20makes%20fans%20crazy%20about%20sports&sc=1, accessed 5/13/13.

50 www.youtube.com/watch?v=tDMIb0k2Mqk, accessed 5/13/2013.

Sponsorship activation

SPONSORSHIP FEATURES

What industry execs are saying...

"Unique and ownable inventory secured to address a specific business opportunity. Differentiation is key in such a cluttered category. Marketing partnerships and corresponding inventory are only as valuable as the business opportunities they are intended to address."[1]

Manager, Marketing Communications, State Farm

Research on industry executives confirms that exclusivity is regarded as the most valuable sponsorship asset, but it is also important to think about how those sponsorship assets will be activated and leveraged.

Sponsorship properties must offer more than marketing "potential" to sponsors; they must offer specific assets which can be exploited for marketing purposes. Sports properties need to take inventory to review the assets they have to offer to sponsors which will be of marketing value, most commonly referred to as sponsorship "benefits."[2] Sponsors, on the other hand, need to identify which assets are most important to them. More importantly, sponsors and properties both need to understand how marketing *potential* can be converted into marketing *results*.

Sponsorship benefits must be activated into an effective sponsorship program, which can then be leveraged to achieve the desired marketing and business outcomes. In conjunction with the sponsorship strategy – *what* you want to say and *whom* you want to say it to – sponsors must figure out *how* to say it. Prioritizing and choosing sponsorship benefits should be aligned with sponsorship strategies and activation plans, all of which should be aligned with sponsorship goals.

Categories of sponsorship "benefits" typically include:

Exclusivity. In general, the fewer the sponsors the more valuable the sponsorship. It is assumed that cluttered environments create a challenge for sponsors to meet their objectives.

Exposure. Exposure benefits seem to be declining in importance to sponsors, according to a recent survey of sponsorship executives,[3] but exposure-related sponsorship benefits remain an integral component of many sponsorship packages. Exposure can be generated for sponsors in numerous ways.

> *On-site signage.* Sponsor logos that are integrated into the event itself – on uniforms, equipment, signs in the venue – are seen by attendees, which helps them develop an association between sponsor and property.
>
> *TV broadcast.* On-site signage or logo exposure is often visible during televised broadcasts, vastly expanding the reach of the exposure and generating large numbers of impressions. Televised broadcasts tend to be the biggest contributors to the overall number of impressions and, therefore, often set the baseline for the value of a sponsorship.
>
> *Advertising.* Sponsor logos can be included in advertising done on behalf of the property, which could include all advertising media: TV, print, radio, direct mail, and digital.
>
> *Promotions.* Sales promotions conducted by the sports property could also include sponsor logos, generating further impressions.

Logo and trademark rights. Rights to use a sports property's logos and trademarks represent a great example of marketing potential. Being able to use a property's logo in a sponsor's marketing communications holds great potential value, provided the sponsor puts these rights to good use. It is not automatic and, in fact, many sponsors fail to appreciate what is involved in putting these assets to use and their sponsorships fail because of it.

Tickets. Tickets to events are a common sponsorship asset offered to sponsors for corporate hospitality and client entertainment purposes or sometimes for consumer incentives in promotions. The greater asset underlying tickets is access, especially if it is unique. Sports properties are becoming increasingly creative in developing access to their properties above and beyond tickets that are publicly available.

Database of contacts. Most sports properties collect databases of the fans and consumers from sales transactions from tickets and/or merchandise, Website visits, and promotions. A quality database of engaged consumers can be of great value to sponsors in developing direct marketing programs.

Image. Sports properties' brand image is an intangible, yet valuable, asset. High prestige properties such as the Olympics can be a valuable asset, which can be leveraged by sponsoring brands.

Vending rights. The right to sell products that are sold at sports events can be of great value to sponsors, especially for pouring rights for beer, soft-drinks and food but is relevant to other product categories as well. Retail outlets for licensed merchandise and apparel has become an increasingly common feature at sports venues.

Creating new inventory

Most of my time at work is spent thinking about...

What we can do from a sponsorship standpoint to bring in new business, increase the sponsorships with our corporate partners that we currently have, and how we can creatively come up with new inventory.

Executive Director, Valero Texas Open

The biggest opportunities for incremental revenue generation on the property side are generally found in sponsorship. Additional seating inventory for ticket sales requires an investment in infrastructure and media rights tend to be locked up in long-term deals. Additional sponsorship revenue, however, requires additional sponsorship value, the foundation of which comes by increasing the assets a property has to offer.

Increase signage. Perhaps the simplest way to create new inventory is to add opportunities for additional signage. The Indianapolis Motor Speedway (IMS) landed additional sponsors by adding signage opportunities on a retaining wall and the back of its video board. There is a balance, however, between creating value for sponsors and being intrusive on the fan experience with added commercial presence. The IMS's chief sales and marketing officer noted, "In the past, we were very concerned about the event we put on for our fans, but we have begun to make the event more friendly for our partners."[4]

Increase number of venues. Adding new venue infrastructure – additional seats, new venues, etc. – can be prohibitively expensive. The PGA Tour addressed that problem by licensing golf courses in its network of Tournament Players Clubs (TPC). TPC represents a true marketing "partnership" in that the participating clubs benefit from the PGA name in their efforts to drive business (e.g., increase the number of rounds played), and the PGA Tour gets to provide additional inventory for sponsors.[5]

Create new events. What do you do if your team does not make the play-offs? If you are the New Jersey (now Brooklyn) Nets, you sell sponsorships to the post-season anyway. The Nets created events, such as lunch with the Nets dancers, a play-off viewing party with players, and a 3-on-3 basketball tournament, which they then sold to T-Mobile as part of a "Stay Connected" sponsorship which ran for three weeks after the regular season ended.

In many cases, sports properties are taking existing inventory and turning it into an "event." The NFL branded its opening weekend as "NFL Kickoff," launching a celebration and concert in 2002, which has now grown to a $50 million plus marketing extravaganza.[6] The NHL modified its product by creating a series of outdoor games, first dubbed the "Winter Classic," then renamed the "Coors Light NHL Stadium Series" as the number of annual outdoor games increased and Coors was signed as a title sponsor.[7] The NHL's outdoor games garner higher television ratings, which adds to the sponsorship's value. The German Hockey League (DEL) has followed suit and staged a "Winter Game" of its own at the Nuremberg football stadium, which generated the league's highest television ratings for a game.[8]

Create new media. New media content provides properties with additional sponsorship inventory, whether it is "new" media (i.e., digital) or traditional media, such as print or television. The NFL's New York Giants, for example, launched *New York Giants Health Monitor*, a health and fitness magazine, which helped to add health and medical sponsors to their roster.[9] Content was customized to the Giants, featuring training tips from Giants staff and articles about tailgating, and distributed via 10,000 local doctors' offices. The magazine could then provide a foundation for a broader health and medical platform.

While traditional print media can be costly to produce, and traditional television incurs buying air time in addition to production costs, digital media presents an attractive low-cost alternative. The challenge with creating new content in digital media is in generating an audience. Even when content is compelling, fans need to find it. Cost and reach are often in tension: low-cost efforts are challenged by low reach, and high reach can incur additional costs.

Roush Fenway Racing creates marketing services group

We view this as an evolution. Historically, the sport was about selling paint on the car. That model in my view isn't sufficient anymore, and we've spent a lot of time and effort to shift away from that and make sure we can offer comprehensive marketing programs that happen to be centered around a sport as opposed to being a sport that has some marketing benefits.[10]

President, Roush Fenway Racing

Create new ideas. The marketing value in sponsorship is not necessarily in the tangible inventory, such as signage. As the president of Roush Fenway Racing argues, it is not about the "paint on the car" but how that exposure can be leveraged to achieve marketing and business goals. In this regard, some of the most valuable items of "inventory" that sports properties have to offer are good ideas. Sports properties, sponsors, and sponsorship agencies alike tend to seek "strategic thinkers" who can innovate and create new inventory. What that inventory will look like largely depends on future professionals in the industry, like you.

Frequently, sponsors are seeking activation ideas that fans can have fun with. While there are some sports properties and sponsorship relationships that are more serious in nature, the Olympics for example, most sponsorship-linked marketing efforts seek to make fan experiences more fun and enjoyable. NASCAR fans, in one study, were more likely to say they were motivated to participate in a sponsor's promotion for "fun" than for merchandise or prizes.[11]

If the goal of brainstorming ideas for sponsorship activation is fun, then the brainstorming itself should be fun. If the people coming up with the idea are not having fun with it, how can they expect fans to? In curling, "hurry hard" is a term used to tell sweepers to sweep harder and faster. When USA Curling executives were brainstorming ideas for fundraising and sponsorships, one staff member joked that "hurry hard" would be a good name for a condom. Laughable at first, the more it was discussed the more feasible it became. Eventually, with the help of sponsor Kodiak Technology Group, "Hurry Hard Condoms" became an anchor for an effort to generate awareness for the IOC's HIV and AIDS prevention program.[12]

ACTIVATION AND LEVERAGING

Job duties: Vice President, Marketing and Partnership Activation – Detroit Lions[13]

■ "Works closely with Corporate Partnerships to ensure the family brand integrity is maintained throughout all elements of partner agreements and activation.

■ *Responsible for conducting and generating creative new ideas through activation meetings with creative team to develop ideas to sell marketing partnerships, generate new partnerships and increase partner spending*

■ *Develops full understanding of the marketing and sales objectives of marketing partners* to create up-selling and cross-selling opportunities, directly increasing revenue for any and all areas of the franchise (marketing partnerships, tickets, etc.)." (emphases added)

The term 'partnership' tends to be overused, but the intent is to reflect an investment in sponsor success on the behalf of the sponsorship property. Here, the partnership ethos is institutionalized in the job description: the candidate for this position must understand sponsors' objectives and develop activation programs.

Sports sponsors are often called "corporate partners" rather than sponsors. Though "sponsor" is often the more accurate term, "partner" is meant to express an approach that works toward the goals of both property and sponsor. As the job description for the Detroit Lions VP of marketing and activation indicates, it is important to maintain "brand integrity" for both the property and the sponsor.

"Hurry Hard" condoms might be okay for USA Curling but probably not for the USOC. Charmin toilet paper brand's use of "skid marks" activating a motorsports sponsorship might play well in NASCAR,[14] but not in F1. Even then, Charmin's deal, in which banners featuring tire skid marks on the backside of white, men's briefs, was forged with a racetrack, not the sanctioning body itself.

After identifying an activation strategy that aligns sponsor and property brands, the program needs specific marketing tactics. Sponsors can bring sponsorship assets to life using any or all marketing tools. "Pull" strategies usually aimed at brand goals typically include public relations and advertising. "Push" strategies typically include sales promotions, direct marketing, and personal selling. Tactically, each marketing tool can target specific sponsorship and marketing goals, but attention must be paid to how tactics can be integrated into a cogent program.

The principle underlying attempts to integrate different media and marketing tools into a cohesive whole is *synergy*, the idea that the whole is greater than the sum of the parts; that marketing tools work better *together* than they would *individually*. Each marketing tool – advertising, sales promotions, PR – might work well as a stand-alone tool, but synergistically they would be even more effective when working together.

Sponsorship managers must determine the best *promotion mix* to attain their goals. They must decide which marketing tools to use, in what combination, in what sequence, and how much to spend on each, all with an eye toward achieving their overall sponsorship and marketing goals.

Public relations

Leveraging paid and owned media to drive earned media is going to continue to grow in importance.[15]

Chief Marketing Officer, MillerCoors

Sponsor-based PR

In order to increase the return on their sponsorship investments, many sponsors seek to leverage sponsorship assets to earn media rather than to pay for it. As sponsorship rights fees and pressure to produce greater return continue to increase, earned media should grow in importance according to MillerCoors' CMO. Public relations efforts associated with sponsorships can garner substantial publicity, which has a value in and of itself, but PR can also help to make other communications tools more effective, especially advertising and sales promotions.

While PR efforts can generate significant exposure for sponsors as a stand-alone marketing tool, they can also be integrated into a more comprehensive sponsorship program by leveraging and supporting other sponsorship marketing tools. Procter & Gamble's (P&G) Olympic sponsorship is widely recognized as among the more successful Olympic marketing campaigns. A poll of sponsorship professionals in the UK identified P&G as the TOP Olympic Games sponsors that got most traction in the marketplace for the London 2012 Olympic Games, receiving more than double the number of votes than second-place finisher Coca-Cola.[16]

Digital campaigns can be a very cost-effective method of distributing content, which make digital platforms very attractive to marketers. The challenge is to drive traffic to digital domains. P&G put together a very compelling, and emotionally charged, series of "Thank You Mom" videos in which Olympians thanked their moms for all of their support during these athletes' careers. According to P&G's news release, "The 'Raising an Olympian' tributes consist of two- to three-minute documentary-style videos that share the journeys of several Olympians in becoming world-class athletes, as seen through the eyes of their

227

moms."[17] In the UK, Hill+Knowlton Strategies engaged high-profile ambassadors such as runner Paula Radcliffe and "key mummy bloggers." In the US, gymnast Jordyn Wieber and swimmer Ryan Lochte joined their moms on NBC's TODAY show, where Ike Lochte, Ryan's mom, broke down in tears after Ryan said, "My mom has been there through everything, and she's been there through thick and thin, and she's supported me my whole entire life and I love her."[18] According to one report, P&G's videos, which were later turned into television commercials, garnered more than ten million views on YouTube before they ever aired on television.[19]

The PR efforts build anticipation leading up to the Games in a way that makes P&G's television commercials an event themselves. By the time of the London Games' opening ceremonies, the number of views for P&G's videos reportedly exceeded 53 million.[20] In this case, public relations helped to generate a buzz around television advertising, likely increasing the attention consumers paid to it, and then the advertising created a buzz which then led to more exposure. That is, there was a synergy between P&G's public relations and advertising efforts.

Public relations techniques are also frequently used to create a buzz around sponsors' promotions connected to a sport, helping to generate awareness and interest. Conversely, many sponsors' promotions are themselves media-worthy. In cases where sponsorship budgets are tight and paid media is not an option to generate awareness for a sponsor's promotion, contests, games, and sweepstakes can be designed with their ability to attract publicity in mind.

Property-based PR

> There's a reason every driver takes time to thank their sponsors after winning a race. It's because they really mean it. Because without sponsors, NASCAR simply wouldn't exist.[21]
>
> CEO, NASCAR

In a true "partnership," sponsors and properties would work together to create value for sponsorships. That is not always the case. Most often, articulating a sponsorship message is left to the sponsor. Sponsors can tap into a range of PR tactics: news releases, branded content, social media, and other media placements. As properties have to justify increasing rights fees, however, some are taking a proactive approach in educating their fans about sponsors' contributions to their sports.

NASCAR fans are nearly twice as likely to be loyal to sponsors than NFL fans.[22] It is especially curious because there is a lot of overlap between NASCAR fans and NFL fans, yet NASCAR fans who are also NFL fans are still more loyal to NASCAR sponsors than NFL sponsors.[23] Why?

One of the distinguishing characteristics of the way NASCAR goes about sponsorship as compared to other sports properties is the way that stakeholders at every level of the sport, from drivers to the NASCAR CEO, talk about the contribution that sponsors make to the sport. How often do you hear a NASCAR driver thank a sponsor after winning a race? Almost always. How often do you hear an athlete from another sport thank a sponsor? Almost never.

It could be argued that motorsports' structure lends itself to sponsorship promotion on the property side. Sponsors are integrated into the action with logos on the cars and the "driver" sponsorships are actually team sponsorships so there are no conflicts between team and individual sponsorships, as is the case with many team sports. Structure, however, is not a guarantee. As sports business reporter Anthony Schoettle noted about driver interviews after the 2013 Indianapolis 500, "I was astounded how many times I heard the drivers who were standing in front of a TV audience of nearly 5 million people say almost nothing about their sponsors."[24]

NASCAR builds value for sponsors by implementing a comprehensive communications program that ensures fans understand what sponsors mean to the sport; and appreciate it. As Schoettle added:

> Anyone who has been around motorsports for any length of time, especially the drivers themselves, realize how critical corporate sponsors are to the sport. No sponsors, no racing. It's that simple. That's why NASCAR drivers have been conditioned like Pavlov's dogs to mention their sponsors every five seconds.[25]

The importance of sponsorship dollars to the financial model of sports is not limited to motorsports or professional sports. The entire spectrum of sports properties, from grassroots to professional and across different sports, have an interest in ensuring sponsors receive value: satisfied sponsors are more likely to renew and increase the size of their deals. Properties can weave positive sponsorship messages into their fabric with a deliberate, coordinated communications program, which is both a deliberate, structured communications plan as well as an outpouring of an authentic cultural tradition.

Property-based sponsorship articulation supports public relations' primary strength as a marketing tool: it is more credible than advertising. When sponsors talk about how much their companies do for a sport, it is boastful. When a property stakeholder does it, it is humble and appreciative, especially when it is sincere.

Advertising

Along with public relations, traditional advertising is still among the most frequently used activation tools by sponsors. Among marketing tools, PR and advertising are generally more effective in delivering reach. Sponsorship-linked advertising can be used: (1) to activate sponsorships by communicating a sponsorship message; (2) to communicate a brand message more effectively; and (3) to increase the effectiveness of other sponsorship-linked marketing tools.

Sponsorship message. Logo exposure alone is not an effective technique for building fan awareness of sponsorships. Fans might make tacit assumptions about the relationship between a property and brand, but there is no clear relationship. Sponsors seeking to build equity in a sponsorship often turn to advertising to let fans know that they are involved with a sports property with varying degrees of detail about the nature and motivations for the involvement.

Sometimes sponsors simply add "Proud sponsor of..." to their existing brand advertising, which saves on added production costs and maintains a consistent brand message, but has less emotional impact on fans. In addition, these ads are suitable for non-sports audiences whereas themed advertising runs the risk of alienating non-fans. Alternatively, sponsors can develop advertising that is produced specifically with the sports property in mind, drawing on the various sponsorship elements to provide greater detail about how the sponsor is involved (e.g., sponsorship level), and more importantly, why.

Brand message. Aflac insurance is a well-known brand that has lacked brand knowledge about its main product, supplemental insurance, which helps cover expenses not covered by medical insurance (e.g., living expenses while you are sick). It is not a very exciting topic for most people, so how can Aflac capture consumers' attention long enough to receive a message that they normally would not be interested in? The decidedly un-sexy product category – supplemental insurance – is compounded by the existing challenges all advertisers face with the ease of consumer advertising avoidance.

Sponsors' brands can address advertising and brand challenges by acquiring sponsorship assets with which they can produce themed advertising and deliver it to targeted audiences. For Aflac, that meant signing sponsorships with NASCAR and NASCAR driver Carl Edwards, then producing advertising featuring Carl and the Aflac duck racing in a NASCAR race, with the duck driving.

Sponsors using themed advertising can influence fans' thoughts, feelings, and behaviors. In a national online study of 1000 NASCAR fans, nearly half (48.6 percent) of all fans and nearly three-quarters (73.7 percent) of "super" fans agree that they like advertising more when it features NASCAR or a NASCAR driver (see Table 14.1). Similar levels of fans reported being more likely to pay attention and remember themed advertising. For Aflac, leveraging their NASCAR sponsorship assets in advertising directed at NASCAR fans helped to deliver their brand message of communicating the uses and value of supplemental insurance, a message which would otherwise be more difficult to get through.

Unlike Super Bowl advertisers, very few of whom link their ads to the sport, game, or teams involved, advertisers for the Daytona 500, NASCAR's season opener and biggest race

Table 14.1 Sponsorship as an advertising catalyst

Percent agree	Total	"Super" fans (top quartile of media usage)
I like advertising more when it features the sport of NASCAR or my favorite NASCAR drivers.	48.6	73.7
I am more likely to pay attention to NASCAR sponsors' advertising when it's about NASCAR.	41.8	68.4
I can recall a lot of NASCAR sponsors' advertising that is related to NASCAR.	37.8	63.2

Source: SRS NASCAR Sponsorship Study 2009 Season.

of the year, are likely to build new creatives specifically for the event. During the broadcast of the 2007 Daytona 500, at least 12 companies debuted NASCAR themed advertising for the race. The key variables here are size of the audience and engagement with the programming. The Super Bowl boasts the biggest audience of any US program but many viewers, perhaps even most, of the Super Bowl are not football fans. In contrast, most viewers of the Daytona 500 are NASCAR fans. Sponsors need to balance the increased production costs for new creative with the audience size and engagement, as fan audiences need to be big and engaged in order to justify the increased production costs in addition to the sponsorship rights fees.

Integrate with other marketing tools. Sales promotions that leverage sponsorship assets can deliver greater engagement with brands. The challenge with sponsorship-linked sales promotions is delivering scale, or big numbers of fans, because sales promotions require advertising and/or PR to generate broad awareness. According to a study of NASCAR fans, the number one reason fans did not participate in a sponsor's promotion was a lack of awareness (see Table 14.2). While social media is an increasingly popular medium for generating awareness of sponsors' promotions, mass media advertising's main strength continues to be its ability to reach mass audiences.

Baby Ruth, the candy bar brand, ran a "Take Me Out to the Ballgame" contest during the 2008 MLB season.[26] Fans were invited to submit videos of themselves singing "Take Me Out to the Ballgame," with the winner being invited to sing during the seventh inning stretch at the All-Star Game in Yankee Stadium. In order to publicize the promotion, Baby Ruth created a 15-second television commercial with a guy in a baseball bobblehead costume playing a ukulele and singing off-key.[27] The ad is fun, meant to capture the spirit of the contest. In addition to being informative, the ad is entertaining so the brand can engage fans while delivering information about the details of the contest.

Sales promotions

Sponsors benefit from sales promotions because they tend to be linked more directly to sales than advertising or public relations. Sales promotions can also be interactive, yielding

Table 14.2 Sponsorship-linked sales promotions' need for awareness

Reasons why some people do not participate in sponsors' promotions

	Percent
I'm generally not aware of NASCAR sponsors' promotions	47.8
NASCAR sponsors' contests are too hard to win	37.0
I don't understand how NASCAR sponsors' promotions work	27.0
NASCAR sponsors' promotions don't save me any money	20.7
I don't like NASCAR sponsors' promotions or contests	7.6
None	23.7

Source: 2007 Season SRS NASCAR Sponsorship Study.[1]

Notes
1 National telephone survey of 1000 NASCAR fans.
Base: Did not participate in sponsor's promotion and data from 2006 NASCAR study.

greater fan engagement than one-way communications such as advertising. Sponsors can use the full array of sales promotion tools to activate their sponsorships:

Product sampling. Sponsors often provide product samples at live events, which often offer an environment that can heighten the experience. Food and beverage brands are a natural fit for live events sampling, especially considering weather conditions (i.e., hot drinks/cold day, cold drinks/hot day). In my research experience, food and beverage brands that sample consistently record the highest sponsorship awareness at events – they can provide a lot of samples to a lot of people. Other product categories need to be a bit more creative in sampling. Paul Mitchell hair products, for example, creates on-site hair salons, providing styling for fans in attendance.

Coupons. Coupons are the most widely used sales promotion because of the direct link to sales. Get a discount, buy the product. In 2012, the NBA began the "NBA Team Sponsorship Activation of the Year Award," with the inaugural winner the "3-Point Hot Shot Promotion" partnership between local restaurant chain Tijuana Flats and the Orlando Magic.[28] The promotion gave Magic fans the opportunity to get a free taco if the Magic hit 10 or more three-pointers in a game, which they did 16 times during the season. One of the benefits of working with the Magic was the communication assets of the team: social media, in-arena signage, and television broadcasts, all in addition to point-of-sale at the Tijuana Flats locations. In addition to the direct link to sales, the Magic and Tijuana Flats could track the bounce-backs and link sales to other customer data, which helped refine future marketing efforts.

Branded products and packaging. The 2013 winner of the NBA's sponsorship activation award went a step further than offering a discount or coupon and created a branded product. The Portland Trail Blazers' partnership with Burgerville included a "Blazers Burger" named after the team. Like Tijuana Flats' sponsorship of the Magic, the promotion featured a discount on the burger, which the team promoted through TV, radio, digital, in-arena, and point-of-sale. Beyond traditional advertising, the Blazers integrated the promotion into the team's assets via product placements and branded content created by the team. The ability to integrate promotions into content is a major advantage of sponsorships relative to traditional advertising.

Integrating promotions into property assets

Instead of doing typical advertising, we really integrated it into our assets. Instead of doing just TV commercials, we had product placement and the same thing for our website. We integrated it into our videos instead of just banner ads.

VP, Corporate Partnership Sales and Service, Portland Trail Blazers

---

Sponsors can integrate property assets into their products without a complete rebranding by branding the packaging, especially for fast-moving consumer goods (FMCGs). Team logos on beer and soft drink cans are commonplace when in season. In the run-up to Indian cricketer Sachin Tendulkar's milestone hundredth "century" (one hundred or more runs in a single inning), Coca-Cola rolled out 6.5 million "Sachin" cans, the first time a celebrity adorned Coca-Cola packaging in India.[29] The rollout of the cans coincided with a mass media campaign featuring Tendulkar in Coca-Cola advertising.

Point-of-sale displays can also be used to increase sales, whether in conjunction with packaging or other promotions or as a stand-alone promotion. Timely, well-crafted point-of-sale displays can help products acquire more and more prominent shelf space in stores.

Premiums. Advertisers cannot buy space in someone's bedroom or office. Well-crafted premium items, however, can earn a presence for a brand in these places as well as in consumers hearts and minds. In keeping with a partnership model, premium items help both to drive ticket sales for events and connect a sponsor with the property, as the Seattle Mariners' marketing director asserts.

Coca-Cola often can be in offices, but usually the brand's presence is restricted to vending machines. Often, sports-related premiums can become collectibles. Cracker Jacks have historically included baseball cards in their boxes, many of which have gone on to become valuable collectors' items. Indian collectible company Collectabilia sold out of Sachin Tendulkar signed Coke cans at a price of 500,000 rupees. One hundred signed Coke cans commemorating Tendulkar's "100th 100" (one hundredth cricket century) were framed and mounted. Where do you think they are displayed now?

A great giveaway can create lines at the ballpark as well as added value and affinity with the Mariners brand. It doesn't matter if it's a Little Leaguer or a CEO. The right collectible or gear creates that moment at the ballpark when the fan thinks, "Wow, this is really cool. I want to put this in my office. I want to wear this." That's something that no other form of advertising can offer. Sports is about creating moments, and I think giveaways help fans celebrate those moments well beyond the event they attended.[30]

Director of Marketing, Seattle Mariners

Games, contests, and sweepstakes. According to some research, sports fans are more hedonistic than utilitarian when it comes to their motivations for participating in sponsors' promotions, meaning they are in it more for the fun than for the money. Among NASCAR fans who participated in sponsors' promotions, the most frequently mentioned reason for participating was "It's fun" (see Table 14.3), much higher than potential monetary savings.

By offering prizes that would otherwise be unavailable, such as behind-the-scenes access, sponsorship-linked sales promotions can attract incremental participation from consumers who would otherwise not participate in the promotion. Unlike sales promotions in general, where "cash is king,"[31] sports fans tend to prefer incentives that are related to the sport. NASCAR fans, for example, are more likely to choose a trip to a race or a behind-the-scenes access than a car or equivalent cash prize (see Table 14.4).

Table 14.3 Reasons why fans participate in sponsors' promotions

	2008	2007
It's fun	69.3	63.2
I want the NASCAR-related merchanise	66.9	57.1
They offer NASCAR-related prizes that aren't otherwise available to fans	64.1	52.9
It saves me money	49.0	34.8
It's easy to enter and win	48.6	37.4
None	8.4	12.3

Source: 2007 and 2008 SRS NASCAR Sponsorship Study.

Note
Basve: Participated in sponsor's promotion.

Table 14.4 Sweepstakes prize preference

Which of the following SWEEPSTAKES PRIZES appeals to you the most? By avidity

Promotion type	Total	Casual	Average	Big
An all-inclusive trip to a race	27.9	27.5	26.3	29.0
Behind-the-scenes VIP access at a race	27.2	13.0	23.0	
A new car	22.7	24.6	23.5	21.8
An equivalent cash prize	21.7	34.8	26.3	15.9

Source: 2006 SRS NASCAR Sponsorship Study.

Note
Base: Prefer sweepstakes.

Direct marketing

An additional benefit of sponsorship-linked sales promotions is the ability of sponsors to acquire consumer information for future marketing efforts, especially for more efforts linked to the sponsorship. While direct marketing efforts can be more effective when targeted to a

> What industry execs are saying...
>
> If I'm at a football game, what the heck do I care about life insurance? You have to build a bridge to [the consumer] with a dialogue that is authentic to them. You don't want to bring a financial adviser to football games to talk about 401(k)s. People have been drinking beer in the parking lot for the last three hours.
>
> SVP, GMR Marketing
>
> The main goal of client entertainment and corporate hospitality is to build and maintain relationships. Sports settings are rarely conducive to negotiating and closing a deal on-site.

qualified audience, such as known fans of a sports property, they can work as a mass effort as well. Cingular, a now-defunct wireless company, had their sponsorship agency conduct tests on a potential direct mail campaign which featured NASCAR driver Robby Gordon. The company found that product offers coming from the driver tested best and ran the campaign as a mass mailing, which yielded a much higher response rate than average.[32]

Experiential marketing. One of the big advantages of experiential marketing is its ability to reach consumers who might not be available by other media. More importantly, perhaps, experiential marketing provides a physical, interactive environment that can help fuel emotions and build relationships. Sports are a visceral experience: sights, sounds, and smells are a big part of the sports experience, whether it is the smell of burnt rubber at a racetrack or freshly cut grass at a baseball stadium. Experiential marketing helps sponsors build more intense emotional relationships with fans by enhancing fan experiences.

Sponsors' exhibits at live events are most effective when they are enjoyable for fans. That means the focus of the experiential marketing campaign should be on the sport, not the brand. Experiential marketing at NASCAR races has become so extensive that the rows of sponsors' exhibits come close to resembling a carnival midway. Nearly three-quarters (73.3 percent) of fans attending races visit the sponsors' exhibits before the race. Among those fans, 72 percent say that sponsors make attending the race more enjoyable. That fan enjoyment translates into positive marketing outcomes for sponsors, as fans who visit sponsors' exhibits are significantly more likely to say they purchase a product or service *specifically* because the company or brand has a sponsorship in NASCAR.[33]

Personal selling

Corporate hospitality: More than big shrimp

It used to be about big shrimp. It was about getting people tickets and then getting them back to the hospitality so they could dip the shrimp in the cocktail sauce. But everybody started realizing that a suite just wasn't enough anymore.... We went from serving good food, then great food and drinks in a tent, to having current and former players and celebrities in the tent making speeches. I want to see what the next level is. Is it some sort of participation?[34]

President, Octagon North America

Corporate hospitality connected to sponsorships is a marketing investment that supports personal selling. Like client entertainment in general, corporate hospitality programs help to build and maintain relationships with important clients, especially for companies focusing on business-to-business. As such, standard client entertainment principles and techniques apply. However, the sponsorship component adds the ability to deliver a branded experience to VIP guests.

The bar has been raised for the execution of corporate hospitality programs. As Octagon NA's president said, it is about more than big shrimp. SportsMark, for example, leveraged

Bell Canada's sponsorship of the Vancouver 2010 Olympic games with a comprehensive corporate hospitality program, which featured:

- event technology solutions
- hotel
- custom designed premiums
- transportation
- tickets
- top-notch food and beverage
- special events
- cultural tours and activities
- technology symposiums
- staffing management.

Bell's program entertained more than a thousand guests, who were led on behind-the-scenes tours in which tour guides were trained to discuss Bell's contributions to sponsored athletes. According to SportsMark, 95 percent of guests rated the program as "an experience of a lifetime."[35]

CASE: BUILDING SPONSOR LOYALTY – THE NASCAR WAY

> There's a reason every driver takes time to thank their sponsors after winning a race. It's because they really mean it. Because without sponsors, NASCAR simply wouldn't exist.
>
> Brian France, Chairman, NASCAR

NASCAR is legendary for its fans' loyalty to sponsors. And for good reason. In its landmark study of sponsor loyalty among NASCAR fans in 1994, Performance Research found that 71 percent of NASCAR fans "almost always" or "frequently" choose NASCAR sponsors' products over non-sponsors' products, simply because of the NASCAR sponsorship. NASCAR fans' loyalty to sponsors has been confirmed by more recent research (see Table 14.1).

NASCAR's success in developing fan loyalty to sponsors is not attributable to a "loyalty gene" in NASCAR fans' DNA, but rather the result of a sophisticated and concerted communications program directed at its fans from every level of the organization, from the NASCAR CEO to the pit crew.

Even casual observers would notice how often drivers mention sponsors in media interviews. It's a practice so common it's almost reached the point of parody. It's also a stark contrast from athletes in other sports who rarely, if ever, mention sponsors in media interviews despite the fact that *all modern professional sports rely on corporate money to survive* (with the exceptions of boxing and professional wrestling, if you consider that a sport). In fact, many sponsorship contracts in NASCAR include financial incentives for drivers to mention sponsors during media interviews.

NASCAR fans understand that sponsorship is a marketing effort and that sponsors are trying to promote their brand and sell their products. But there's also a *culture of appreciation* at every level of NASCAR, from fan to CEO, which evokes sincere emotions. NASCAR drivers really do appreciate their sponsors because they're acutely aware that without the sponsor, they don't race. Fans understand that, too, primarily because drivers tell them in a sincere and consistent voice.

EXERCISE

The application for the VP, Marketing and Partnership Activation at the Detroit Lions requires answering the following question: "What components lead to the most successful activations? Please describe an activation where you feel you were the most successful."[36] How would you answer that question? Which activation would *you* pick, regardless of sport or sponsor?

THREE MAIN TAKEAWAYS

1   Most sponsorship "benefits" listed by sports properties are really features which need to be activated in order to become benefits.
2   The growth potential for sponsorship is limited only by sponsorship executives' imaginations – there's a constant need to create and innovate new sponsorship inventory.
3   Sponsorships are most effective when combining appropriate promotional tools: advertising, PR, sales promotions, direct marketing, and personal selling.

RECOMMENDED READING

www.powersponsorship.com. Kim Skildum-Reid's sponsorship blog is a great resource. I also strongly recommend her "Toolkit" books, which include a lot of sample forms and checklists.

NOTES

1   (2012). Activation highlights and trends in sponsorship. www.sportsbusinessdaily.com/Journal/Issues/2012/10/01/In-Depth/Conference-panelists.aspx?hl=activation%20highlights&sc=1, accessed 5/16/13.
2   As I will explain in the chapter about sponsorship sales, I think this is a misuse of the term.
3   12th Annual IEG/Performance Research Sponsorship Decision-Makers Survey. www.performanceresearch.com/2012-IEG-Study.pdf, accessed 5/14/13.
4   Mickle, T. (2012). "Aggressive" Indy shows revenue strength. www.sportsbusinessdaily.com/Journal/Issues/2012/05/21/Facilities/Indy.aspx?hl=%27aggressive%27%20Indy&sc=1, accessed 5/16/13.
5   Show, J. (2009). TPC adds Blue Monster, Stadium Course at PGA West. www.sportsbusinessdaily.com/Journal/Issues/2009/10/20091005/This-Weeks-News/TPC-Adds-Blue-Monster-Stadium-Course-At-PGA-West.aspx?hl=tpc%20adds%20blue%20monster&sc=0, accessed 5/16/13.
6   Lefton, T. (2009). Marketing activation for NFL Kickoff will top $50M. www.sportsbusinessdaily.com/Journal/Issues/2009/09/20090907/This-Weeks-News/Marketing-Activation-For-NFL-Kickoff-Will-Top-$50M.aspx?hl=nfl%20kickoff%20&sc=1, accessed 5/16/13.
7   (2013). Coors Light to title sponsor NHL Stadium Series; League confirms Soldier Field game. www.sportsbusinessdaily.com/Daily/Issues/2013/05/02/Leagues-and-Governing-Bodies/Coors-NHL.aspx, accessed 5/16/13.

8 (2013). DEL Winter Game nets top ratings, most-successful DEL game on ServusTV yet. www.sportsbusinessdaily.com/Global/Issues/2013/01/08/Media/Media-ratings.aspx?hl=DEL%20winter%20game&sc=0, accessed 5/18/13.

9 Lefton, T. (2008). Four NFL teams sniff out sponsor money in tight times. www.sportsbusinessdaily.com/Journal/Issues/2008/10/20081013/Marketingsponsorship/Four-NFL-Teams-Sniff-Out-Sponsor-Money-In-Tight-Times.aspx, accessed 5/14/13.

10 Mickle, T. (2013). Roush Fenway adds marketing services group. www.sportsbusinessdaily.com/Global/Issues/2013/01/08/Media/Media-ratings.aspx?hl=DEL%20winter%20game&sc=0, accessed 5/18/13.

11 DeGaris, L., West, C., and Dodds, M. (2009). Leveraging and activating NASCAR sponsorships with NASCAR-linked sales promotions. *Journal of Sponsorship*, 3(1): 88–97.

12 (2009). Curlers hawking "Hurry Hard" condoms. www.cbc.ca/sports/curling/story/2009/12/04/sp-curling-condoms.html, accessed 5/20/13.

13 NFL Team Jobs. http://footballjobs.teamworkonline.com/teamwork/r.cfm?i=49194, accessed 10/19/2012.

14 Mickle, T. (2013). Go with it: Charmin taking "skid marks" message to Charlotte NASCAR fans. www.sportsbusinessdaily.com/Journal/Issues/2013/05/06/Marketing-and-Sponsorship/Charmin.aspx, accessed 5/22/13.

15 Belzer, J. (2013). The (r)evolution of sports sponsorships. www.forbes.com/sites/jasonbelzer/2013/04/22/the-revolution-of-sport-sponsorship/, accessed 5/14/13.

16 (2012). Survey reveals P&G was Olympics' most effective sponsor. www.sportsbusinessdaily.com/Global/Issues/2012/11/06/Marketing-and-Sponsorship/PG-sponsorship.aspx, accessed 5/23/13.

17 (2003). P&G recognizes what it takes to "Raise an Olympian." http://news.pg.com/print/node/2003, accessed 5/30/13.

18 Eugenios, J. and Dube, R. (2012). Olympic hopefuls' moms on supporting star athletes: "I love my job." http://todayinlondonblog.today.com/_news/2012/05/08/11597679-olympic-hopefuls-moms-on-supporting-star-athletes-i-love-my-job, accessed 5/30/13.

19 Ukman, L. (2012). Olympic sponsorship winners and losers. www.sponsorship.com/About-IEG/Sponsorship-Blogs/Lesa-Ukman/August-2012/Olympic-Sponsorship-Winners-And-Losers.aspx, accessed 5/23/13.

20 Ibid.

21 NASCAR. *Team Sponsorship Guide 2005*.

22 Broughton, D. (2012). NHL sponsor loyalty numbers move to top tier. www.sportsbusinessdaily.com/Journal/Issues/2012/06/18/Research-and-Ratings/NHL-Sponsor-Loyalty.aspx?hl=sponsor%20loyalty&sc=1, accessed 5/3/2013.

23 DeGaris, L. and McDaniel, S. (2011). Selling corporate sponsors more than a sign?: The impact of property-based sponsorship articulation in meeting sponsorship-linked marketing objectives. Paper presented at the American Marketing Association Winter Educators' Meeting, Austin TX, February 2011.

24 Schoettle, A. (2013). Indy 500 drivers' failure to mention sponsors inexcusable. www.ibj.com/the-score-2013–05–30-indy-500-drivers-failure-to-mention-sponsors-inexcusable/PARAMS/post/41638, accessed 6/2/2013.

25 Ibid.

26 http://mlb.mlb.com/mlb/fan_forum/babyruth/index.jsp.

27 www.youtube.com/watch?v=DJ_X-gHObbI.

28 Magic win NBA Sponsorship Activation of the Year Award. www.nba.com/magic/news/magic_win_nba_team_sponsorship_activation_of_the_year_award_2012.html, accessed 5/14/2013.

29 Bhushan, R. (2011). Tribute to Tendulkar: Coca-Cola to roll out 6.5 million "Sachin" cans as part of 100th century celebrations. http://articles.economictimes.indiatimes.com/2011–07–18/news/29787447_1_coca-cola-coca-cola-india-vp-coca-cola-cans, accessed 6/4/2013.

30 Deutsch, J. (2012). Merchandise a powerful activation tool for teams, sponsors. www.sportsbusinessdaily.com/Journal/Issues/2012/05/28/Opinion/From-the-Field-of-Marketing.aspx?hl=merchandise%20a%20powerful&sc=1, accessed 5/31/2013.

31 Johannes, A. (2008). Champagne tastes: Marketers are offering consumers more and better rewards, survey shows. www.chiefmarketer.com/promotional-marketing/incentives/champagne-tastes-01092008, accessed 6/4/2013.

32 King, B. (2009). Sweet spots. www.sportsbusinessdaily.com/Journal/Issues/2009/06/20090622/SBJ-In-Depth/Sweet-Spots.aspx?hl=sweet%20spots&sc=1, accessed 6/4/2013.

33 Dodds, M. and DeGaris, L. (2011). Using mobile marketing to engage NASCAR fans and increase sales. *Sport Management International Journal*, 7(1): 63–75.

34 Show, J. (2008). Creating experiences that pay off. www.sportsbusinessdaily.com/Journal/Issues/

2008/06/20080623/SBJ-In-Depth/Creating-Experiences-That-Pay-Off.aspx?hl=creating%20experiences%20that%20pay%20off&sc=1, accessed 6/4/2013.

35 Bell Canada Vancouver 2010 Olympic Games. www.sportsmark.com/studies_Olympic_Games_03.php?mp=3&opc=19, accessed 6/4/2013.

36 NFL Team Jobs. http://footballjobs.teamworkonline.com/teamwork/r.cfm?i=49194, accessed 10/19/2012.

Sponsorship measurement

Measurement remains sponsorship's biggest challenge as a marketing tool. Measurement challenges are not unique to sponsorship because accountability remains one of the top priorities for marketers in general, not just those involved in sponsorship. Sponsorship, however, presents unique measurement challenges.

As a comparatively new marketing discipline, sponsorship does not have an established record of measurement. Serious research about sponsorship has been going on for about the past 20–30 years, and even then without a lot of resources behind these efforts when compared to more established marketing tools like advertising. Historically, spending on sponsorship research has fallen well below the marketing industry guideline of 1–3 percent of the marketing budget.

Sponsorship is also "multi-faceted," meaning it combines advertising, PR, and sales promotions, plus the sponsorship itself. Sponsorship measurements need to consider not only each piece of the program, but how those pieces interact with each other. Sponsorship faces all of the challenges faced by integrated marketing communications (IMC) with the added dimension of the contribution of sponsorship. Because sponsorships are integrated, then so too must sponsorship measurements be integrated.

The multi-faceted nature of sponsorship has made standardized measurements elusive. There has been no "silver bullet" or "magic pill" that solves the sponsorship puzzle, and sponsorship experts do not believe the "Holy Grail" will be found anytime soon, if ever. The main problem caused by the lack of a standardized measurement is that there is no "rate card" for buying sponsorships. Unlike advertising, where media is bought and sold with fairly precise audience measurements, sponsorship rights fees have no such standard, making pricing, buying, and selling sponsorships more difficult.

The other problem, equally significant, is that sponsors are left to wonder whether or not their sponsorship is worth the money, even after the price has been negotiated. Internally, sponsorship executives need to justify their programs. Sponsorship salespeople need to justify their fees. Sponsorship agencies need to show how they add value to sponsorship programs with activation ideas.

While sponsorship has continued to grow rapidly during recent decades, I believe that there is yet a lot of untapped potential for sponsorship as a marketing discipline. And I believe that the potential can be tapped with more, and more rigorous empirical research that supports sponsorship effectiveness.[1]

MEASUREMENT APPROACHES

Although most sponsorship executives have long given up on a standard measure of sponsorship effectiveness, the lack of a standard measure does not preclude a systematic approach. And since sponsorship is multi-faceted, sometimes a multi-faceted measurement approach is appropriate.

- *What is the media value?*
- *What is the marketing value?*
- *Did I meet my objectives?*
- *What is the financial value?*

Media value

Measuring the value of media exposure was a very popular technique for evaluating sponsorships early on. Pioneered by Joyce Julius in 1985, measuring the media value of sponsor exposure drew on the well-established models of advertising measurement. Since advertising costs are well established and widely accepted, aligning sponsorship values to advertising equivalencies has given some legitimacy to sponsorship fees.

But sponsorship and advertising are not equivalent. Advertising can accomplish much more than simply placing a logo; it can communicate a message, deliver a tone, and provoke an emotion. Consequently, exposure-based evaluation tends to be discounted heavily when calculating values, though the precise amount "discounted" tends to be generated somewhat arbitrarily.

On the other hand, sponsorship is much more than simply logo identification. Sponsorship is not equivalent to advertising, but sponsorship programs can include advertising; and public relations; and sales promotions; and elements of personal selling. Therefore, there has been a growing disillusionment with exposure evaluation as *the* method of sponsorship evaluation. But let's be careful not to throw out the baby with the bathwater.

Table 15.1 Daytona 500 sponsor exposure estimates

Rate card	Sponsor/driver exposure time	Value
$132,357/30-seconds $4411.90/second	M&M's/Kyle Busch 17:09 (1029 seconds)	$4,500,138
	AMP Energy/Dale Earnhardt Jr. 15:18 (918 seconds)	$4,050,124.20
	DuPont/Jeff Gordon 14:44 (884 seconds)	$3,900,119.60

Sources: Joyce Julius, Image Impact.[1]

Note
1 www.joycejulius.com/PressReleases/pr_Feb_11_2010.htm, accessed 6/25/2013.

Media exposure tells us *something* about a sponsorship's effectiveness, just not *everything*, and certainly not what the financial return on a sponsorship might be. Joyce Julius has been measuring sponsor exposure during NASCAR television broadcasts for almost 30 years. Televised NASCAR races are a good example of media exposure because sponsors' logos are visible and identifiable during much of the broadcast.

Calculating advertising equivalencies is fairly simple. First, you look at the rate card for a 30-second television commercial. For example, the average cost to air a 30-second spot for Sprint Cup race telecasts was $132,257 (see Table 15.1), which translates into $4411.90 per second. Then, you measure the amount of time that the sponsor's logo was visible during the broadcast. Digital technology has allowed companies that do this type of work to be very precise about the amount of time and the legibility of the logo. To obtain an advertising equivalency dollar figure, multiply the rate card rate by the amount of time the logo is visible.

Advertising equivalencies capture a lot of attention because they put up some pretty gaudy numbers (see Table 15.2). Advertising equivalencies totals often run into the billions.

Table 15.2 2010 Sprint Cup sponsor exposure

Sponsor	Exposure value (in millions)
Sprint	$272.2
Chevrolet	$121.3
Toyota	$78.0
Ford	$64.8
Lowe's	$52.8
Budweiser	$51.6
AT&T	$46.6
DirecTV	$36.1
FedEx	$35.9
Nationwide	$35.0

Source: Image Impact.[1]

Note
1 Sprint Cup exposure. www.sportsbusinessdaily.com/Daily/Issues/2010/12/Dec-21/Research-And-Ratings/Sprint-Cup-Exposure.aspx?hl=sprint%20cup%20exposure&sc=1, accessed 6/25/2013.

The problem here is that nobody in the sponsorship industry really takes those numbers seriously, though they do get taken into account at a discount. Discount rates for advertising equivalencies probably run between 5 percent and 20 percent, give or take. That is the irony about being so precise about calculating exposure time: the discount rates are often a "big fat guess," as one sponsorship expert says.[2]

But the discount rates for advertising equivalencies are more than a "big fat guess"; they are based on professional judgment, which is still highly subjective but more than a random guess. It is possible to calculate the value of media exposure in a sponsorship, but that depends on how it interacts with other variables that predict sponsorship effectiveness.

Exposure, for example, is a strong predictor of sponsorship awareness, which in turn is related to activation effectiveness, which enhances brand image, which is related to increased sales. The importance of media exposure depends on the elements in the sponsorship mix, such as how and how much a sponsor is activating.

Return on marketing investment

Advertising equivalencies are also popular as a technique for evaluating sponsorships because marketers need to choose among a wide array of different marketing options. Sponsorship has a marketing value relative to other marketing options. So, for example, say it takes $20 million dollars in advertising to gain a percentage point in brand awareness for a particular brand, like Samsung. Can a sponsorship be more effective at increasing brand awareness than advertising? If a $10 million sponsorship can deliver the same results as $20 million in advertising, would you say that the sponsorship is "worth" $20 million? For marketers looking to get the most out of the marketing dollars, these are real choices. Choosing the best option is not always readily apparent.

Marketers also must figure out how to get the most out of what they are currently doing. So, can a sponsorship increase the effectiveness of other marketing efforts? If it does, then does that add "marketing value"? Sprint, for example, was estimated to have spent $23.22 million on advertising during NASCAR race broadcasts during the 2012 season, according to Nielsen.[3] Sprint is the title sponsor of NASCAR's top series, the Sprint Cup. Does the sponsorship make the advertising spend more effective? Suppose Sprint's sponsorship doubles the effectiveness of Sprint's $23.22 million advertising campaign, what is the marketing value of the sponsorship? $23.22 million? In this case, the more a sponsor spends on advertising, the greater the value of the sponsorship.

Of course, sponsorship's ability to increase advertising effectiveness depends on how advertising effectiveness is defined. There is a small but growing body of evidence that supports the proposition that sponsorship increases the effectiveness of marketing communications. Intuitively, it makes sense. There is a large body of evidence that shows support for a positive relationship between fan involvement and sponsorship attitudes: the more involved the fan, the more positive are the attitudes toward sponsors.

Marketing measurement is not physics. As with valuing media exposure, measuring the marketing value of sponsorship relative to other marketing options depends on other elements in the sponsorship mix as well as available non-sponsorship options. The overall approach, however, can be persuasive in demonstrating sponsorship value and guiding marketing decisions.

243

Chicago White Sox corporate partnership brochure

Quick hit

■ 85 percent of White Sox attendees are more likely to notice an offer or advertisement when it contains the White Sox name or logo

Source: FanTrak Survey taken by White Sox Attendees, 2012 season

The Chicago White Sox, for example, feature data in the corporate partnership brochure that shows how the White Sox name and logo increases advertising effectiveness among fans. In a survey of White Sox attendees, 85 percent of respondents said they were more likely to notice an offer or advertisement when it contains the White Sox name or logo. Similarly, a survey of NASCAR fans found that fans are more likely to participate in a promotional game, contest, or sweepstakes if it is related to NASCAR (see Figure 15.1). More avid fans are more likely to participate in NASCAR-related promotions: nearly half (49.4 percent) of "super" fans in the study (the top 25 percent based on fan behaviors) said they were "a lot more likely" or "definitely would" participate in a promotion if it were linked to NASCAR.

Return on objectives

Many sponsors tend to focus on a return on sponsorship objectives rather than a return on investment because demonstrating a conclusive link between sponsorships and financial

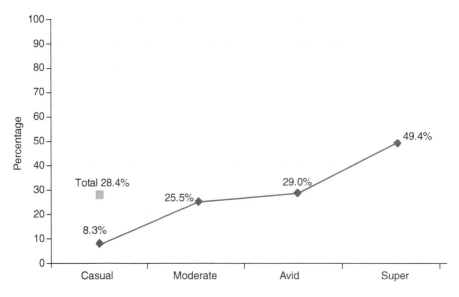

Figure 15.1 Likelihood to participate in promotion if related to NASCAR by fan avidity percent: A lot more likely or definitely would (source: SRS NASCAR Sponsorship Study).

returns has been elusive. Typically, sponsorships are just one promotional effort among many, and promotions are just one "P" out of the traditional four "Ps" of marketing (product, price, place, and promotion). In addition, there are external factors that influence sales: economic conditions, politics, demographic shifts. There is a measurement gap between marketing efforts and sales so measuring sponsorship effectiveness according to sponsorship goals is a more valid method than measuring sales, which can be influenced by a lot of other factors.

While most sponsorships have the ultimate goal of increasing sales and profits, most sponsorship managers identify sponsorship objectives along the way. Fast-moving consumer goods companies, for example, might be interested in sponsorship-linked sales promotions that can demonstrate increases in retail traffic among consumers, and increased shelf space or display prominence among retailers. Sponsors with B2B goals might be more interested in the quantity and quantity of clients entertained at corporate hospitality functions.

Return on investment

Sponsorship is not alone in facing ROI challenges as other marketing communications, especially advertising, face similar issues of accountability. While measuring sponsorship objectives is a more valid method for measuring sponsorship, the return on investment is more important. Marketing communications effectiveness, brand awareness, and brand image are all important to the extent that they translate into sales and profits, and that is not automatic. Linking sales to sponsorship programs has been sponsorship's "Holy Grail" in that it is the most important measure of effectiveness but has thus far proven to be largely elusive, though there is a small but growing body of research that links sponsorships to product sales.

WHAT TO MEASURE

Measurement "dashboards." Since sponsorship is "multi-faceted," sponsorship measurement should address the most important components of the program. Many sponsors have adopted a "dashboard" approach in which they piece together measures of the sponsorship's most important goals. Effective sponsorship goals should be measurable, but then they must be measured.

Integrating measurements. The major limitation of the dashboard approach is that the measures are treated as independent when they are related in practice. Some sponsorship experts advise that sponsorship measurement should focus exclusively on marketing goals,[4] but it is also important to measure sponsorship goals, like exposure, awareness, and favorability because those sponsorship components are antecedents to the end goals of brand image and sales. While sales are ultimately the most important measure, sponsorship managers must understand the path to sales and both the inter-relationships and unique contributions of different sponsorship components.

In this respect, sponsorship measurement is a valuable research tool. By understanding how different components contribute to the desired goals, sponsorship managers can allocate resources more efficiently.

Benchmarking. Practically speaking, one of the main questions sponsorship managers have about research is: "Is this good?" Take achieving 30 percent unprompted sponsorship awareness for a particular deal, for example. Is that good?

One approach would be to compare results to similar sponsorships. Do other sponsors achieve similar awareness levels? If the average awareness level for sponsors in other categories is 50 percent, then maybe it is not very good, though you would still have to consider other variables, especially brand prominence and activation efforts. There are many factors to consider but benchmarking against other sponsorships can be helpful.

The other main approach would be to benchmark your own results. If awareness was 20 percent last year and 30 percent this year, then 30 percent looks pretty good. Sponsors who neglect to establish benchmarks before the sponsorship begins can have difficulty in gauging the effects. Establishing baseline measures of awareness, image, and brand preference among a target audience can provide evidence of a sponsorship's contribution to reaching marketing goals.

Reach

Audience size. Media consumption and live attendance provide a baseline for sponsorship value so TV ratings and attendance figures (actual, not reported) provide a baseline measure of sponsorship effectiveness. By establishing the parameters of the "sponsorship universe" for a particular deal, audience size, along with conversion rates, can provide an indication of the potential magnitude of sponsorship effects.

Demographics. Demographics help to estimate the overall demand potential for a sponsor's product, and provide an indication of marketing efficiency in reaching a target. Since most brands have a good idea who buys their products or services (or at least they should), they can "match" their target markets with the sponsorship audience. The better the demographic "fit" between property and sponsor, the more likely that the sponsorship program will be more efficient and effective.

Strategically, demographics can help to plan sponsorship activation programs. For example, about half of Major League Baseball fans are female, but most sponsorship activation programs are targeted to men. Sponsors who target activation programs toward women might seize an opportunity to tap into a traditionally underserved market.

Exposure. Though often maligned as a sponsorship research tool, media exposure is related to other more important outcomes and a worthwhile and inexpensive sponsorship measurement. Exposure measures can capture "indirect" sponsorship effects. Often, people are affected by marketing communications even when they do not consciously remember them. Sports fans might like sponsors more even when they cannot consciously identify the brand as a sponsor.

Fan involvement

Octagon is one of the world's biggest sports marketing agencies. The company's mission statement is: "We use passion for sports and entertainment to deepen the emotional connections between our clients and their target audience."[5] Fan passion, fan involvement, fan avidity, and fan identification are all terms that reflect the intense emotional relationship people have with sports. Since sponsorship attempts to tap into that passion for commercial purposes, it is important to measure fan involvement.

Since fan passion is at the core of sponsorship programs, it is important to measure, not as an end in itself but as a means to an end. Some research agencies have put together versions of a "passion index," attempting to rank fans according to different dimensions of passion. While the importance of different components of fan passion depends on sponsor objectives, fan passion should be measured along cognitive (thinking), affective (feeling), and conative (doing) dimensions:

- *Thinking*. How much do fans know about their sports? How much do they remember about events?
- *Feeling*. How much do they like their sports? Do they "love" their sports? Is the relationship enduring or fleeting? What are the emotions associated with being a fan: elation, frustration, indifference?
- *Behaviors*. Though all thinking and feeling are often strongly related to doing, most often behaviors are the most important component of fan involvement, mostly because marketers need to be able to gain access to fans to be effective.

Activation

Activation is widely recognized as among the most important components of sponsorship, but also the least likely to be measured, though it is gaining the attention of more academic and practitioner researchers. From a practical standpoint, sponsors need to make decisions about activation spending so they need to know what works. Sponsors can choose from the full range of marketing communications (advertising, PR, sales promotions, etc.) in any combination so they need to decide how and how much to spend on each tool.

Overall, most sports fans are receptive to sponsors' efforts, according to an industry study of 2750 US adults.[6] However, the propensity to participate in promotions varies among different sports fans. Younger fans are more likely to be receptive to sponsors' promotional efforts, as are fans of particular sports, notably NASCAR. And, according to the study, 25 percent of all sports fans are not receptive to sponsors' efforts at all.

This viewpoint comes from the perspective of making the sponsorship successful.

- How can favorable attitudes toward the sponsorship best be leveraged into increased brand equity and sales volume?
- Which are the most effective elements of the promotional mix in achieving desired sponsorship outcomes?

However, sponsorship assets can also make marketing communications more effective. The "lift" marketing communications receive from sponsorship assets can be measured by asking the following questions:

- Do sponsorship relationships increase the effectiveness of other elements in the promotional mix? For example:

- Does sponsorship increase advertising effectiveness, especially among targeted audiences?
- Do fans pay attention to, like, and remember advertising more because of a sponsorship?
- Are fans motivated to enter contests or sweepstakes because of sponsorship-related prizes?
- Are sales promotions more fun because of sponsorship assets?
- Is the sponsor's message being communicated effectively?

Awareness

Traditionally, awareness has been a popular technique for measuring sponsorship effectiveness. More recently, however, there is a growing recognition among both practitioners and academics that awareness is just one component of sponsorship success and there are other, more important measures.

Awareness continues to be popular in large part because it is easy to measure, though awareness levels vary according to how they are measured.[7] Awareness can be unaided or unprompted as in:

- Please name a sponsor of XYZ property.

Awareness can be prompted by industry category:

- Please name a bank that sponsors XYZ property.

Or, awareness can be measured by prompted recognition:

- Did you know that ABC bank is a sponsor of XYZ property?

Unaided or unprompted awareness is the most valid technique. Prompted awareness introduces more chance for error but does tell you something of value.

Sponsorship awareness on its own does not hold much value for most sponsors, excepting those whose primary goal is increasing brand awareness. The big question about sponsorship is, so what? Therefore, the value of sponsorship awareness lies in its relationship to other, more important, sponsorship outcomes, and those relationships vary by sponsor and property, making integrated measurement vital.

In the case of a primary car sponsor of a NASCAR sponsor, for example, sponsorship awareness can be directly linked to increased sales. NASCAR fans know, appreciate, and like sponsors who sponsor their favorite driver (i.e., the brand is on the car), and that awareness combined with the positive attitudes can lead to enhanced sponsor image and increased sales. Admittedly, primary car sponsorships are somewhat unique in the sports world: team sports do not offer such opportunities to link to a property so closely. With other sponsorships, however, sponsorship awareness can be linked to increased marketing communications effectiveness, which is in turn linked to enhanced brand image and increased sales. The relationship can be indirect but important nonetheless (see Figure 15.2 for a proposed model).

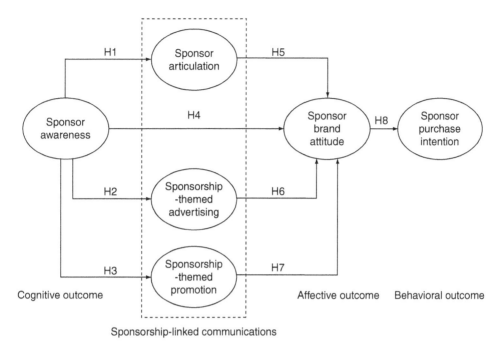

Figure 15.2 Indirect relationship between awareness, brand, and purchase intent.

Liking

There are two main questions about sponsorship and "liking": (1) Do fans like the sponsorship?, (2) Do fans like the sponsor's brand more because of the sponsorship? These questions are closely related.

Liking the sponsorship itself is important to the extent that liking the sponsorship translates into liking the sponsor. Academics often refer to this process as "image transfer," a kind of brand osmosis in which the positive attitudes of the property transfer to the attitudes toward the sponsor. Some industry research supports this view, as one industry researcher found that consumers who are "delighted" with a sponsorship have much higher levels of brand advocacy for the sponsor.[8]

Sales

One of the simplest methods of measuring the effects of sponsorship on sales is to look at "before" and "after" sales figures. Peak Antifreeze and Motor Oil signed sponsorships in NASCAR and the NHRA (drag racing), for example, and sales increased 5–7 percent within a year after the deals began. Executives at Peak noted that the "do-it-yourself guy" is 50 percent more likely to be a motorsports fan, so the sponsorships looked to be an efficient vehicle to reach their targets. The sponsorships were leveraged with promotions generated with a partnership with the "Duck Dynasty" reality show, an A&E network show about a family business that makes duck hunting equipment. Peak executives also point to the sponsorships in their success as a result of being introduced to NAPA, an auto parts retailer.

While pre-test/post-test sales data can be compelling, it is not very precise, mostly because there are a lot of other factors that can influence sales year-to-year. In a difficult economy, are more people doing their own oil changes? Are car owners paying more attention to oil changes because they are putting off new car purchases? In addition, the sponsorship are not Peak's only marketing efforts. What else did they do in that year that might have influenced sales? Did competitors' prices increase, decrease, or stay flat? Did Peak prices increase, decrease, or stay flat?

Real-world settings are not laboratories so it is impossible to control for everything in practice, but it is possible to apply some statistical controls to see if sponsorship effects can be isolated. An academic study[9] controlled for price and advertising spending effects in their examination of the effects of Coca-Cola's Olympic sponsorship on soft drink choices in American households. Drawing on household scanner data from a three-year period, the authors found a significant short-term sales increase for Coke over Pepsi during the Games. Again, there is support for the relationship between sponsorship and sales but there is no direct link between increased sales and specific sponsorship components. The main benefit of this approach, however, is the precision with which sales data are measured.

There is a fair amount of research that links sponsorship to product sales by measuring the relationship between brand preference and fan avidity, with the idea being that sports fans are exposed to sponsorships that non-fans are not, so an increase in brand preference within a fan base is an indication that the sponsorship is working. For example, one study found that action sports spectatorship, age, and gender have a positive effect on brand use for Mountain Dew.[10] While this study provides some support for Mountain Dew's sponsorship effectiveness, it is a single snapshot in time so it is not possible to identify any increases. In addition, there is no comparative basis between fans of action sports and non-fans. It is possible that brand preference increased overall, or among related population segments like the youth market, not just with fans of action sports.

Scarborough Sports Marketing adds the benefit of tracking brand preference over time and comparing to a general population. Sponsors can implement a benchmark that tracks annual changes in brand usage, and compare fans and non-fans. Alaska airlines, for example, had a substantial advertising presence with the NFL's Seattle Seahawks. Tracking usage of Alaska Airlines over a period of three years, Scarborough was able to demonstrate an increase in brand usage among Seahawks attendees, radio listeners, TV viewers, and fans, and compare those Seahawks fan segments to the Seattle market in general, finding that while there was an overall increase in usage among Seattle adults, it was far outpaced among Seahawks attendees.

These studies have limited implications for ROI, however, because the researchers do not address the "how much" question of consumption.[11] Are action sports fans drinking one more Mountain Dew per year, or per week? Are Seahawks attendees flying Alaska Airlines once a year or once a month?

CASE: LINKING SPONSORSHIP TO SALES

In order to gain some perspective about sales volume attributable to specific sponsorship components, an industry study looked at the relationship between sponsorship activation

Table 15.3 Average weekly soft drink servings consumed

Statement	Do not agree	Agree
I like [SOFT DRINK BRAND]'s advertising more when it features the sport of NASCAR or my favorite NASCAR drivers.	2.42	6.26***
It is fun to participate in [SOFT DRINK BRAND]'s promotional games, contests, or sweepstakes when they are related to NASCAR.	2.53	6.70**

Notes
*** $p < 0.001$.
** $p < 0.01$.

efforts and self-reported consumption levels for a major soft-drink brand.[12] Fans in the study who reported positive views toward activation efforts reported more than double the amount of soft-drink servings consumed in an average week (see Table 15.3). Fans who agreed that they like the brand's advertising more when it features the sport or a driver drank 6.26 servings per week, compared with 2.42 servings for fans who do not like themed-advertising more.

The advantage of this approach is that it ties sponsorship components directly to sales. One of the limitations, however, is that self-reported sales are not as accurate as scanner data. And while it is impossible to conclusively measure the exact amount of sales attributable to a specific marketing effort, the statistical relationships can be robust and persuasive.

A recent trend in sponsorship entails sponsors looking to pare down assets and de-emphasize exposure, while focusing on promotional activation directly tied to sales. In a tight economy, sponsors understandably want to reduce costs and increase sales, so efforts not directly linked to sales are more likely to be cut. One of the interesting findings in this study was that favorable attitudes toward advertising was a strong predictor of sales, which suggests that sponsors looking to increase sales should look at brand-building promotional tools in addition to efforts more directly targeted at sales.

EXERCISE

A large consumer brand is considering becoming a sports sponsor but is hesitant because brand executives are concerned about measurement. Write a brief memo that outlines how sponsorships can be measured.

THREE MAIN TAKEAWAYS

1 The lack of a single, comprehensive sponsorship measure does not preclude a rigorous, systematic, and effective measurement approach.
2 Approaches to sponsorship measurement include estimating media value, comparing sponsorship to other marketing options, measuring the fulfillment of sponsorship objectives, and measuring financial return.

251

3   Sponsorship measurement should include audience analysis (reach and involvement), activation effectiveness, and outcomes (cognitive, affective, and behavioral).

RECOMMENDED READING

Davis, J. (2011). *Advertising Research: Theory and Practice*. Upper Saddle River, NJ: Prentice Hall. Sponsorship measurement is often unfavorably compared to advertising, mostly because Nielsen provides reliable measures of audience size and characteristics which establish prices. Measuring the effectiveness of advertising, however, can be as elusive as sponsorship. In that respect, sponsorship is often held to a different standard than advertising.

NOTES

1 As a sponsorship research consultant, I understand this is self-serving but I believe in my product.
2 Skildum-Reid, K. (2012). *The Corporate Sponsorship Toolkit: Using Sponsorship to Help People Fall in Love With Your Brand*. Australia: Freya Press.
3 Karp, A. (2012). Jimmie Johnson tops Keslowski in driver exposure value; Sprint TV ad spend down 8%. SBD.
4 Skildum-Reid. *The Corporate Sponsorship Toolkit*.
5 www.octagon.com/#!/home, accessed 6/1/2013.
6 Broughton, D. (2012). Research segments fans by lifestyle, not sport. www.sportsbusinessdaily.com/Journal/Issues/2012/07/23/Research-and-Ratings/Team-Epic.aspx, accessed 9/10/2014.
7 Tripodi, J.A., Hirons, M., Bednall, D., and Sutherland, M. (2003). Cognitive evaluation: Prompts used to measure sponsorship awareness. *International Journal of Market Research*, 45(4): 435–455.
8 Cameron, N. (2009). Understanding sponsorship and its measurement implications. *Journal of Sponsorship*, 2(2): 131–139.
9 Cho, S., Lee, M., Yoon, T., and Rhodes, C. (2011). An analysis of the Olympic sponsorship effect on consumer brand choice in the carbonated soft drink market using household scanner data. *International Journal of Sport Finance*, 6: 335–353.
10 Bennett, G., Ferreira, M., Lee, J., and Polite, F. (2009). The role of involvement in sports and sport spectatorship in sponsor's brand use: The case of Mountain Dew and action sports sponsorship. *Sport Marketing Quarterly*, 18: 14–24.
11 Ibid, p. 22.
12 DeGaris, L. and West, C. (2013). The effects of sponsorship activation on the sales of a major soft-drink brand. *Journal of Brand Strategy*, 1(4): 401–410.

Chapter 16

Sponsorship sales

CHAPTER OUTLINE

1 Sponsorship sales elements
   a Prospecting
   b Needs analysis
   c Presentation
   d Advantages
   e Closing

2 Sponsorship proposals
   a Linking features with benefits
   b Exposure benefits
   c Promotional rights benefits
   d Tickets/events benefits

Sponsorship revenue tends to be the biggest opportunity for growth among sports properties. Ticket sales are upper bound by facility constraints and media rights tend to be locked in for long periods. In contrast, sponsorship programs are flexible with no hard limit on size or scope. Properties can increase sponsorship revenue by adding sponsorship categories, creating new sponsorship inventory, or increasing the size of current sponsorships.

The growth opportunities for sponsorship revenue lead to a very competitive marketplace, as all sponsorship properties compete for limited sponsorship budgets. Sponsors with big budgets tend to get inundated with proposals, sometimes numbering hundreds per week. In some cases, sponsors will determine their needs and seek out the appropriate sponsorship properties, but for the most part the responsibility for initiating sponsorship programs is most likely to fall upon the property so sponsorship sales executives need to find ways to break through the clutter.

Director of Sponsorship Sales, Tacoma Rainiers (minor league baseball)[1]

Do you think you have what it takes to land the big partner? Do you thrive under pressure? Are you motivated and competitive?

Responsibilities

- Responsible for the direct sales of partnership and advertising packages that may include the following: arena signage, radio, television, internet and game program advertising, season tickets, group hospitality, parking, merchandising opportunities, promotions, events, and others elements.

  Fulfillment reports, which demonstrate the value received by sponsors, are important tools for renewing sponsorship accounts.
- Responsible for generating and developing new business through lead lists, name collection activities, cold calls, networking events, speaking engagements, etc. . . .
- Assist in the fulfillment aspect of all partnership accounts. Works closely with Corporate Partner Services on execution, relationship building and renewals.
- Works in tandem with Corporate Partner Services staff on renewing established partnership accounts from year to year.
- Keep accurate sales files, customer services files, call reports, appointment schedule reports, prospects reports, etc. Maintain weekly communication on all activity reports.
- Prepare sales proposals. Work closely with graphic design staff for specific elements of proposals.
- Assist with the development of team sales databases.
- *Learn partner objectives, sales, marketing & community development initiatives.*
- *Make partnership fun. Make the decision maker look good and make the relationship easy for them (take the work out of their hands).*
- Consistently promote the team and seek to develop business relationships. (emphases added)

This is a good list of typical sponsorship features. Note the unspecified "other" category, which is often what it takes to land the "big partner."

This is a good list of prospecting activities: as noted in the final bullet point, effective salespeople are in the constant pursuit of relationships.

Understanding sponsor objectives and their current programs provides sponsorship salespeople with the necessary foundation to create effective programs and deliver the right solutions. Making your client look good to his or her boss is a great way to get and keep business.

SPONSORSHIP SALES ELEMENTS

Prospecting

The first step in selling sponsorships is to determine who you want to sell to. Some experts argue that the most effective technique in identifying sponsorship prospects is to think about industry categories rather than specific companies,[2] although the actual thought process could go in the opposite direction. Sponsorship sales executives might think first of how their properties would fit a specific brand and then identify benefits for the product category as a whole.

Networking. Sponsorship seekers should begin by leveraging their own relationships. Properties can look at their vendor lists and see where the organization spends money. Spend a lot of money on technology? Leverage that account into a two-way partnership. Many owners of professional sports teams also operate other business concerns and control sizable family assets, all of which can be leveraged for the benefit of the sports property when seeking sponsorships.

The principle can extend to non-profit organizations, too. When *Right to Play*, a non-profit that uses play to help educate children facing adversity, was looking for a Global Partnerships Manager, the job responsibilities included "Pursue Board Members and Senior Management for partnership leads."[3] Sponsorship can conflict with philanthropy because the board members of non-profits are also likely to be senior-level executives at target companies.

As with ticket sales, one of the quickest ways to increase revenue is to cross-sell or up-sell existing clients. So, if you were to be hired by the NBA to sell sponsorships in China, it might make sense to start with sponsors who are active in North America and try to cross-sell NBA partnerships in China. For existing partners in China, it might make sense to develop plans to grow sponsorships (up-sell) as the NBA continues to grow in China. New business relationships can take a long time to develop so leveraging existing relationships can be an effective first step.

Product categories. While all sponsorships should be customized to meet the needs of sponsors, certain product categories tend to be active sponsors.

- *Mega-brands.* For many huge brands – Coke, Pepsi, McDonald's, Budweiser – ubiquity is part of their brand identity. They need to be everywhere, and sponsorship's ability to integrate brands into compelling content gives these brands a unique opportunity to maintain a presence where it otherwise might be excluded.
- *Sports brands.* Brands closely associated with sports, like Nike and adidas, maintain their prominence through highly visible sports partnerships. Historically, Nike favored individual sponsorships but continues to become more active with team and league sponsorships. Sports clothing brands consistently rank among the top spending industries globally, according to *The World Sponsorship Monitor*.
- *Fast-moving consumer goods.* Soft-drinks, snack foods, and personal care item brands tend to look to sponsorship for its ability to drive traffic at retail. Sponsorships provide a platform upon which to develop integrated marketing communications programs, using advertising and public relations to make sales promotions more effective, for example.
- *Financial services.* Regulatory requirements that limit banks' ability to grow market share by acquisition have led banks to do more consumer marketing. In addition to sponsorship's ability to provide hospitality opportunities for the "mass affluent," banks and other financial services increasingly look to sponsorship to reach mass consumer markets.

- *Auto.* The automobile industry is among the largest advertising spenders and often leverages its marketing muscle in sponsorship deals. Auto brands frequently tap into live events and promotions in order to involve local dealers and provide incentives for prospective buyers to test drive vehicles.
- *Telecommunications.* The telecommunications industry is highly competitive and huge. In addition, telecommunications companies often target younger consumers who can be difficult to reach via traditional media, so sponsorships can provide access to a difficult-to-reach segment.
- *Travel.* Airlines and hotels are endemic to big events that attract a lot of visitors. For example, Thomas Cook, a UK-based travel company, leverages its sponsorships to market sports travel and accommodations for fans.
- *Beer.* Beer is endemic to the sports experience for many fans. Try this thought experiment. Imagine a "beer prohibition" for baseball. No beer advertisers or sponsors. No beer sold at the stadium or consumed while watching on TV. What does it look like?
- *Gambling.* Gaming sponsors are somewhat muted in the US sports landscape because sports gambling is illegal in most places in the country. Internationally, however, gambling companies have a strong presence in sports, though widespread sponsorship has raised some concerns. In response to a charge that the Australian Football League (AFL) was "getting drunk" on gambling revenue, the league's commissioner responded, "The reason we're involved with gambling agencies is not for the revenue. It's so we've got access to information to protect the integrity of the code."[4] While the bulk of sports gambling in the US is done underground, gambling brands, especially websites, are eager to compete for a multi-billion dollar global market.
- *Retail.* Retailers often benefit from having their sponsorships subsidized by brands that they carry. Consumer good brands are eager to get priority shelf space and locations within stores and retailers benefit from cross-promotion with other sponsors to help drive traffic to their stores.

Non-traditional sponsors. Sports properties look beyond traditional sponsorship industry categories in order to increase sponsorship revenue despite limited or declining sponsorship budgets, especially during down economic periods. As there are no ready templates for new categories, this takes a lot of ingenuity. As an executive for the NFL's St. Louis Rams' sponsorship agency said during the recent financial crisis, "Traditional sponsors aren't spending – you have to look hard for new money."[5] Accordingly, the Rams, who are located in Missouri, signed the US Border Patrol as a sponsor.

Finding potential sponsors. Sponsor directories, such as Repucom's *The World Sponsorship Monitor* and the IEG Sponsorship Sourcebook, compile lists of current sponsors, their relationships, and contact information. For business which may not currently have sponsorships or not be listed in sponsorship directories, business directories such as Hoovers provide comprehensive lists. Many regional business journals provide company lists of companies within industry categories. Internet searches, of course, can cast a wide net. As many businesses come and go, either changing addresses, starting up, or going out of business, in-person, door-to-door prospecting can also be a productive technique depending on the nature of the targets.

Sponsorship's buying center. After US Figure Skating's prime "kiss and cry" area went without a sponsor for several years, the organization hired sponsorship sales agency Van Wagner to help. Van Wagner e-mailed the brand manager for Puffs' facial tissue, who connected Van Wagner to Puffs' media agency MediaVest. Subsequently, Puffs' advertising agency Publicis and media planning agency Carat joined the discussion. Already there were five different organizations involved and, for sponsorship, this was a fairly streamlined process. Puffs handled the deal independently without parent company P&G or its numerous other brands. The deal focused on media, so public relations and promotions were yet to be involved, not to mention Puffs' sales staff and corporate hospitality opportunities.

The Puffs case is fairly typical in that most sponsorships are spearheaded by executives with expertise in advertising or public relations, though sales and other marketing sub-disciplines are involved. As some sponsorship experts note, sponsorship budgets are being raised within companies by "passing the hat around" different departments.[6] Therefore, many sponsors, even very large ones, do not necessarily have one person serve as a focal point for sponsorships. Even when there is a sponsorship manager, large deals must climb the corporate ladder for approval. A motorsports sponsorship manager, for example, might need approval from a VP of sponsorships, who reports to the VP of marketing, who must get budgets approved by the CEO.

Needs analysis

Sponsorship spans across many industries and marketing disciplines. This creates a huge challenge for sponsorship sales executives because if they wish to understand their clients, they have to become experts in everything. Gaining expertise across industries and marketing disciplines also makes sponsorship sales a great path to career development, as sales executives gain valuable skills, experiences, and contacts. Developing that expertise, however, takes a lot of time and effort.

Researching prospects. Sponsorship expert Kim Skildum-Reid suggests that the information search about prospects should begin with the company website, then proceed to Google, and research databases.[7] Company websites sometimes contain sponsorship guidelines, which may or may not be useful, but most contain information about products and services and yield some insight into the overall identity of the company. After reviewing the company website, Skildum-Reid suggests sales executives move to an Internet search, looking for examples of advertising and other marketing efforts to identify the prospect's key message. Lastly, Skildum-Reid's favorite research tool, something which will make a lot of professors very happy, is ABI/Inform Full-Text Online. Fortunately for students, most university libraries provide access to a full range of research databases.

It is also a good idea to try to find out information about individuals whom you would plan to contact. LinkedIn profiles can provide detailed work history, which can provide some valuable perspective. Job histories, awards, achievements, and even personal interests can yield some insights into what a prospect might be receptive to.

Asking questions. Secondary research is just a starting point. The most valuable information about prospects comes from the prospects themselves. The Chicago Cubs, for example, devote their first meeting with a prospect to trying to understand what the prospect needs, and then create a proposal based on the results of the meeting rather than walking in with a proposal.[8] How do salespeople find prospects? What kinds of questions should they ask?

Questions should be aimed at finding out about the prospect's marketing goals, strategies, and tactics. In particular, it is important to learn about priorities and evaluations. Sponsorship salespeople take on the role of marketing consultant, diagnosing problems and proposing solutions. Broad, "grand touring" questions can provide direction for follow-up questions:

- What are your biggest challenges?
- What is working well? What isn't?
- What are your top priorities?

However, busy executives do not appreciate having their time wasted. Do not ask questions which could easily be answered with a brief search on the Internet. Do your homework on the prospect individually, the brand, the company, and the industry.

Asking informed questions.[9] One of the best ways to impress a prospect is to ask a "good" question, which by the way is a great way to get noticed by industry guests who speak to your class. What is a "good" question? Mostly, good questions are based on a knowledge of the prospect.

- *Questions about the individual.* Knowledge about a prospect's prior work history can be helpful in gaining perspective. "I see where you switched from the property side to the brand side. What's that experience been like for you?"
- *Questions about the company.* Having done research about a company, you can skip right to a follow-up question. "I see where market share declined slightly last year. What are your thoughts about turning that around?"
- *Questions about other marketing efforts.* Preliminary research should include getting a grasp of what the brand is currently doing, which can inform questions to gain more insight. "A lot of your advertising seems to emphasize trust. How do you see that playing out in a sponsorship?"
- *Questions about the industry.* If you are pitching soft-drink brands, it might be a good idea to read *Beverage Digest* or some other trade publication to learn about what is going on in the industry, which helps to put potential sponsorship programs into context. "I see where Pepsi's CEO says that the next 3–5 years will be a crucial period for carbonated soft drinks [CSDs]. What do you think about the future of CSDs during this time?"

Ignore "lesson #2." In *Scarface*, Frank Lopez's "lesson number two" is "don't get high on your own supply." As we have seen, one of the main benefits of corporate hospitality and client entertainment is to gain intelligence. If a salesperson is seeking to gain "inside" information about a prospect beyond what is published, close personal contact can be a big benefit. To that end, sponsorship properties can benefit by provide some "product samples" to prospective sponsors. Sponsorship properties sell corporate hospitality and client entertainment; they should use it, too.

Presentation

F-A-B selling. Feature-Advantage-Benefit selling is a "textbook" technique, in that it is included in many sales textbooks.[10] Many sponsorship proposals often list their sponsorship features as "benefits," erroneously in my opinion. I do not wish to quibble about semantics but the terminology here is important. Strictly speaking, features are product characteristics, such as fan characteristics, property brand image, logo exposure (e.g., signage), and marketing rights. Sponsorship advantages are how those features will be used and why they are superior to alternatives. Benefits are something that promotes well-being.

F-A-B selling

- A **feature** is a prominent part or characteristic. Features are *what it is*.
- An **advantage** shows superiority. Advantages are *what it does*.
- A **benefit** is something that promotes well-being. Benefits are *why it's important*.

Signage is a product feature, which may or may not lead to benefits for a sponsor. Effective sponsorship sales presentations must connect sponsorship features to marketing and business goals, i.e., the "benefits" that sponsors seek (Table 16.1). Sponsors are most interested in attaining their marketing and business goals. Sponsorship presentations must address these concerns. Effective sponsorship proposals establish a strong link between features and benefits.

Advantages

Sponsorship salespeople should sell benefits, but in order to do so need to make a connection between features and benefits. The link between sponsorship features and benefits is the advantage of the proposed sponsorship. In F-A-B selling, advantages are what the feature does. As a comparatively new marketing tool compared to advertising and sales promotions, often there is a greater need to explain to prospects how sponsorship works. Basically, sponsorship

Table 16.1 Sponsorship features and benefits

Sponsorship features	Marketing benefits	Business benefits
Exclusivity	Awareness	Increase sales
Exposure	Knowledge	Reduce costs
Logo and trademark rights	Liking	Increase productivity
Tickets	Purchase intent	
Database of contacts	Purchase	
Image		
Vending rights		

salespeople need to tell prospects how their sponsorships can be used. Property-side representatives are well-positioned to explain the sponsorship's advantages because they (should) know the property well. And for even the most seasoned of sponsorship professionals, there is a need to provide authoritative proof that sponsorship will be effective.

Sponsorship. Often, sponsorship salespeople will have to sell the idea of "sponsorship" as a marketing tool before they can sell a specific sponsorship. Sponsorship salespeople need to make the case that sponsorship is more efficient and effective than alternative marketing tools.

- *Efficient targeting*. Sponsorship offers an alternative to mass media marketing by delivering targeted audiences. Sports fans tend to be more affluent than the general population, for example, so sponsors seeking affluent audiences can reach a higher percentage of affluent consumers through sports sponsorship than other marketing vehicles.
- *Increased engagement*. Sponsorship is often said to "pull at the heartstrings" or "touch the soul." While some of the jargon tends to be hyperbolic, there is an element of truth. Sports fans love their sports. Sponsorship salespeople need to demonstrate how they can help sponsors tap into that passion.
- *Integration*. Sponsorship provides a built-in platform upon which brands can integrate across media and marketing communications. While comprehensive integration across media and marketing communications often involves coordinating different entities, effective sports sponsorship programs facilitate integration for brands.

Sports sponsorships. Sports continues to attract by far the largest share of sponsorship revenue relative to arts, culture, music, and fairs/festivals. Mostly, that is a reflection of audience sizes and media opportunities but sports offer other advantages relative to alternative sponsorship properties.

- *Access*. Sports properties can often provide behind-the-scenes access not available to other properties.
- *Fans receptive to marketing*. Sports fans are likely to be more receptive to marketing efforts and a commercial presence.
- *Integration into the content*. Sponsors can be integrated into the content of the property.

Your property. Sports audiences differ along important characteristics, such as age, gender, and income, so some sports have some basic advantages built in. Even within sports, properties differ with respect to advantages they offer to prospective sponsors.

- *Brand*. Standards include things like performance, excellence, and tradition. It does not hurt to include these attributes if they are accurate but it is important to focus on what makes a property different. What is compelling about your property? What is important? How would you make a difference to your sponsor that other properties would not?
- *Features*. Do you offer additional, different, and exceptional sponsorship features? Many sponsorship properties claim to "go the extra mile" but provide little tangible details

about what that means. If your features are industry standard, consider creating new ones. Adding inventory is one of the best ways to increase value, which is especially relevant during a down economy when there is a lot of pressure to justify fees.

■ *Performance.* Winning never hurts, but on-field performance does not necessarily equate with sponsorship performance. Yet, many sponsorship proposals discuss on-the-field performance without connecting it to sponsorship benefits. Do championships lead to more loyal fans? Sometimes but not always. Does winning increase attendance and TV ratings? Maybe. Does winning create a strong brand? Possibly. Perhaps more importantly for sponsorship salespeople, winning is something under which they have no control. The sponsorship department does not draft players or make trades. Sponsorship performance, however, is something under their control.

■ *Service.* I asked a long-time client, a major NASCAR sponsor, what she valued most in their sponsorship. She replied that the driver the company sponsored had only missed one hospitality event in a multi-year agreement, and that was because of a major snow storm, and he called hours in advance (from the airport) to keep the sponsor informed of the status. As a sponsorship salesperson, can you demonstrate that your organization will go the extra mile to ensure results for the sponsor?

A "consultative" approach to sponsorship sales means that a salesperson assumes the role of marketing services consultant. As the Chicago Blackhawks say in their sponsorship brochure, they deliver: "Turn-key, impactful programs customized to meet your goals and objectives." Increasingly, sports properties are hiring activation managers to assist in this role.

Closing

Effective sponsorship sales presentations should make closing as simple as asking for the business. Closing on a sponsorship sale, however, requires convincing a prospect that the benefits promised will be delivered. Even when prospects are personally convinced that the sponsorship is a good deal, they often need something to take to their boss(es) to support their decisions.

Along with integration, corporate marketers have mentioned accountability as a pressing challenge. Linking features with advantages and benefits conceptually can create a convincing case, but it is often not enough in an era of increased accountability. And, as we have seen, there is fairly widespread dissatisfaction among sponsors about research and data provided by properties.

Market research conducted by a professional firm can be expensive, prohibitively so for many smaller sports properties. But even small sports properties or properties not willing to invest in research can provide factual support for their sponsorship proposals.

■ **Guarantees.** Sports properties can guarantee features of the sponsorship proposal, such as athlete/coach appearances, attendance, or media ratings.

■ **Company results.** Sports properties can cite a track record of sponsorship performance, not just competitive results on the field of play. Do players and coaches show up to events? Does your sponsorship department deliver "turn-key" programs?

■ **Testimonials and case studies.** Testimonials from current and past sponsors are anecdotal but can be persuasive. Showing how a sponsor used your property to deliver business results can help prospects develop ideas about how they might use the property for their brands.

Independent research results. In the absence of empirical research, sponsors can rely on "water cooler conversations" or "feelings around the company"[11] to make decisions about their sponsorships. "Gut feeling" can be an important element in making decisions about sponsorships as seasoned sponsorship veterans can have a very good intuitive feel about what works and what does not. But without systematic, rigorous research, those feelings are anecdotal at best. As most sponsors do not have dedicated research budgets for their sponsorships, sports properties who supply research to sponsors can provide a valuable service in addition to supporting the sponsorship sales effort.

■ **Third party validation from a credible source.** Both sponsor and property have vested interests in their sponsorship relationship, with all sides wanting the sponsorship to work, which can influence how research is structured. An independent third-party without a dog in the fight can provide a more objective assessment.
■ **Generalizable results.** Systematic, rigorous research can be generalized to similar situations. While testimonials and case studies can provide insight into how a sponsorship *might* work, systematic research, while itself never absolutely conclusive, can provide more support for how it *does* work.
■ **Sponsorship strategies.** Market research can provide strategic direction for both new and existing sponsors. Being able to discuss the relative merits of a sweepstake versus a premium for a promotion, for example, can be of great assistance to sponsors in developing their programs.

SPONSORSHIP PROPOSALS

"Send me your deck."

Sponsorship brochures. "Send me your deck" is a common response from a prospective sponsor who shows interest in a property. Most properties have a sponsorship "deck," or printed presentation of their sponsorship opportunities for prospects who might have an interest. Often, sponsorship decks or brochures can be accessed via property websites.

Most sponsorship brochures focus primarily on an overview of sponsorship features, as providing more information about advantages and benefits is difficult without knowing about prospective sponsors' specific goals. Sponsorship brochures typically provide some basic demographic info about the property's audience, then a detailed list of media opportunities with perhaps a brief mention of other activation concepts, such as sales promotions and themed advertising.

Sponsorship brochures are more effective, however, when they provide some insight into sponsor benefits, not just the features. Some brochures make effective use of testimonials to demonstrate how their sponsorships might be used. The Sydney Roosters of Australia's

National Rugby League (NRL), for example, provide a page of partner endorsements immediately after an introductory page summarizing the club and its history (see Sydney Roosters
Partnership Endorsements box below). With the testimonials, the Roosters are able to highlight some key benefits of the sponsorship – access and personalization, in particular – which
otherwise might be difficult to communicate, much less document with support.

National Rugby League (NRL) Sydney Roosters Partnership endorsements[12]

Steggles (chicken and turkey products):

> "A key initiative we are immensely proud of is the Steggles Roosters Charity
> Nest. Since its inception, we have raised in excess of $620,000 for children's
> charities in New South Wales and Queensland."

Trackmaster (apparel):

> "We currently sponsor Jared Waerea-Hargreaves who has been a great
> ambassador for my business and has formed a strong bond with my family and
> staff. Our customers enjoy being entertained at the Roosters matches and
> having access to the players and coaching staff that they otherwise would not
> have access to and this gives them an added sense of ownership of the team.
> The network of people that I have met through partnering with the Sydney
> Roosters is unparalleled in business and sporting circles."

Vic's Meat (Australia's leading distributor of grass and grain-fed beef):

> "There was an obvious synergy to this sponsorship with my businesses located
> in the homeland of the mighty Sydney Roosters, but the partnership has been
> about much more than that. One aspect I have enjoyed most is the personal
> relationships that have developed between myself, my staff and the players.
> The boys will often come down to our weekly Vic's Meat Market Day, we are
> able to offer ticket give-aways to our database and provide a link between our
> customers and our great team."

Sponsorship brochures can be effective in providing some background about sponsorship
opportunities but will close a sale on their own. In this extremely competitive sponsorship
environment, sponsorship salespeople need to personalize and customize proposals in order
to even gain consideration. Sponsorship is not a shelf product so "cookie-cutter" proposals
will not persuade sponsors, no matter how glossy and polished the brochure is.

Initial contact. Sponsorship salespeople need to be concise and to the point if they are
to rise above the cluttered marketplace. The most common form of initial contact is e-mail,
but like sponsorship brochures, a mass e-mail which clearly is not customized is not likely
to gain a response. As sponsorship experts Collett and Fenton argue, sponsors are never

"interested in sponsoring"; they are interested in marketing and business benefits. Therefore, they recommend a personalized approach led by creative ideas relative to the prospect's brand and company. "I have a way for you to reach car owning college graduates who change their cars every three years," for example.[13]

While initial contact should be customized, it is possible to take a systematic approach. Basically, the initial contact should explain, preferably in one sentence, how the property will actively engage an attractive audience to achieve desired results. E-mails are easy to delete without opening so the subject line needs to say as much as possible, as concisely as possible.

Full proposal. After gaining initial interest and finding out what a prospective sponsor is looking for, sponsorship salespeople must develop full proposals and put a price on the package. According to one industry source, most sponsorship proposals fall short on meeting sponsoring brand needs.[14] Therefore, there is an opportunity for sponsorship salespeople to distinguish themselves from competing "cookie-cutter" proposals.

Proposal sections. Sponsorship proposals typically include the following headings. Ideally, sponsorship advantages and marketing and business benefits should be integrated throughout the proposal.

- *Summary*. Carlsberg suggests that sponsorship proposals, "Try to deliver the benefits at an early stage; the longer the pitch, the more likely a negative response."[15] In internal strategy sessions, my long-time colleague Don Hinchey would always push me to provide the "three main takeaways" at the beginning of a presentation. I found it helpful to begin with the conclusions and then spend the presentation supporting my assertions.
- *Property description*. Many sponsorship proposals spend *way* too much time describing their property, in my opinion. Often, a brief history and overview will suffice.
- *Audience description*: demographics, purchasing habits, etc.
- *Exposure*. Provide details about sponsor identification opportunities.
- *Activation concepts*. Creative activation concepts are a sure-fire way for your sponsorship proposal to break through the clutter. According to one account, a Coca-Cola marketing executive once said he was looking for "something that adds color to my day."
- *Marketing and business benefits*. Ultimately, enhanced brand image and increased profits are most sponsors' goals. Sponsorship proposals should maintain that focus.
- *Total cost*. A lot of sponsorship deals fall through because, too often, prospective sponsors are not told the difference between sponsorship rights fees and the total cost of the sponsorship *with activation*. Personally, I believe sponsorship salespeople would be more successful if they were to pitch "turn-key" programs with no added expenses, which can often be quite substantial. Imagine, for example, being pitched on what you were told was an $8 million title sponsorship, only to find out that the total cost with activation would be more like $25–$30 million.

Linking features with benefits

Effective sponsorship proposals must establish clear links between sponsorship features and benefits to sponsors (Table 16.2). In sum, proposals should explain what the sponsorship is, what it does, and why it is important, while offering proof to support the claims.

Audience

Attractive audience demographics are often featured prominently in sponsorship proposals without explicitly stating how appealing demographics benefits sponsors. Broadly speaking, sports audiences allow more efficient and effective marketing programs. Attractive demographics are more efficient because they allow marketers to reach targets more efficiently. Syndicated research, such as Scarborough or Simmons, for example, can show how motorsports audiences index highly in sponsors' product categories and/or brand preferences.

Sports audiences can be more effective because they are more receptive to sponsorship-linked marketing programs. Sports fans like advertising more in general; they are more likely to participate in sponsors' promotions; and they are more engaged in sponsorship-linked advertising. Increased efficiency and effectiveness helps to reduce marketing costs and yields more bang for the marketing dollar.

Exposure benefits

Sponsorship features which provide exposure are usually most prominently emphasized in proposals. While exposure value is often overstated, it does provide benefits to sponsors. Logo exposure, for example, is linked to sponsorship awareness, generating increased awareness for the brand and building equity in the sponsorship, which can then be leveraged with other promotions (Table 16.3). Logo exposure in sponsorships is often much more cost-effective than generating awareness through other promotional tools, such as advertising, thereby reducing marketing costs. As integration across media is a pressing challenge for corporate marketers, logo placement across media channels (e.g., TV, print, Internet) provides a built-in integrated program, which is a more effective communication option than one-off communication efforts.

Table 16.2 Proving the links between sponsorship features, advantages, and benefits: audience characteristics

Feature	Advantage	Benefit	Proof
Attractive demographics	Reach targets more efficiently	Reduce marketing costs	Syndicated research (Scarborough) Custom survey
Audience attitudes	Audience more receptive to advertising	Reduced marketing costs	Consumer survey

Table 16.3 Proving the links between sponsorship features, advantages, and benefits: exposure

Feature	Advantage	Benefit	Proof
Signage	Generates awareness and recognition via exposure more efficiently than advertising	Enhance brand image	Logo exposure measures, sponsorship awareness surveys
	Builds equity in sponsorship, which can be leveraged via other promotional tools	Reduce marketing costs	
Logo placement across media	Integrates media (e.g., TV, Internet, print)	Enhance brand image	Consumer survey
	Increases recall	Reduced marketing costs	

Promotional rights benefits

Promotional rights are perhaps the most under-utilized asset in sponsorship proposals, in spite of the demand for creative marketing programs among prospective sponsors. Sponsorship-linked marketing communications are stronger predictors of increased brand image, purchase intent and sales, than sponsorship awareness and exposure. Yet, most proposals allocate much more space to exposure than to promotional programs. Sponsorship proposals should focus on the advantages and benefits of sponsorship-linked marketing communications:

■ Themed-advertising increases consumer engagement: sports fans pay more attention to sports-linked advertising; they like it more; and they remember it more (Table 16.4).

Table 16.4 Proving the links between sponsorship features, advantages, and benefits: promotional rights

Feature	Advantage	Benefit	Proof
Rights to marks and logos	Themed advertising is more effective	Enhance brand image	Consumer survey
		Reduce costs	
	Increase participation in sales promotions	Increase sales	Company results
		Enhance brand image	Syndicated research
		Reduce costs	Consumer survey
	Mobile marketing at races increases fan enjoyment, engages fans with brands	Increase sales	Company results
		Enhance brand image	Consumer survey
		Reduce costs	

Table 16.5 Proving the links between sponsorship features, advantages, and benefits: tickets/events

Feature	Advantage	Benefit	Proof
Tickets to race	Reward employees	Increase productivity	Company results
			Employee surveys
	Build and maintain client relationships	Increase sales	Company results
		Enhance brand image	Testimonials
			Focus groups
			Surveys
Behind-the-scenes access	Create customized events to attract potential clients	Increase incremental sales	Company results
		Enhance brand image	Testimonials
			Focus groups
			Surveys

- Fans are more likely to participate in sports-linked promotional games, contests, and sweepstakes. As sales promotions are often short-term incentives to sales, there is a strong link to increased sales. The sports tie-in makes promotions more fun and engaging, also making sponsorship-linked sales promotions a strong brand-builder.
- Experiential marketing at events is woven into the fabric of the event experience, adding to fan enjoyment and increasing consumer engagement with sponsors.

Tickets/Events benefits

Corporate hospitality can be both a marketing and a managerial tool. As a marketing tool, corporate hospitality gives salespeople a tool with which they can build and maintain customer relationships. As a management tool, hospitality can be used to reward employees and increase profitability.

CASE: SPONSORSHIP "BENEFITS"

Like many sports properties, the NHL's Chicago Blackhawks posted a corporate sponsorships brochure on their website.[16] These brochures can provide a lot of insight into the relative priorities of sponsorship properties – I strongly recommend comparing and contrasting different approaches. One criticism that I have about most brochures is that they tend to be very "product-focused" – that is, they take a "spots and dots" approach to selling media inventory rather than providing solutions to sponsors' problems.

The Blackhawks brochure, like most sports properties, is very media heavy. The brochure breaks down like this:

- Audience characteristics = 2 pages
- Promotions = 2 pages

267

- Hospitality = 2 pages
- Events = 3 pages
- Media = 11 pages

The body of the brochure is at odds with the stated goals up front, which promise customized programs. To be fair, it is difficult to communicate customization in a brochure being distributed across industry categories.

Chicago Blackhawks: THE BENEFITS OF CORPORATE SPONSORSHIPS

- Associate your brand with one of the most popular and recognizable logos in sports.
- Reach an upscale, affluent audience with an average annual household income of over $101,000.
- Highest income per capita of all major sports leagues.
- Consistent advertising campaign covering Q1 and Q4 (October–April).
- *Turn-key, impactful programs customized to meet your goals and objectives*.
- Provides a great platform to connect with consumers during their leisure time.
- Immerse your brand in an environment about which the consumer is most passionate: Blackhawks hockey.
- Sponsorship sends a message that your brand is strong and vibrant and that you are continuing to invest in it. (emphasis added)

The Blackhawks have a great brand and their fans are an affluent demographic, one that many brands would be interested in. Blackhawk fans are also passionate. While advertising opportunities are clear and abundant in the brochure, how programs are customized to leverage fan passion into sponsorship goals is not clear, nor is there any proof provided, not even testimonials or company results.

The cornerstone of Blackhawk sponsorship effectiveness – "turnkey, impactful programs customized to meet your goals" – is left unclear. Take a look at the Blackhawks sponsorship brochure, or one like it. What are your suggestions to provide proof of sponsorship features leading to sponsor benefits?

EXERCISE

Needs analysis. Conduct a needs analysis similar to the exercises in Chapters 7 and 11, but this time choosing a top sponsorship category.

THREE MAIN TAKEAWAYS

1   Sponsorship salespeople must understand sponsor goals and current practices in order to create customized programs.

2   Sponsorship proposals should include sponsorship features, advantages, and benefits, with a heavy emphasis on benefits to the sponsor.

3   Effective sponsorship proposals require proof of assertions linking sponsorship features to sponsor benefits.

RECOMMENDED READING

2012–2013 Chicago Blackhawks Sponsorship Brochure. http://blackhawks.nhl.com/v2/ext/ Fliers/1213-Sponsorship-Brochure.pdf, accessed 6/17/2013.

NOTES

1 Director of Sponsorship Sales, www.milb.com/content/page.jsp?sid=t529&ymd=20071203&content_ id=327340&vkey=team4, accessed 6/10/13.
2 Collett, P. and Fenton, W. (2011). *The Sponsorship Handbook*. San Francisco: Jossey-Bass.
3 Global Partnerships Manager – Right to Play. http://aroundtherings.com/GoldenOpportunities/Job%20 posting%20-%20Global%20Partnerships%20Manager%20Nov%202012.pdf, accessed 6/11/13.
4 We're responsible on betting: Andrew Demetriou. www.theaustralian.com.au/sport/afl/we-are-responsible-on-betting-andrew-demetriou/story-fnca0u4y-1226647617722, accessed 5/21/2013.
5 Lefton, T. (2008). Four NFL teams sniff out sponsor money in tight times. www.sportsbusinessdaily.com/ Journal/Issues/2008/10/20081013/Marketingsponsorship/Four-NFL-Teams-Sniff-Out-Sponsor-Money-In-Tight-Times.aspx, accessed 6/12/2013.
6 Collett and Fenton. *The Sponsorship Handbook*.
7 Don't send a sponsorship proposal until you read this. http://powersponsorship.com/dont-send-a-sponsorship-proposal/, accessed 6/10/2013.
8 Ukman, L. (2011). By necessity or choice, Chicago Cubs take different approach to securing sponsors. www.sponsorship.com/About-IEG/Sponsorship-Blogs/Lesa-Ukman/May-2011/By-Necessity-or-Choice,-Chicago-Cubs-Take-Differen.aspx, accessed 6/10/13.
9 For more details, see Washo, M. (2004). *Break into Sports Through Ticket Sales*. Rutherford, NJ: MMW Marketing LLC.
10 Futrell, C. (2008). *Fundamentals of Selling: Customers for Life Through Service*. Boston: McGraw-Hill Irwin.
11 Collett and Fenton. *The Sponsorship Handbook*.
12 Sydney Roosters 2013 Corporate Partnership Guide. www.roosters.com.au/site/_content/document/ 00003527-source.pdf, accessed 6/19/2013.
13 Collett and Fenton. *The Sponsorship Handbook*, p. 183.
14 Ibid, p. 180.
15 Ibid, p. 191.
16 2012–2013 Chicago Blackhawks Sponsorship Brochure. http://blackhawks.nhl.com/v2/ext/Fliers/1213-Sponsorship-Brochure.pdf, accessed 6/17/2013.

Index

Page numbers in *italics* denote tables, those in **bold** denote figures.